HOW
SOCIETY
MAKES
ITSELF

About the Author

Howard J. Sherman is Professor Emeritus of Economics at the University of California, Riverside, and is Visiting Scholar in Political Science at the University of California, Los Angeles. He has published 17 books, 70 journal articles, and 27 articles in edited books. Included are books on radical and Marxist political economy, macroeconomics. comparative systems, sociology, and methodology of social science. He has served on the editorial boards of the *Journal of Economic Issues* and the *Review of Radical Political Economy*.

HOW SOCIETY MAKES ITSELF

The Evolution of
Political and Economic
Institutions

Howard J. Sherman

M.E.Sharpe
Armonk, New York
London, England

Library of Congress Cataloging-in-Publication Data

Sherman, Howard J.
  How society makes itself : the evolution of political and economic
institutions / Howard J. Sherman.
     p. cm.
  Includes bibliographical references and index.
  ISBN 0-7656-1651-3 (hardcover : alk. paper) — ISBN 0-7656-1652-1 (pbk. : alk. paper)
  1. Social evolution. 2. Social institutions—History. 3. Social history.
4. Economic history. I. Title.
  HM626.S494 2005

  306'.09—dc22   2005009434

Printed in the United States of America

The paper used in this publication meets the minimum requirements of
American National Standard for Information Sciences
Permanence of Paper for Printed Library Materials,
ANSI Z 39.48-1984.

∞

BM (c)   10   9   8   7   6   5   4   3   2   1
BM (p)   10   9   8   7   6   5   4   3   2   1

Dedicated with love to
Barbara Sinclair, Lisa Sherman, and Paul Sherman

Contents

Preface

I always have been fascinated by the dramatic changes that have occurred in human social relationships and institutions, such as the emergence of various forms of family and government. How and why did human society change and evolve into entirely new types of institutions? Because these changes affect everyone, they should be of great interest to everyone.

My intention has been to write a book that would appeal to a broad readership. It has not been written for experts, although I have consulted experts' works on each issue. Most experts specialize in one issue, but this book covers all issues that arise in social evolution. While experts may find little of interest in their own areas of expertise, they may learn something in reading the other sections. The book cuts across all of the social science disciplines and history. Thus, in addition to being of interest to general readers, the book is designed to be used as an introduction to social evolution in any of the relevant disciplines. I hope that readers will learn the basics of social evolution, and that they will enjoy reading this book as much I enjoyed researching it.

Note on Language

The term, America, applies equally to North, South, and Central America. So when the term is applied only to the United States, the rest of the Americas often feel insulted, and rightly so. On the other hand, the terms, U.S. and United States, are often awkward to use. So in cases where it makes the writing flow better, this book uses America or Americans to refer to the United States or the U.S. population. The terms Central and South America are used to refer to those areas. The author hopes this apology will suffice to remove any unintended insult.

Acknowledgments

I would like to thank a number of people who gave me excellent constructive criticism, thus eliminating many of my mistakes. They are Sharman Babior, Robert Brenner, Richard DuBoff, William Dugger, Robin Hahnel, Michael Kearny, Patricia Kolb, David Kotz, Nancy Levine, Reynold Nesiba, Phil O'Hara, Robert Pollin, Lisa Sherman, Paul Sherman, Ira Sohn, and Barbara Weins-Tours.

HOW
SOCIETY
MAKES
ITSELF

– 1 –

Prehistoric Communal Institutions in the Middle East

Our sun and planets evolved over an enormous amount of time. The Earth was originally uninhabitable by life as we know it. Over billions of years, however, the earth evolved and eventually changed into an environment in which we can survive. These geological changes in the earth are revealed in its layers of rocks. For example, some rocks show plant fossils from a million years ago or reveal a volcanic eruption caught forever at a given moment.

When the environment permitted, life evolved at spots where all the necessary elements happened to be together. All other life has evolved from the simplest virus-like creatures that lived at least three billion years ago. Charles Darwin showed how nature selects from the existing individuals the ones best suited for survival under particular conditions. Eventually this type of individual has the highest reproduction rate and that fact leads to a change in the species. This process of change is called natural selection. Thus new species evolved, including human beings.

At the time our first humanoid ancestors evolved on grassy plains, they made simple tools and weapons from pieces of wood or stone or bone. Remnants of early humanoids have been dated to 6 or 7 million years ago, but the exact time of the earliest humanoid is still controversial. Those who had better brains could use tools and weapons more effectively, thus improving their chance of survival. This process led to slow enlargement of the brain. Humanoids with a larger brain could improve the use of tools. An erect stance allowed these humanoids to hold tools while running, so their survival chances were improved.

The new species of homo sapiens (our present species) became dominant about a 100,000 years ago. Eventually, the older humanoid species disappeared, but there is much debate about whether homo sapiens wiped out the old types, or simply interbred with them, or if the earlier humanoids just died out. The earliest type of society developed by homo sapiens endured most of the last hundred thousand years, so other types of societies are a relatively new invention.

How do we know anything about societies that existed tens of thousands of years ago? Many societies of the past three to four thousand years had written languages, so scholars can translate their documents and learn a great deal about them. But earlier societies were prehistoric (meaning before written history) and had no written language. Two kinds of evidence are available on the earliest human societies.

First of all, archaeologists have dug up the earliest dwellings and graves, containing weapons, tools, and ornaments, as well as skeletons. From this evidence, archaeologists deduce an amazing amount of information. For example, by comparing the value of different houses or of different objects found in graves, archaeologists can estimate the degree of economic inequality in the society.

Second, in the past two centuries, anthropologists have studied existing societies that resemble the prehistoric societies, though the numbers of such societies have steadily declined. One problem in using this kind of evidence is that we cannot say for sure whether existing societies that resemble the prehistoric ones behave exactly the way prehistoric ones did. Moreover, the evidence is contaminated because these societies have been in contact with more advanced societies. If no one else, the anthropologist has contacted the communal society and therefore changed it. Nevertheless, in the past two centuries, anthropologists have accumulated an immense amount of reliable information on the earliest type of society.

Features of Prehistoric, Communal Society

To understand prehistoric institutions and how they changed, it is useful to examine four aspects of that society. The four pillars of that society were technology, economic institutions, social institutions, and ideology.

First, what is meant by technology? We think of technology today as modern gadgets and machines, but it means far more than that. Technology is the way that human beings produce goods and services. Technology includes the knowledge of how to do things, the available skills of different types of workers, the amount of production by each type of present equipment, and the quality of land and natural resources available.

The technology of the early communal societies was used for hunting or fishing and gathering fruits and vegetables. Their technology was based on a knowledge of simple stone or bone or wood tool making. Since they lived off of hunting and gathering food, these small groups had to roam over a large amount of land to find their food supply. The total labor force of each group was small, estimated at 5 to 35 people.

Second, economic institutions are defined to mean the ways that people interact in the economy. An economic institution is not a thing; it is a set of relations between people doing economic activities. For example, the institution of slavery is the relation between slaves and masters. The main prehistoric economic institution was the family. It was an extended family of brothers and sisters, cousins, aunts, uncles, parents, and grandparents. There was a division of labor between men and women—and a division of labor between young and old. Men, usually as a group, did most of the fishing and hunting. Women, usually as a group, gathered fruits, nuts, and vegetables. The division of labor between genders, however, was far from absolute because the men probably often gathered fruits and vegetables, while women probably hunted small animals. These two collective groups delivered their food to the whole band. The whole band consumed the food as their right. This little collective group was isolated from other groups and seldom met the other groups.

Such family-based, collective or communal societies existed for 90 to 95 percent of human history. No one word describes all aspects of their existence, but the term "communal" emphasizes the collective nature of their economic institutions. Since everyone worked together and everyone consumed the product, the prehistoric communes had no use for the market. Thus, the communes were non-market societies. The reader is reminded that such early, family-based communes had little or nothing in common with the utopian groups called communes in the nineteenth and twentieth centuries.

Third, the social institutions are defined to be all noneconomic ways that people interact together, such as the political process, the family, or religious organizations. The earliest institutions were very simple. There was no separate government. Most decisions were made collectively.

Table 1.1

Four Features of Early Communal Society

Technology	Earliest stone tools; hunting and gathering
Economic institutions	Common ownership by extended family
Social institutions	Consensus of group
Ideology	Community togetherness and equality

There were no separate, organized religious institutions. The whole community took part in various magical ceremonies, though one person usually led them. There was no separate education system. Education consisted of learning from your parents and the rest of the band by following their example. There were no separate media. News was spread by everyone around the campfire.

Fourth, ideology is defined to mean a more or less coherent system of ideas about how society works and how we should behave in it. We may believe that an ideology is good, like democracy, or bad, like the idea of burning witches. Everybody, however, has some ideology. Ideology is simply a particular viewpoint that integrates many of one's ideas. The communal social ideas (or ideology) reflected their life and environment. If the earliest groups behaved like similar small bands of people discovered in the nineteenth and twentieth centuries, then they valued cooperation among all individuals in the band. They also had a set of superstitious beliefs, which were centered around animals and natural forces, such as lightning.

The four features of communal society are summarized in Table 1.1. These features raise a lot of intriguing questions. For example, when one asks how they fit together in the social whole that was prehistoric communal society, the tale becomes more exciting.

How the Four Basic Features of Society Interacted

These four categories—technology, economic institutions, social institutions, and ideology—will be useful in understanding society as a whole. At first glance, there seem to be hundreds of unrelated aspects in a society. They must be seen in a framework, such as these four categories, to understand how society functions.

Figure 1.1 **Illustration of six interactions**

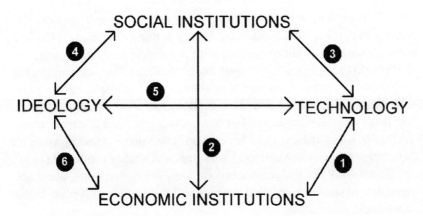

These four aspects of society are not independent of each other. Rather, it will be seen that each of the four is determined by the other three. For example, technology has provided quite reliable birth control devices. This new technology has changed our ideas about sex. Thus, technology can affect ideology.

A simple schematic picture of these interactions is presented in Figure 1.1.

1. economic institutions with technology,
2. social institutions with economic institutions,
3. social institutions with technology,
4. social institutions with ideology,
5. technology with ideology, and
6. economic institutions with ideology.

We will explore how each of these interactions plays a vital role in understanding the early communal society.

Economic Institutions and Technology

The technology of the prehistoric communal society has been defined by four main points. First, it used land for hunting and gathering. Second, there was a small labor force. Third, production was based mostly on simple stone, bone, and wooden tool making. Fourth, physical capital, which just means the equipment and materials being used, consisted only of these simple tools. Communal economic institutions were described as nothing but an extended family acting collectively. How did the communal institutions interact with the simple tools they used?

With this simple technology of bone, stone, and wooden tools, the prehistoric communal society was able to hunt animals, gather plant resources, make leather and fiber implements, clothing, and shelters. The tasks were accomplished but there was a low level of productivity. Technology was at such a low level that if everyone worked together all day, there was only enough food, clothing, and shelter produced for everyday survival. For this reason, no one could specialize in any one trade, since that would have reduced the production of needed supplies below immediate, daily needs.

The description of economic activity and productivity in this chapter relies on archaeological evidence from the Middle East. We know from studying recent bands (small simple societies) that every group devoted some time to leisure activities and recreation. More leisure time is found in early societies that lived in easier environments, such as a fertile Pacific island with a pleasant climate all year.

Because there were no specialists, no one focused his or her thoughts on how to improve tool-making technology. In fact, the prehistoric communal people did not dream that their tools could be radically improved. Moreover, the economic institution of the family encouraged people by peer pressure to work at a reasonable pace, but it did not encourage people to do anything differently than the family had always done. When the family is just above the starvation level, it cannot take chances with new ways of doing things that might result in death by starvation for most of the family. For all of these reasons, technological progress was very, very slow. In tens of thousands of years, there was very little improvement.

Each band of people was forced to form a communal group to protect themselves from large carnivores, as well as to hunt large animals, such as the mammoth. An individual who left the communal group usually died quickly. One institutional consequence of the low technological level was that, if there was a clash with another band, it made no sense to keep a prisoner as a slave because a slave could only produce enough to survive. Therefore, a prisoner from another band was either integrated into this band, or killed and left behind, or killed and eaten. Although it was rare, cannibalism made economic sense to some bands, but slavery did not. Only in a few exceptional cases, such as intensive fishing under good conditions, could slaves produce more than their own needs.

Each small community was separate from the others, so there was little or no trade with other communities. There was no market exchange because there was rarely anything to exchange. Since there was no exchange, there was also no money. The reason for the isolation was that each person required about half a square mile or more for adequate food supply, though they often moved in a nomadic life style from place to place following the food supply. Since it was a family, and since everyone worked collectively to bring in the food, the food was distributed to everyone. People had almost no private possessions, except for an animal skin as clothing and perhaps some simple implements. This information comes from the archaeological data on the Middle East from approximately 100,000 to 10,000 years ago.

Thus, the economic institutions included the extended family; the collective production of the food supply; no division of labor, except partly between men and women and partly by age; no specialists; no market; no money; no significant amount of wealth; and the collective consumption of the food supply. These economic institutions did not encourage technological experimentation, but tended to promote the use of the same technology century after century. Since there was little or no change in the available technology, there was no need to change these economic institutions. The entire set of economic institutions and the available technology fit together perfectly at a very low level, while change was incredibly slow.

Social Institutions and Economic Institutions

Given these technological forces and the economic institutions, the other institutions that were necessary to maintain the community were also very simple. No group of managers or complex corporate structure was needed to run the repeated economic tasks of hunting and food gathering by a small group of people.

No separate government structure was needed in the political sphere to run such a small, highly integrated group. The simple tasks of governance and major decisions could be and were made by the group as a whole. There was a direct democracy because all adults participated in the group. There was no need to vote for representatives.

Since society was not complex and everyone knew what was happening, there was little opportunity for getting away with crimes of violence or theft. With very little crime, there was no need for police. The group as a whole punished or expelled anyone guilty of crime. Expulsion was an extremely serious punishment because it was very difficult to survive alone.

The total amount of personal wealth was a few tools, weapons, and ornaments that could easily be reproduced and carried. There was thus little reason for theft by individuals. Nor was there reason for war by communities, except skirmishes over hunting grounds. A bigger war was not profitable. Moreover, war wasnot possible in much of an organized way over the vast spaces roamed by the different families. So there were no armies or navies.

According to studies of similar bands still in existence today, life was mysterious to people with limited scientific knowledge. Therefore, there was a widespread belief in magic. But there was no organized religion and no full-time priests. One reason was that there was no surplus above basic necessities to feed groups not engaged in production. Everyone had to work for the community to survive.

There was no sexist discrimination. As noted earlier, men tended to do most of the hunting, while women usually focused on gathering food because pregnancy and childcare often did not allow them to go on long hunting trips. But it is quite possible that women often produced more resources for the groups than men did. The food gathering was often more important for the food supply than was the hunting, which was often unsuccessful. Women carried very heavy loads at least as often as men did.

There was no racial discrimination within the group because everyone was a family member. There was certainly ignorance of other families and wariness about all strangers. This was a result of the isolation, an isolation imposed by the need for each group to roam a very large area for its food supply. Different bands occasionally met, mainly to find suitable mates outside the immediate family.

Of course, these social institutions also helped mold the economic institutions. The education and communication systems, in which all of one's learning and news came from other family members, meant that all of the views reinforced the existing system of an extended family working cooperatively. The magic ceremonies involved the entire family, so they also reinforced the family unit as the center of activity. The whole group made the most important economic decisions, such as where to go next to look for food.

Social Institutions and Technology

We have already discussed how the technology of prehistoric communal societies consisted of a small labor force, large areas of land for hunting and food gathering, a few simple tools as capital, and an unchanging fund of technological knowledge. These facts had important implications for social institutions. Hunters and gatherers had fairly stable populations. Their low level of technology and perilous existence meant that even a high birth rate was balanced by a high death rate.

Not only were there no radio, TV, or cable, but they were not needed for spreading news and education within the family. Because there was no long distance communication, hunters were more constrained to work as a group within sight or calling distance of each other. No chiefs had the right to have their children inherit their power. So the low level of technology enforced a rough equality of power and wealth.

In turn, the social institutions of the extended family, education by the family, news exposure within the family, and magical ceremonies within the family all tended to reinforce and support the economic institutions of cooperation among family members.

Social Institutions and Ideology

The extended family was not only an economic institution, but was also the most important social institution. As described in detail above, living within the extended family meant that it constituted one's early training and conditioning, education, exposure to news, and religious experiences. No wonder that the family dominated one's ideology and behavior. In similar isolated communal groups living today, the prime importance of the extended family is perhaps the most important idea or ideology in every individual's mind—the family is everything.

This potent ideology of the all-important family lasted for thousands of years. It was taken for granted and almost never questioned. Everyone agreed that the extended family was the proper and only possible economic institution. Therefore, this ideology was very powerful and went unchallenged. The ideology of the importance of the family helped shape the way this society behaved in every aspect of life.

The group was collectivist in its thinking, meaning that it was taken for granted that everyone must work together just to survive. Expulsion from the group usually meant death. The collectivism was not an outlook thought up by philosophers or politicians. Rather, the collectivism of the family was a result of dire economic necessity as the only way the group could survive.

For people in that era, economic necessity meant having enough food and shelter. Economic necessity shaped the main communal institutions, such as working together. Economic necessity also shaped their ideology, the idea that it is good to have cooperation in the extended family. Then that ideology of cooperation became a powerful force holding the group together for tens of thousands of years.

It was noted that the work that women did was roughly equal to that of men in importance to the survival of the family. It is no surprise that this experience was reflected in the myths that portrayed men and women as roughly equal. There were no sexist myths about the inferiority of women. Economic necessity and institutions shaped this egalitarian ideology of men and women, but those ideas of equality then shaped the democratic institutions for eons.

Technology and Ideology

The small labor force meant that everyone knew everyone else extremely well and made the ideology of cooperation seem natural. The simple stone tools produced little envy for the wealth of others. Other people had very little except their tools and ornaments.

Moreover, the use of the same simple tools for eons meant that people came to think that this way was the only way that things could be done. After a long time, people trust these tools and ways of doing things and they come to distrust any change.

These ideas—forming a strong ideology—reinforced habits and formed rigid traditions. But one should not assume that the belief that there should be no change in technology was merely a superstitious impediment to progress. Rather, for tens of thousands of years, it represented reality and the best available wisdom. Prehistoric communal people did not look for brand-new technology, but they did spend much time learning how best to use the technology they had. It was this belief in the unchanging technology that pushed them to do their best with what they had. You and I could not shape stone tools as well as they did without years of practice.

In the prehistoric communal period of technology, which covered most of human existence, most myths had to do with nature. Nature was at the center of their lives. Nature was dangerous and full of surprises to prehistoric peoples. So their myths had to do with gods who were embodied in animals, fire, water, thunder, and lightning. Some of these myths encouraged magic rituals to accomplish goals. If a wise person correctly portrayed a mastodon in a magic ceremony consisting of song or dance or pictures, then the band might control it and kill it without losing members of the family. So myths about nature helped to give confidence to the whole band. These myths also served to reinforce the power of those who seemed to know the most about "spirits," animals, the weather, and other mysteries.

Art often meant pictures of the animals, or dances depicting the animals, because that was part of the magic to control them. Science consisted of accumulated detailed knowledge of nature plus magic. In short, all of their ideology helped unify the family and helped it operate successfully for thousands of years. At the same time, the economic and political environment of the extended family, along with the level of the technology, helped shape their ideological views.

Economic Institutions and Ideology

The communal economic institution—consisting of the extended family, along with cooperation and collective action by all—lasted for at least 90 percent of the time that homo sapiens has existed and over 99 percent of the time since the first hominids came out of the trees. As noted earlier, it was not planned by philosophers, but was pure economic necessity, since people could not survive alone. Not only the ideology of the extended family but also the ideology of cooperation and collective action by all were taken for granted. Any dissenter was handled harshly. Although the ideology at first represented necessity, it came to be a habit of thinking, and then a rigid tradition.

13

The ideas of cooperation and collective action within the extended family did tend to hold back progress, but they were not silly ideas. Remember that this belief in cooperation and collective action was what allowed the society to survive for countless ages and was the glue that held it together. Since these ideas were vital to survival under these circumstances, any other social ideas (a different ideology) would have led to societies that would not have survived and would not have reproduced. Thus, their ideological beliefs helped to enforce the unchanging technology, as well as the economic, social, and political institutions that lasted for most of human existence.

Conclusion

This chapter showed how the four categories of technology, economic institutions, social institutions, and ideology are a useful tool to examine human societies. Their interaction in prehistoric communal societies explained why those societies survived. Yet their interaction also explained why these societies did not change for an incredibly long time.

Suggested Readings

All of the facts in this chapter are discussed in detail in the suggested readings. This section does not provide the latest books and articles for specialists. Rather, the suggested materials provide the reader with some books that will be easy to read, useful, and in some cases fun to read. None are obscure or difficult books that would interest only specialists. A few more difficult books are identified as advanced or scholarly, so the reader is warned. The same approach—expanding the facts in interesting and pleasant books or articles—will be used in all the Suggested Readings sections in this book. Note that all citations in the text are partial, but full citations are in the References at the end of the book.

Early communal societies are beautifully, but precisely, described in Jared Diamond, *Guns, Germs, and Steel* (1997). A good introduction to the geological evolution of the Earth is Edmund Blair Bolles, *The Ice Finders: How a Poet, a Professor, and a Politician Discovered the Ice Age* (1999), which is very pleasant reading. A book that explains the disappearance of the dinosaurs and reads like a detective novel is Walter Alvarez, *T Rex and the Crater of Doom* (1998).

There are hundreds of books on Darwin and evolution, but by far the best is Stephen Jay Gould, *Ever Since Darwin* (1977). Gould was one of the best writers in science. A scholarly collection of articles on the role of women in prehistoric societies is by Frances Dahlberg, editor, *Woman the Gatherer* (1981).

The entire history of writing on social evolution, including Suggested Readings focusing on anthropology, is presented briefly in the Appendix.

– 2 –

From Communal Equality to Slavery in the Middle East

This chapter tells the story of social evolution from the earliest communal societies to the first complex, class-divided civilizations.

How Communal Ideology and Institutions Led to Improved Technology

The technology available to early communal societies was shaped by the prevailing ideology, economic institutions, and social institutions. Even after Homo sapiens became the clear winner among various types of humanoids about a hundred thousand years ago, little or no technological change occurred during the next eighty or ninety thousand years.

As we saw, the basic economic institution was the extended family; the dominant ideology said that the technology could never change; and the way of life in fact did not change. These facts perpetuated a tradition that no change was possible and that no change was good. As a result, for tens of thousands of years, people with about the same brain capacity as you or I kept on using crude stone tools, gathering fruits and vegetables, and hunting, just as their ancestors had done.

Although the same economic techniques were used for eons, the human institutions were different than the animal ways had been. Humans made tools and used them in their food gathering and in their hunting. Language and speech were also very important differences between humans and other animals. Over thousands of years, people learned a great deal about tools, plants, and animals. Therefore, in spite of very traditional societies, imperceptible changes crept into their tool making, hunting, and gathering.

Eventually, after a very long time, human institutions and ideology allowed humans to make three great discoveries, all somewhat linked together. The three great discoveries were better tools, the invention of agriculture (farming and herding), and the invention of effective pottery. All three together were called the Neolithic revolution.

When and where did the Neolithic revolution begin? As a very broad generalization, one can say that it began around 10,000 B.C.E. (Before Common Era, that is, before year 1 of our present calendar) in the Middle East. But the details are complex and there is much controversy over it. There is some evidence that a few crops were planted in Syria and Palestine as early as 13,000 B.C.E., and a little later in Mesopotamia, especially around the Euphrates River in Iraq. But it was several thousand years later before there was full-scale farming.

In China, probably independently, there is evidence of some planted crops as early as 11,000 B.C.E. Full-scale farming in China, however, started thousands of years later. The only other independent beginning of agriculture was far later in Central and South America, with the potato coming from the Andes and corn (or maize) from Mexico. The Neolithic revolution—including new and better stone tools and pottery, as well as agriculture—spread from these three areas. From the Middle East it spread east into India and west into Africa and Europe. The Neolithic culture moved all around the Mediterranean and then slowly up the Danube, but took thousands more years to spread west to the Atlantic.

How exactly did this long process unfold in the areas where it began? First, the crude stone tools were improved very, very slowly over thousands of years. Eventually, Homo sapiens developed easier and more consistent techniques for making tools. They also figured out how to improve tools in many ways, such as making them with sharper cutting edges. Although this does not sound like much, most anthropologists consider it a revolution. It was a revolution from the Old Stone Age to the New Stone Age. The move from the Old Stone Age to the New Stone Age did bring major results in increasing productivity in hunting and food gathering, but also helped strengthen the possibility of new and different economic activities.

In a few exceptionally favorable environments, especially some river valleys in the Middle East, China, and the Americas, a very simple sort of agriculture emerged. Agriculture consists of both farming and herding, so we must follow the story of how food gathering changed to farming, and then how hunting changed to herding.

The revolution in the human way of life from food gathering to farming was very slow because it included many stages, such as weeding around favored plants, protecting the plants from other animals, and learning how and when to plant crops. All of this human activity eventually, over thousands of years, changed the environment of these plants and resulted in their genetic modification by natural and human selection. Therefore, different dates are given for the coming of farming, not only because of different evidence, but also because it matters exactly which point in the process you are trying to date.

The Middle East, China, and the Americas had fertile river valleys and just the right plants for a transition to farming. So climate, distribution of easily domesticated plants and animals, and geography played a big role in determining which locations would make the change from food gathering to farming. It also appears that geography helped determine the areas to which farming spread as people and news disseminated from the original areas. Europe and Asia really form one big continent, with nothing blocking the way of communication, except distance, mountains, and deserts that people went around. Thus, farming spread along the entire latitude from the Middle East to India (and perhaps China) in one direction and to northern Africa and southern Europe in the other.

Farming in North and South America began with severe disadvantages compared with the Middle East. For instance, the alpaca and llama of the Inca civilization in Peru were far inferior beasts of burden and of nourishment than were the cattle, sheep, goats, pigs, and horses found in Eurasia. Similarly, the corn (or maize) of Central America was more difficult to cultivate and nutritionally inferior to the wheat, sorghum, and rice of Eurasia.

To further complicate matters, the spread of knowledge of farming by the movement of ideas from one village to another (called diffusion) was much more difficult in the Americas. The narrowness of Central America made a blockade between North and South. Apparently, plant domestication and civilizations appeared independently in both North and South America. Another blockade to diffusion of farming was that spreading farming practices to the North or South was much more difficult than spreading farming practices to the East or to the West. The reason is that the weather changes from North to South, so the agriculture that works in one latitude may not work in another.

Thus, geography played an important role in determining the location of the earliest farming and the directions of its spread. Of course, geography remains an important part of the story of institutional change. Geography, however, is mostly a constant factor because the geography of mountains and continents has hardly changed in the past ten thousand years, except for human-made ecological disasters. Therefore, after the beginning of farming, further changes in institutions must be explained mostly by factors other than geography.

It was observed that the transition to farming did not happen overnight, but took thousands of years. The details of the scenario seem to have been something like this. When women did their age-old activity of gathering fruits and vegetables, they sometimes pulled the weeds to allow certain plants to grow that they especially favored. Eventually they learned how new plants came from the old, so they could even plant new ones if they wished. When women learned how to plant their favorite fruits and vegetables and protect them from weeds or from other gatherers, they were then practicing the beginnings of farming. Moreover, human processes, such as harvesting techniques, influenced the genetics of plants. For example, if you collect the seeds of native grasses, chances are you are selecting seeds that tend to stay on the stalk longer. Thus, if you replant them, you are selectingfor those varieties of grasses.

With the simple stone tools, or even the improved ones, farming was very difficult, with low productivity. Nevertheless, the earliest farming meant an enormous increase in the food supply as well as the certainty of that supply. Using jars from newly developed pottery, people could put more food away for winter to prevent starvation in cold climates. Also, it meant that people became more dependent on these labor-intensive crops instead of what grew wild.

People ate all the grains, such as wheat, oats, barley, and rice, but also sugar. Later, in the great cities of the slave empires, while the elite ate meat, the grains and sugar were fed to the masses of servile people. (Much, much later, sugar played an important role in the industrial revolution of the nineteenth century. See Mintz, *Sweetness and Power,* 1986.)

Since women had most of the burden of gathering fruits and vegetables, they developed most of the earliest farming techniques and became most of the earliest farmers. Men, however, did most of the hunting and therefore had the main role in developing the techniques of herding animals. The process of changing from hunting to herding took a very long time. A number of steps were involved and these happened very gradually over thousands of years. First, men learned to follow a herd as it moved. Next, they had to fight off other predators. After that, men had to find ways to tame a herd. Finally, men had to find ways to keep the herd in some area where they wanted it to be. When men became herders, they increased the food supply greatly. These herders now produced far more food than the same number of hunters had produced.

When farming and herding became the dominant way of life for society, productivity increased dramatically. So it is reasonable to describe this process as the first agricultural revolution. As we shall see, this revolution had several effects, helping to change the productivity of labor, division of labor, the size of the population, and the economic institutions.

From Collective Labor to Division of Labor

In the early communal period, everyone worked together. The women collectively did most of the plant gathering, while men collectively did most of the hunting. Except between men and women as a whole, there was no division of labor and no specialists doing separate tasks. This resulted in very low productivity. Productivity is defined here simply as the product per worker. Productivity thus means the amount that each person is able to make and bring to the table.

The agricultural revolution in farming and herding changed all of this and greatly increased productivity. When the herding and farming increased productivity, people could produce a surplus over immediate food needs. So it became possible to have some people specialize in certain tasks. The specialists could be fed with the surplus food in exchange for their talents. Those people who specialized in tool making further improved the efficiency of tools and weapons. As tools improved, the productivity of farming and herding improved. So this was a cumulative process, with the surplus from agriculture allowing specialization in tool making, while better tools in turn helped agriculture.

Division of labor affected many other processes. For example, some people could now specialize in making pottery, while others could specialize in weaving. In the construction of buildings, specialists from many crafts could work together to do things much faster than before. The reason for the improvement was that each knew their craft better than any one person could have known all the crafts.

Higher productivity also meant that some people could specialize in mathematics, astronomy, accounting, healing, or even fortune telling. This was the beginning of intellectual specialization. Most of the intellect workers were employed by the elite and justified every action of the elite. Therefore, it was also the beginning of specialists in ideological propaganda in the service of those who had vested interests in the new society.

From Nomads to Big City Dwellers

Farming meant that people would end their nomadic existence, at least for a year or two at a time, to harvest the crops they had sown in a particular place. Some people still roamed the countryside between the time of planting and the time of harvesting, but more and more chose settled living. The tendency to a settled existence gave more stability to their economy.

It should be noted that people did not just choose to go into agriculture. One reason for leaving hunting in favor of agriculture in many areas was over-hunting and the extinction of game. This cannot be proven, but it is a fact that most of the larger animals disappeared at about the same time that humans began to live in North America. Most of the large animals also disappeared at the same time as humans appeared in Australia.

The higher productivity of agriculture meant that there could be a far larger population per square mile than in the old hunting and food-gathering societies. Greater population density meant that people began to live in villages. Over the centuries, villages became small towns and towns became large cities. The economic unit grew from the small band to the large tribe to entire empires.

How New Technology Undermined Communal Institutions and Led to the Rise of a Transitional Economy

The rising productivity of agriculture, including farming and herding, slowly undermined the old economic institutions of collective production in an extended family. Not only did the higher productivity lead to more population and growth of towns, but it also led to the first small accumulations of goods and wealth. Eventually, it led to economic inequality between rich and poor. The division between rich and poor was followed by political inequality between the powerful and the powerless.

There was, however, no overnight jump from the collective governance of the small communal economy to the wealthy slave owners, kings, and emperors of later times. Rather, those who had more wealth slowly gathered more economic and political power. Eventually, these differences between people made obsolete the old communal band of brothers and sisters working in solidarity in collective activities.

A transition began toward an economy with more private ownership, more specialists, division into rich and poor, and division into ruled and rulers. All of these are discussed below.

From Collective to Private Ownership

In the transitional period, some activity was still collective, but some now became private. As a few people amassed more private wealth, while others remained poor, the differences in affluence also led to differences in influence. At the same time, the population of the economic unit grew from dozens to hundreds and then to thousands. The larger population meant that some governing body had to make decisions.

Those with a good reputation for leadership, as well as enough money to employ warriors, took political power. In the old system, people might become temporary leaders of hunting groups if they showed merit, or a temporary leader of the food gathering group if they showed excellence in that occupation. But now there were permanent chieftains for tribes of thousands. And these chieftains usually managed to have their sons inherit their power. This was shown in detail for the Middle East in Diamond (1997). So far the story is one of widening differences in economic wealth and widening differences in political power. After a while, the chieftains could tell the people: "I direct, and you do as I say." Usually, the same people held both wealth and power. Yet this was still a fluid situation. There was not one class that owned all the wealth and another that worked for it under some kind of coercion. The differences began very gradually with no class system set in concrete. There may have been inheritance of the rule in one family, but others could aspire to a higher level.

Moreover, as was shown by traditions, myths, religious stories in later tribes with writing, and even in the traditions of the early Roman republic, there was still a view among many that equality is a good thing and the tribe should return to it. There were many conflicts between those holding to the old principles of equality and those who now wanted individual power. Those who advocated equality were for a return to the old ways. The advocates of equality often struggled long and hard, but they lost to those with power in the class-divided civilizations that survived.

From Skirmishes to War

In the early communal period, there was communal ownership of land and communal production of food, but there was barely enough food to eat and few personal goods to own. In the transitional period, there was wealth in the form of buildings, belongings, fertile land for farming, and herds of animals. This wealth meant that it was profitable to raid a village or town for loot. Since that had not been true earlier in the communal period, war had not shown its ugly face. There had only been brief skirmishes over hunting land and brides for marriage alliances. When, however, there was wealth to be gained by conquest, there were significant wars.

From Communal Equality to Slavery

Wars meant not only looting any wealth that could be moved or taking over fertile land, but also taking prisoners. A prisoner in the early communal period could not produce a surplus of food beyond his or her own needs, so the prisoner was useless as a slave. Therefore, the prisoner was either killed or integrated into the group. There were a few extremely rare cannibal groups, who ate their prisoners. Within the band, there was solidarity and equality, but hostility toward other bands occurred in squabbles over hunting grounds or brides.

With a higher productivity of farming and herding in the transitional period, a prisoner could produce a surplus. Therefore, great humanitarian progress was made by ending the killing of prisoners—and ending the occasional cannibalism. Higher productivity also meant, however, that the winning side found it profitable to make slaves of prisoners of

23

war. The slaves worked for their masters. They produced a surplus, which could be eaten by their masters. Was the old situation of approximate equality with very low productivity and killing of prisoners better or worse than the new situation of much higher productivity, vast inequality, and the cruelty of slavery? All we can say is that this was the path of change in some areas. It illustrates the fact that one cannot assume that change produces a "better" society.

For better or worse, the new technology and higher productivity of agriculture meant the final end of the early communal economic and social institutions. (Only a few isolated small-scale societies never changed from their hunting and gathering technologies.)

There was no longer merely some inequality among farmers or herders as in the transitional economy. Now, some people owned slaves and some did not. Moreover, there was now a class of people who were slaves. Thus, the community became differentiated into permanent classes of top dogs and underdogs. As differences arose over economic rank, the old bonds of the extended family frayed and became far less important than class divisions. There were now dominant classes and subordinate classes and innumerable subclasses.

Masters and Slaves

In some areas, such as ancient Greece, the largest subordinate class was the slave class. This group was given little to eat, bits of clothing, dirty and cramped shelters. They worked for the benefit of the master class from dawn till dusk. The master class had agricultural slaves to produce a large surplus over the immediate needs of the estate, so they had profits on which to live in luxury. In addition, the estate owners had domestic slaves to cater to their every whim. The slaves did the cooking, made the clothing, minded the children, and were forced to fill the sexual needs of the male masters.

It is important to understand, however, that these were not simple two-class societies, but rather very complex ones. Even at the beginning of class-divided societies there were other types of forced laborers, sometimes more numerous than slaves. There were many kinds and degrees of forced or subordinate labor, some very onerous and some with a lighter burden. For example, some laborers were not owned in body as the slaves were, but had to give service to a master a certain number of days per year. In Western Europe, slavery was the dominant form of labor in ancient societies, but other types of forced labor became the dominant form in medieval, feudal societies.

In addition, the masters also employed free workers, including warriors to fight, craftspeople to make things, and officials to collect taxes. Kings also made sure that the priests in their employ emphasized the major religious belief of the time that kings were gods or sons of gods, thus upholding their right to power. Beneath the master class and their employees were the slaves, who could now produce enough—due to higher productivity of farming and herding—to provide gourmet food, sumptuous clothing, and luxurious shelter for the master class, as well as food, clothing, and shelter for the underlings of the master class.

The population of the economic and political unit moved from hundreds to thousands to hundreds of thousands, ruled by a king and nobility. All of this was due to the greater productivity of herding and farming, the use of vast numbers of slaves, and the division of labor into many specialties. For example, some artisans made maps, while others made saddles. Each specialist was far more proficient in his or her specialty than earlier unspecialized workers had been.

While the rough equality and solidarity of the early communal period was destroyed, the community was maintained and enlarged. It was, however, a very different kind of community, with new social and political institutions. Some now could exert more influence than others. And some could become specialized as leaders and rulers.

The old hunting and gathering band with rough equality in an extended family, and even its last vestiges in the transitional tribal society, vanished. But it did not go without a struggle. People who had not acquired wealth and slaves preferred the old communal institutions. But Pandora's box had been opened and there was no way to close it. As farming and herding became a fact, they allowed far greater profitability to those with slaves, so the owners of slaves slowly acquired more wealth and power. Soon, society had its rulers and its ruled.

There also emerged a class of independent farmers. At the end of the transitional period, the class of independent farmers was quite large in most places, but their numbers declined for reasons we shall see below. Usually, such independent farmers became a small minority in class-divided societies.

In Greece and Rome, the independent farms tended to die out for several reasons. First, there was competition from large plantations with slaves. Second, the men from the independent farms were often drafted into the army for long periods of time. Third, the independent farmers sometimes had to pay considerable taxes, but they did not have enough money to pay the taxes while they were in the army. The ruling group was forced to draft independent farmers into the army because the slaves would not fight for their masters, so this was the only way to raise an army. Since many soldiers lost their farms to pay taxes, this policy eventually lowered the number of free farms.

Greece and Rome were mainly slave societies, but in the cities they also had workers who were not formally subservient. These workers were free to produce and sell their goods and services at any price they could get. Because of the dominance of slave workers, independent workers could ask only low prices and therefore usually remained very poor. In Rome, they were given some free bread at times and they were also given free entertainments, called circuses, to keep them happy. These circuses were grisly affairs in which men killed each other or killed animals or were killed by animals.

Women: From Equals to Pieces of Property

In the early communal society, men and women were generally in rough equality, but that changed markedly with the introduction of slavery. Women were clearly subordinate in Greek and Roman society. The basic reason was that men had been the warriors, so the prisoners of war belonged to them. As slaves became important, the status of the men who owned them also rose. They became masters of people in the economy, and their economic power and wealth allowed them to become rulers of the society. Only men above a certain level of wealth could become members of the Roman Senate.

Men used the slaves primarily in agriculture. This was no longer the light agriculture begun by women and conducted by women for a very long time. This was new agriculture with much better and heavier implements that could now be made. These heavy plows required either slaves or animals such as oxen to pull them. Since men were also the herders, they naturally took control of the animals as well when these animals were used in agriculture. As men came to dominate production under slavery, they also came to dominate women.

Gender Myths and Slavery

The institutional structure was one in which men ruled slaves and slaves produced wealth. Women were said by myths to be inferior in order to rationalize their subordinate position. Furthermore, to pass on private property in ancient Rome, it was important to determine a legitimate heir. This was done by prohibiting women of the ruling class from having sex freely with men other than their husbands. Hence the law prohibited such sex by women of the ruling class. If a ruling class woman had sex with a slave, she was punished in various ways, while the death penalty was used against slave men. Ruling class men could have sex anywhere they found it without punishment, but husbands used every possible way to prevent their wives from having sex with other ruling class men.

As a consequence, myths and legends that became popular were about the wonders of virginity and abstinence from extramarital sex by women, though not by men. It was in this way that a double standard for sexual behavior arose, in which women were severely restricted to monogamous marriage, but men could do as they pleased. Thus, the social mores and beliefs completely changed from the rough equality of the communal period as the new subordination of women emerged.

Under the laws of the Roman slave society, a woman who was the daughter of one of the master class was completely under the control of her father; she had no rights of her own no matter how old she was. When she got married, control was transferred to her husband; she still had no rights of her own. Women of the slave class belonged to their master. So the slave women suffered under a double burden. She was exploited as a worker who was paid no money and had no rights, but she was also exploited sexually by her master.

Technology and Division of Labor

The new agriculture was highly productive compared with the earlier light agriculture. With the new agricultural productivity, more specialists were possible because of the surplus of food. Thus, there were specialists in tool and weapon making, who were able to greatly improve the tools and weapons of Rome. It is interesting that these specialists were often slaves. Then there were police and soldiers to guard all the new wealth. The police and soldiers also had to keep the slaves under control. They intimidated the slaves with terror and ruthlessly put down all slave uprisings.

There was also a class of priests, whose job was to advocate religion and lead religious practices. Priests, like soldiers, were paid out of the agricultural surplus by the ruling elite because the elite found these priests to be very useful. In some religions, such as the ancient Egyptian, the priests declared that the ruler was himself a god and could do no wrong. Mark Twain once observed that in every war, the priests on both sides declared that their side is morally superior and racially superior to the other side. Thus, each side can call on God to help them kill their enemies. Twain even wrote a satire called "The War Prayer," in which a priest prays to God to kill all of his people's enemies.

Later, in the feudal period of Europe, priests declared that kings were divinely appointed by God, so everyone should obey them. During the American slave period, Southern clergy said that slavery was divinely ordained, while Northern clergy declared that God and morality demanded the abolition of slavery. Religion has often played a positive role in society. For example, sometimes religion was the only source of education. Religion also often played an ideological role in favor of retaining the existing institutions or in favor of revolution against the existing institutions.

Government and Slavery

The change from communal to slave economies meant a big change in government. There was no separate government in the earliest communal period, only decisions by the leading members of the family. Sometimes someone was chosen temporarily to lead the groups in hunting or food gathering. After the Neolithic revolution, there was a long transitional period in government with increasing power going to chiefs. The eventual result was the emergence of a large, strong government with a slave economy. One task of government was to protect private property, especially property in slaves, by using force to control slaves and put down their revolts.

In addition to starting wars to acquire more slaves, as well as repressing the subservient classes and stopping bloody slave revolts, large governments were needed for the expansion and growth of the entire community. For example, in fertile river valleys, such as the Nile, the government had to control irrigation schemes, build dams or other means to control flooding, and establish laws for orderly landholding after a flood. But even these community service functions often had a class angle as well. For example, the Nile was controlled in ways that satisfied the landowner class, but paid no attention to the interests of the slaves.

The group that was governed was now far larger than a family. Although family interests were important for each individual, the ties that held the elite together in the governing system were mainly economic interests, not family ties. Of course, in Egypt and later in Rome, the close family of the ruler was on a much higher level than the families of the other nobility.

In the early communal society, the community as a whole decided on the use of force against an individual in the community or against outsiders. They made harsh but relatively democratic decisions. In a slave society, such as ancient Rome, the use of force was monopolized by the ruling elite of the master class. The use of force had to be authorized by the government, but that government was made up exclusively of the master class and contained no slaves. For most of its existence, the powerful Roman Senate had legal restrictions for membership that required a level of wealth attainable only by a small group. Since much wealth was in slaves, they had a common interest in repressing the slaves.

Economic Institutions Under Slavery

The surplus produced by the slaves in agriculture and herding was used not only for the luxury living of the master class, but also to employ all kinds of specialists, including police, judges, and soldiers to uphold the government. The government also employed scribes to record taxes as well as to write stories about kings' victories. This propaganda in favor of the kings was among the first uses of writing.

Once metal tools were invented, the master class employed craftspeople to make weapons, jewelry and other ornaments, pots for food, and pipes to carry water. This division of labor into many narrow specialties further increased productivity. There was now enough productivity to build large palaces and other monuments and to construct large cities. Although technology did not progress rapidly, the existent technology was used ingeniously to bring many comforts to the homes of the elite. The homes of the poor, by contrast, were tiny in size, lacked running water, plumbing, and other conveniences.

Such civilizations, based on slave labor and the labor of other subservient classes, with specialists and division of labor, with heavy agriculture and large cities, and with craft production, all followed the emergence of agriculture. Thus, they probably arose first in Mesopotamia. From there, they spread to Egypt, Greece, Rome, and then to most of Europe. This type of agricultural society also evolved independently in China, and much later, in Central and South America among peoples such as the Aztecs, Mayas, and Incas.

To support such societies on an ideological basis, even philosophers, such as Aristotle, proclaimed that it is natural for some people to be slaves and some to be masters, while it is also natural for women to be subservient to their fathers and husbands. It should be noted that philosophers received their living from the male nobility, who took it from the surplus produced by the slaves.

There was also a change in the ethical values of people after communal life changed to slavery. Under early communal conditions, solidarity was vital, so the highest ethical value was working for the good of the whole group of men, women, and children. In class-divided societies, it is every man for himself and woman's duty is to support her man without asking questions.

Since some people had more wealth, others envied them. The way of life of the elite was copied as much as a person's resources allowed it. The laws, however, did not allow the subordinate classes to look exactly like the elite, so there were severe penalties for adopting too much of the dress code of the elite.

Traditions, however, remained a long time after their basis had disappeared. So in early Greek and Roman society, there were remnants of tales about the good old communal life and tales of heroism in its favor. But most of the Romans in the later days of the empire came to have a completely individualist view, which claimed that only their own welfare counted.

Racist Myths in Slavery

The ancient Romans had conquered much of the known world and considered themselves superior to everyone else. They thought of the Germans as ignorant barbarians, while the Greeks were thought to be soft and decadent. The Romans made slaves of all the groups under their control. The case of the Greeks was most ironic, since they had previously considered themselves to be superior to all the surrounding peoples. The Romans used Greek slaves for much of white-collar labor, from accounting to artistic works.

The ideology of racial superiority was very useful to the master class, first in Greece and then in Rome. Racism is defined as the ideology that one group is superior by birth to another group. Racism meant that the masters felt it was perfectly proper and legitimate to enslave other peoples. Racist ideology was so powerful that some of the slaves were also convinced of their inferiority. And racism meant that free Roman farmers felt that slavery was proper and supported it. Because of prejudice, free Roman farmers continued to support slavery even though slave plantations began to out-compete the independent farms and those farms often went bankrupt. The free Roman farmers were the backbone of the Roman army for a long time, so their loyalty to the Roman state was very important. Racism helped to cement that loyalty.

The masters had a vested interest in the racist myth that the slaves were inferior beings, so they reinforced it by every means possible. The priests of the early religions in Rome preached that the Romans were superior to all others. The philosophers of the ancient world all said that slavery was inevitable and natural; even the great Aristotle argued that proposition. The politicians, such as the Roman Senators, stated in their speeches to the poor population of Rome that they were superior to all other peoples. Therefore, the poor should support the Roman state in its battles with others.

Slavery and Myths of Divinity

In ancient Egypt, there was slavery, so a strong government was needed to prevent slave rebellions. A strong government was also needed to fight with other governments over slaves and ownership of land. The pharaoh was given absolute power and proclaimed to be the divine son of a god. This was done to make the government more powerful. Thus, this myth was strong support for the political and economic status quo.

In order to expand the belief within the context of the religious mythology of Egypt, it was decided to protect the immortal body and soul of the pharaoh by protecting him for eternity in a huge pyramid. The pyramids also added to the awesome and impressive might of the Egyptian government. In order to build the pyramids, thousands of slaves were used as cheap labor. Thus, the government's needs in a class society, the necessary religious myths, and the labor supply afforded by the class relations were all necessary to the building of the pyramids and the new technology that was developed during their creation.

Four Features of Slave-based Society

There are four main features common to the ancient slave-based societies of the Near East, Egypt, Greece, and Rome.

First, technology was based on tools made of bronze and other metals. Most economic activity was agricultural, including farming and herding. Land was divided into large estates of the elite, with massive slave labor forces on each estate.

Second, economic institutions consisted mainly of the use of slaves by masters, with the slaves producing a surplus exploited from them by their masters. The slaves worked mainly in agriculture, but also in domestic work and service work in the cities. There also existed every other conceivable type of unequal labor relations between the dominant group and the subordinate groups, including serfdom, sharecropping, and free worker contracts, all discussed later in this book.

Third, all of the social institutions supported slavery, from a priesthood that extolled slavery to an army and government that enforced it. Elite men were masters and elite women were subordinate to them. Slave women were exploited both sexually and for their labor.

Fourth, the dominant ideology strongly supported slavery, from the religious ideas to the philosophical arguments to the ideas stated by the politicians and the great orators. The ideology included racist prejudice against all foreigners, sexist prejudice against women, and elitist prejudice against all the subordinate groups that did the labor of society.

These four features are summarized very briefly in Table 2.1.

Summary of Steps from Communal Society to Slavery

First, the ideology, social institutions, and economic institutions of the early communal economy all held back rapid technological advance. Yet they were sufficient to promote extremely slow technological progress over tens of thousands of years. Eventually, the communal society pro-

Table 2.1

Four Features of Ancient Slave Society

Technology	Bronze and iron tools; farming and herding
Economic Institutions	Slaves work; masters take product
Social Institutions	Rule by masters in all social institutions
Ideology	Racism. Sexism, Elitist Prejudice

duced new, better stone tools; changed from gathering fruits and vegetables to farming; and changed from hunting to herding.

Second, this new technology created the conditions for the emergence of slavery. The new technology of agriculture meant that people could produce a surplus above their own subsistence needs. The higher productivity of the new agriculture meant that there was some wealth to be conquered by war. War brought prisoners, who were enslaved. The heavy implements used in agriculture of that day were used by the slaves to produce a surplus large enough for their own needs, to support the luxury living of the masters, and to produce huge monuments (such as pyramids) and enormous cities.

Third, the new technology and new economic institutions, forced what was left of the old communal economy to change because it held back further progress. After a long transitional period of mixed communal and private ownership, the old system eventually disappeared and was replaced by slavery and other forced labor. The old ideology, with its ideas of community solidarity of all its members, was destroyed. Remnants of the old ideology lived only in folk tales. Communal political equality gave way to a transitional period of chiefs in large tribes. The tribes then gave way to empires, including very large cities with massive bureaucracies, police, and armies.

Men controlled the slaves in heavy agriculture, which was the main source of food. From their power gained by control of the slaves, men were able to exercise domination over women in society. The transition from early communal institutions, with roughly equal political and economic power among all adults, to slavery, with masters and emperors, led to many bitter struggles. These struggles were between those defending the doomed old communal institutions and those in favor of the new seemingly invincible and eternal slave institutions. Few of these conflicts were described in writing at the time. Writing and literature emerged only during the time of slavery, so the accounts of events were written by members of the master class from their own viewpoint and in their own interest.

In a nutshell, society created new technology. The new technology undermined existing economic institutions and created tensions in the society that could not be resolved peacefully. Some people resisted change, but in a long transition the struggle for change was won by the increasingly powerful master class. Thus, slavery—and other types of oppression—became dominant. This revolution took place over thousands of years, but in the end it changed all of human life.

Suggested Reading

We know much about slave civilizations from their own writing and also from archaeological evidence. The most pleasant and fascinating introduction to archaeology is *Gods, Graves and Scholars* by Ceram (1951). It deals with the exciting discovery of some slave civilizations, including Troy, ancient Egypt, and ancient Crete.

Many books in anthropology and archaeology deal with the transition from the rough equality of communal bands to the slavery of the ancient civilizations. The most wonderful to read, however, is Diamond, *Guns, Germs, and Steel* (1997), which is clear and up-to-date in its facts, but written in a popular style that fascinates readers.

– 3 –

From Slavery to Feudalism in Western Europe

This chapter explores how slavery ended and feudalism emerged as the dominant system in Western Europe.

Ruling the Roman Empire

The political structure of ancient Rome was closely entwined with the slave-based economy. For some time during the second and third centuries B.C.E., Rome was a republic. In the Roman republic, all of the male citizens, which did not include the male slaves, were equal at least in theory. For the minority who could vote, the forms of democracy existed. Later, after titanic struggles and civil wars, Rome became an empire with no democracy. There was an emperor who had most of the power plus a weak Senate composed mostly of the wealthiest slave owners.

Rome followed the same path as many other ancient peoples from small bands of hunters and gatherers into large tribes with powerful chiefs. Eventually, the most powerful tribes became city dwellers with a government that also ruled the surrounding areas. Finally, Rome conquered an empire. The empire was a collection of tribes, cities, and subordinate countries. In the transition from the communal societies, the ruler (chief, leader of the republic, emperor) gained ever more power with the change from temporary leader to hereditary chief, then to king of a city, and finally to emperor with absolute power over an enormous area.

The Roman Senate pretended to function independently for a long time after the republic died, but it surrendered most of its power to the emperor. In both the republic and the empire, the master class did all of the governing, while the slaves had no power.

When Rome was a republic with democratic forms, how could it justify the fact that the slaves had no rights? The answer was embedded in the racist view that slaves were only property, not people and not citizens. This racist view was embodied in all of the Roman laws. So even when there was a form of democracy in ancient Greece and Rome, the slaves, who were the majority of the people in much of this period, had no rights. Of course, women were also excluded from democratic procedures. This was a democracy of an exclusive small minority of elite, slave-owning males, who did all the ruling.

Slavery, Work, and Technology

In the early period of the ancient world of slavery, there was tremendous technological improvement beyond the technology that existed under early communal economic institutions. As spelled out in the previous chapter, when slaves could produce a surplus, that surplus supported all kinds of specialists as well as the master class. Specialization led to further technological development, the building of large cities and monuments, advances in astronomy, wonderful works of art, and a standardized and systematic legal system.

In the ancient slave civilizations, the specialists—who were often slaves—figured out excellent ways of improving life. All of those ways were used by the masters, so their homes were very comfortable places and had many conveniences. They had water piped to their houses and forms of central heating in many cases. The architecture was beautiful. Of course, the slaves were excluded from using most of the comforts of Roman life, even though they had produced it all.

In Western Europe, the Roman Empire and its institution of slavery disappeared in the fourth and fifth centuries C.E. (Common Era, that is, since year 1 of our calendar). The downward trend culminated in the fall of Rome itself to Germanic tribal invaders in 456 C.E. The decline, however, started much earlier. Later, we will discuss the circumstances that led to the decline of the Roman Empire.

There was very little industry in the Roman Empire, so agriculture was dominant and it remained the largest economic sector until the nineteenth century. Agriculture remained dominant even longer in many areas of the world. At the peak period of ancient Rome, 90 to 95 percent of the people worked in agriculture. Most of the agricultural workers were slaves on large plantations. In addition to the masters and the slaves, there were always free farmers in agriculture, though their numbers declined over time.

The cities were tiny islands in a sea of agriculture, yet the cities grew to be enormous and controlled mighty armies. The cities could do these things because they were supported by the surplus flowing from the vast countryside, as well as the labor of the slaves and the craftspeople in the cities. Rome seemed so powerful that people thought that the empire and slavery would last forever. What led to the decline and fall of the mighty Roman Empire?

The great wealth of Rome was all built by the device of slavery. The situation was very pleasant from the masters' viewpoint, though it was awful from the slaves' viewpoint. The problem was that slavery created barriers to further economic growth. Specifically, consider the following problems.

First, one reason for stagnation was the attitude and behavior of the master class. In the ancient Roman Empire the ruling elite did no manual work and often no white-collar work or even professional work, except to govern or lead armies. Slaves produced all of the food in agriculture. Slaves made custom clothing for their masters. Slaves prepared the food for their masters. Slaves were domestic servants, providing everything that was desired by the masters, including sex from the slave women. All heavy work was done by slaves. But also much intellectual work was done by slaves, such as accounting, supervising other slaves, or clerical work. Moreover, some slaves were professional artists, dancers, and musicians.

Since only slaves did actual production, the entire area of economic production came to be seen as a place for slaves. People at the very top of the elite ladder perceived anything associated with the dirty business of making money to be beneath them. The elite had supervisors who handled the slaves on their plantation and sent the profits to the masters in Rome. They had supervisors for every kind of labor as well as treasurers to take care of their money.

So the top elite looked down their noses at anyone who was interested in ways of improving production. With few exceptions, the elite took no part in science or technological improvement. This attitude was one of the reasons that the Romans, after a certain point in their history, did not produce much new technology, though they made advances in governing and war making.

Furthermore, slavery produced a sufficient surplus for all of the masters' needs without further changes in technology. Thus, many plantation owners lived in absentia in Rome. A great many of the plantation owners knew nothing about agricultural technology. Moreover, they usually had enough money that they did not have a driving compulsion about getting more profit from their estates. If they needed more money, in most cases they were more likely to make money through use of the government. For example, a rich Roman could become a colonial governor and loot their province of its surplus in various ways, both legal and illegal. For all of these reasons, the master class allowed technology to stagnate in the later Roman Empire.

A second reason for technological stagnation was that some of the early impetus to improvements came from the free farmers and the free artisans. But farms were slowly taken over by slave plantations as the men were drafted into the army for long periods of time or the taxes were increased beyond their ability to pay. The free artisans had to compete with slaves who were paid the most minimal subsistence and many of them went out of business. Thus, as slavery became more dominant, some of the groups who could have made more technological improvements were greatly reduced in numbers.

A third problem tending to cause stagnation was that the slaves also had little interest in technological innovation. A more productive technique would not have reduced the number of hours or the intensity with which they had to labor. Their hours and intensity of work were not affected because they were always pushed to the maximum, no matter what technology they used. So the slaves saw nothing for them in new technology and, as we shall see, often actively resisted it.

A fourth type of technological problem also resulted from the master-slave relationship. It was not profitable to give the slaves the expensive equipment necessary to increase production. If the slaves were given a large new device meant to improve their productivity, they acted against the introduction of the new technology. They acted this way for very rational reasons. For one thing, if the slaves could sabotage the equipment, this action would give them some rest time. As a stronger reaction, they could turn the new equipment into weapons in order to rise up and kill the masters. Therefore, putting a lot of money into developing new equipment made no sense.

Fifth, slavery meant that it was difficult or impossible to use a complex organization of work, such as many different crops in different fields. Slaves could only be effectively supervised if they all did the same work and if nobody was out of sight. But good agriculture required planting different crops and changing them from time to time. By planting just one crop to make supervision easy, the land eventually became exhausted. The less-productive land was another reason for stagnation with little or no growth.

Sixth, even for simple types of production, a large number of supervisors were needed to prevent slave revolts. The masters were always terrified at the prospect of slave revolts. In fact, the Roman Empire witnessed many small slave revolts at fairly frequent intervals, but there were also some massive slave revolts. During the slave revolt led by the gladiator Spartacus, the slaves defeated three Roman armies sent against them. When they were finally defeated, most of the slaves were crucified.

But if slaves did not get enough to eat and died at a young age, or if they were killed for revolting, or for attempts to escape, it meant that the supply of slaves was often insufficient. This problem became worse and worse over time. This was a vicious circle because the supply of slaves could only be drastically increased by new conquests. On the other hand, slavery weakened the empire, so it became more difficult to make conquests.

For all of these reasons, although slavery at first brought great advances over earlier methods of production, after a certain point was reached, productivity stagnated and output stopped rising. The fact that it was so much more productive than the earlier communal system allowed the system of slavery to last for hundreds of years. But the system of slavery had limits to its progress, which led it to stagnation and eventual fall to invaders.

Slavery and Military Power

In addition to the economic problems, another problem caused in various ways by slavery was the weakening of the army. Slaves could not be put in the army and given weapons because they could use them against their officers and lead even stronger revolts. So, at first, the Roman army was largely composed of free farmers. But, as noted above, the class of free farmers slowly declined. Farmers were forced to spend long years in the army and many were killed fighting. When a soldier came home after twenty years or more, his farm was gone, taken by the government for unpaid taxes, or sold to slave plantations. Even those who stayed home had to compete with the products of cheap slave labor, so a steady stream of free farms went bankrupt. When their owners could not pay debts, they often ended up as slaves themselves (see Anderson, 1974).

At any rate, this factor and others, such as increased corruption and lessened ability to pay the soldiers, weakened the army. Yet the threat of the surrounding Germanic tribes remained or grew as these tribes improved their weapons and strategy after contact with the Romans. These tribes were separate from each other, but were known collectively by the Romans as Germans or Goths. The tribes were all in various stages of the transitional period from equalitarian, communal societies to class-divided societies based on slavery or other kinds of unfree labor. At this period, they were led by chiefs, nobles, and priests, but the common people retained some rights.

After a while, in order to fill out the ranks of soldiers needed, the Romans hired some of the Germanic tribes as mercenaries. But one of their main jobs was to fight other Germanic tribes. They often had little desire to fight others like themselves, so the Roman army became less effective.

Moreover, at the same time that the army became filled with more mercenaries, the central power declined and it had fewer resources to pay the army. Thus various units decided to make money for themselves by taking extra amounts of taxes from conquered areas. Later, they even forced Roman plantations to pay for "protection." Paying for protection really just means paying someone not to attack you—so the army just agreed not to attack as long as this particular plantation paid money to the army.

As the army declined in power, the Germanic tribes advanced further into the relatively affluent empire. Even while the Germanic tribes advanced, the army generals perceived the weakness of the emperor. Therefore, some generals proclaimed themselves emperor. After ruinous civil wars, some of the generals became emperors, until they in turn were overthrown.

Eventually, law and order declined and only military might mattered. The empire was slowly dismembered and each little area became to some degree independent of the Roman emperor. In some areas, there were bands of armed slaves trying to survive. In some areas there were Roman legions looking for loot in any form available. In some areas, the Germanic tribes conquered the region. Eventually, in 456 A.D. even the city of Rome was taken and sacked by a Germanic tribal army, marking an advanced stage of decline.

From Slavery to Serfdom

Even though slavery had existed for many centuries, the decline of safety and productivity in the third and fourth centuries C.E. made slavery less appealing to the elite than other forms of subordination and exploitation. The Roman plantation owners wanted a workforce that would be less likely than slaves to revolt whenever there was an armed attack on the estate and more likely to help defend the estate. They also wanted a workforce that would be more productive than slaves, but would not need a great many supervisors with whips.

On many plantations, slaves were given a little more freedom and graduated to the category of "serfs." A serf is defined as someone who owes service to the lord for a certain number of days a year, but is given his or her own small amount of land for subsistence farming. The serf is bound to the land, must remain there, and belongs to whatever lord captures the land. The serf, however, cannot be bought and sold as a slave, so the serf's children cannot be sold to another master. The serf is subordinate, is exploited, and produces a surplus for the lord, but has somewhat more freedom than a slave.

During the decline of the Roman Empire from the third to the fifth century, some bankrupt free farmers also became subordinate to landlords. They were not called slaves or serfs and even continued to be called "free men" throughout their service, but they were subordinate to the lords and had to provide certain labor services. Serfdom meant varying degrees of subordination to the lord of the estate. There were varying obligations to perform work on the lord's land for a certain number of days a year, to give some kind of payment in goods or other services to the lord of the estate. Finally, a small percentage of slaves, continued to exist through most of the feudal period.

During the decline of the empire, exactly why did the Roman elite change from being slave masters to being lords of feudal estates with serfs? We saw earlier that they had two main goals in getting rid of slavery: more safety and more productivity. Not surprisingly, these were two main reasons why serfdom was attractive to the elite.

First, in economic terms the serf had some motivation to work and provide goods or services to the lord in return for possessing a piece of land. To possess land meant to have a degree of independence and economic stability. That possession, however, would only last as long as the serf worked for the lord, without additional compensation. The right of the lord to have those services or goods in return for letting the serf use some land was strictly enforced, not only by tradition and law but also by the use of force beyond the law. Each lord kept a group of armed men to hold down the serfs and force them to perform labor services.

A second reason why the masters were forced to change from the use of slavery to serfdom was a military one. If the estate or manor was attacked, slaves could seize the opportunity and revolt. Serfs, however, had some interest in the manor because they had their own small plots of land. Therefore, the serfs usually saw the attackers as a greater evil than their own feudal lord. Hence, the serfs could be more of a supporting group in a military defense or at least they were not likely to be another hostile group. So the serfs, under these chaotic conditions, proved to be both more willing to work and far more helpful, or at least less dangerous, in military situations than slaves.

Since the serf could not be bought or sold as a slave, and since the serf had a plot of land that might be enough to feed his or her family, the serf had some incentive to work on the lord's land and not revolt. Yet serfs were still exploited and spent most of their time producing for the lord. Serfs were held down by two mechanisms. First the lord employed his own soldiers who held the serfs down by force. In addition to the use of force, the lords used an ideology to convince everyone of the righteousness of what they were extracting from the serfs. They emphasized the idea that the lord was protecting the serf from roving armed bands.

This concept that the ideal way of life was for lords to protect and serfs to produce was part of the powerful role of tradition in the feudal period. The next chapter will discuss in depth the system of feudalism. Feudalism may be defined briefly as a system based on serfdom, where political power was mainly decentralized from kings to lords of estates, called feudal manors.

In addition to the Roman elite, parts of the empire were controlled by chiefs of Germanic tribes. As they gained wealth, they came to have more power over their followers. So they were attracted to the feudal scheme in which their leading followers became nobles and military supporters, while their less powerful followers became subordinate workers similar to serfs. Since this subordination was happening within their own ranks, it was also natural and convenient to make the conquered Romans or other peoples into serfs. Serfdom had the same economic and military appeal to the former tribal chiefs, who had now become feudal lords, as it had to the Roman elite.

Eventually, by different paths, all of Western Europe became a set of feudal manors, consisting of lords and serfs. There were also "free men" who were similar to the serfs, but with a few more rights. Trade and commerce had completely broken down, both because of economic stagnation and lack of any law and order. Thus, each feudal manor became isolated from the others in an economic sense. They each tried to be completely self-sufficient. Each became a small society isolated from all others.

The most powerful and ambitious lords became kings of large territories. The lesser lords, who owed them allegiance, retained complete power of law and control of all force within their own manors. They only agreed to give military support as necessary. The king was usually just a greater feudal lord, so the king had to raise all the revenues of the kingdom on his own estates.

Feudalism provided the possibility of more productivity from serfs than there ever was from slaves. The possibility of greater productivity, however, did not materialize for several centuries for other reasons. In the chaos of the decline of the Roman Empire, which had held Western Europe together as a unified area including much of the Mediterranean, the great Roman cities declined and some of them disappeared. Since the area was no longer a political unity, trade between distant places was no longer protected by the Roman army. Thus, trade declined for the next several centuries.

Moreover, the Roman level of technology was dependent on vast numbers of specialists available in each city. When the population centers mostly died, while travel became very risky, there were no longer all the needed specialists available in most places. In the isolated feudal manors, only a few types of specialists were usually present. Therefore, the level of technology also declined for centuries. These were rightly called the Dark Ages, penetrated by little "light." Ignorance and illiteracy dominated the scene as each lord tried to protect his own area and ruled over a system of subsistence production for his manor. The old centers of learning died as the Roman surplus disappeared and much knowledge of science was lost in Western Europe.

Conclusions on the Transition to Feudalism

The myth of "inevitable progress" in technology and in civilization was proven false in the fall of Rome. In the modern world, we often take technological progress for granted and think of it as inevitable. Actually, that has not been the case in many areas at various times. One example was the stagnation of technology in ancient Rome for several centuries. Moreover, there was an actual decline of technology in the Dark Ages, following the decline of the Roman Empire.

Rather than being inevitable, technological progress happens only when the social and economic institutions and the dominant ideology encourage it to improve. That was not the case in the late Roman Empire or the early feudal period. Slavery and all of its related institutions and ideology held back technology in the later Roman Empire. The chaos that followed the fall of the empire resulted in the isolation of each manor from all others. This caused a further decline of technology during the centuries of transition to the new institutions that followed.

One can see this in a striking way if one compares the Roman cities of Pompeii and Herculaneum that were buried by a volcano with the castles and villages of the feudal period. The Roman cities were filled with conveniences for the elite and with evidence of high culture and art works. The castles of early to middle feudalism were unpleasant, cold places to live, while the villages of the serfs lacked all amenities. The lifespan of the serfs was short and often miserable.

To summarize, the mechanism by which slavery was transformed to serfdom can be laid out in several steps. First, Roman economic institutions, the dominant Roman ideology, and Roman social institutions were permeated with slavery and its related effects. These institutions and ideology based on slavery resulted in technological stagnation.

Second, that stagnation created powerful tensions in Roman agriculture, Roman trade, and the Roman army. These tensions within the slave-based institutions of Rome were not solvable until slavery was ended and a new system of institutions created.

Third, the fact that the tensions could not be resolved within existing institutions led to the decline of Roman agriculture and weakening of the Roman army. This led to various types of social conflicts, class conflicts between masters and slaves seen in major revolts, as well as class conflicts in Rome between the aristocrats and the poor citizens. There were also ethnic conflicts between the Romans and surrounding Germanic tribes who saw an opportunity to conquer their old enemy. The conflicts between wandering groups of slaves, Roman legions, and Germanic tribal armies produced great insecurity in the economically weakened agricultural estates. These conflicts led to the fall of Rome, which meant that the benefits of the empire—common laws, maintained roads, shared currency, and a military to maintain order—vanished. This led to still lower technology and several centuries of decline. Finally, as a result of these conflicts, the system of feudalism was born, with isolated manors containing serfs, nobility, and armed retainers.

Suggested Readings

There are hundreds of books on the decline of the Roman Empire, but the best one, which deals with both the decline of slavery and the rise of feudal serfdom, is a book by Perry Anderson, *Passages from Antiquity to Feudalism* (1974). Anderson's book contains all of the factual knowledge and theoretical discussions relevant to this chapter. Although many earlier books on the issue have interesting things to say, Anderson includes the best of all of them and lays it out in a concise and readable manner.

– 4 –

From Feudalism to Capitalism in Western Europe

This chapter describes and explains the basic features of feudalism, then shows why it failed and how it was replaced by capitalism.

Four Features of Feudalism

Feudalism differed from the slave systems that preceded it in four major aspects. (1) Economic institutions. Most production on the manor was performed by serfs, while the feudal lords made all economic decisions and owned the product of all labor on the lord's land. (2) Social and political institutions. Power was decentralized from the king to the lords, so all legal, economic, and military power was held by the lord of the manor. Note that a large part of the land and the power was owned by the Church. (3) Technology. The level of technology fell in the early feudal period and rose slowly thereafter. (4) Ideology. The dominant ideas of this period include the divine right of kings and the subordination of women to men. The lord of the manor was supported by the inertia of tradition and sanction of religious teaching.

These brief descriptions of the four features are amplified in the rest of this section.

The economic institution of serfdom was based on the serf's working on the lord's land performing agricultural and other duties for a certain number of days per year. The serfs, however, could work on their own land the rest of the time.

The previous chapter showed that the feudal economic institution of serfdom originated in three different ways: Roman slaves were turned into serfs, Roman farmers were turned into near-serfs, and the common people of Germanic tribes became serfs. The Roman slaves became serfs partly because the landlord felt that the serfs would have a greater reason to defend the land than the slave. This meant that the serfs would be more likely to support their lord in an attack, rather than using it as an opportunity to revolt as the slaves did. The landlords also believed that the serfs would work with higher productivity than the slaves on the lord's land. The reason they might produce more was the threat that they could lose their own land.

The second source of feudal labor came from free Roman farmers. Unlike the serfs, the free Roman farmers remained technically free, but they were coerced to work for the feudal lord in return for the lord's "protection." This was a protection racket in which the lord gouged services and goods out of the peasant to "protect" them from other would-be "protectors," such as Germanic tribal kings. It was not clear, however, that the lords were any better than the tribal kings. In fact, it was clear in much of the feudal period that the most dangerous predator for the peasants were the feudal lords. It was only a fiction that the lords agreed to protect the peasants from other predators out of a sense of Christian duty. At any rate, the status of the "free" peasants on the lords' lands eventually became very similar to that of the serfs. (The relations of lords and serfs were very complex, as discussed more below; and, as is discussed in great detail by Robert Brenner in many articles, including his article in Aston and Philpin, 1985.)

The third source of feudal serfs was the free members of Germanic tribes. After the Germanic tribes had conquered parts of the Roman Empire, the ordinary members of the tribe slowly became mere subjects of their now-powerful chiefs, who soon began to call themselves kings. Eventually, the ordinary tribal members came to have a status similar to the serfs, though they could still technically be free. Both serfs and "free" persons on the estate owed services and/or goods to the lords, while the lords had all the military power to enforce these traditional duties. In brief, the first feature of feudalism, the economic institution of serfdom, had three sources of labor: slaves, free farmers, and Germanic tribal members.

The second feature of feudalism was its social and political institutions. The institutions of the feudal manor included the legal power of the lord to do as he pleased. The lord was typically a "he," although there were a few examples of manors under the management of ladies, rather than lords. Thus, the personal pronoun "he" is clearly the more typical one to use. He had both legal and economic power on his estate and commanded a large military force. So there was no practical difference between military command, political power, and economic power.

The lords used military force to control the serfs, as well as tradition and religious teachings. This meant that the lords could take their traditional dues and services, but could also demand arbitrary new dues. Usually, the extra dues were in the form of goods, which feudal law said was proper. The serfs, however, resisted the dues, sometimes by force, so the lord had to constrain his greed unless he wished to face a major backlash.

Although the lords competed bitterly among themselves, they usually united to put down peasant revolts, thus enhancing the power of each individual lord. For example, during the Reformation, the extensive peasant revolts in Germany were put down violently, with great cruelty and bloodshed. The peasant revolts adhered to religious sects to the left of Lutheranism that advocated equality of all men. Therefore, the Lutheran leaders supported brutal suppression of the revolts. At the time, such religious intolerance was considered normal. Thus, religion and tradition were powerful determinants of who did what in the feudal period. On the other hand, religion itself was shaped by feudal society and many feudal lords were part of the church hierarchy.

The level of technology fell for the first few centuries of feudalism after the fall of the Roman Empire. After that, it rose extremely slowly for the rest of the feudal period. There were many barriers to progress, but not quite as many as under slavery.

Dominant feudal ideas included the God-given right of kings and nobles to rule. Another dominant idea was the subordination of women to men. Both of these ideas were preached by the Catholic religion, the only form of Christianity in Western Europe during the early and middle feudal periods. The Catholic Church had a monopoly on religion, except for small groups of persecuted Jews and Muslims. Its leader, the Pope, had absolute power in the church and considerable power in society. The Catholic Church was the largest single landowner and treated its serfs about the same as did any other feudal lord.

The dictates of Catholic theology were supreme under feudalism, while science was considered subversive. Some scientists were burned alive

Table 4.1

Four Features of Feudal Society

Technology	Iron tools; very slow improvement
Economic institutions	Serfs work; lords take product
Social institutions	Rule by lords in all institutions
Ideology	Christian paternalism, sexism, and racism

for stating scientific ideas that conflicted with church doctrine. Even the great scientist, Galileo Galilei, was forced by the Catholic Church to cease his attempt to prove that the earth revolves around the sun.

The four main features of feudalism are summarized in Table 4.1.

Dynamic Relations of Feudalism

Some of the relationships among the processes of feudal society are obvious and some are not so obvious. First of all, each feudal manor had only one center of power, so the lord had both the political power and the economic power.

There was no separate political sphere in feudalism. Economics and politics were so closely interwoven that for most purposes it made no sense to try to separate them. The economic system worked in part because the lord enforced the services owed to him by the use of force. Of course, over the centuries, tradition came to play a big role. Serfs gave the traditional amount of service and lords demanded the traditional amount of service. Only in crisis situations were the traditions sometimes challenged or overthrown.

Religion also played a central role in feudal society. The church hierarchy was shaped to look like the secular hierarchy, which consisted of lesser nobles, greater nobles, and the king. In fact, the church not only looked like the feudal system, but also was part of it in very concrete terms. The church owned large estates in every country, which altogether added up to more land than was owned by anyone else by several magnitudes.

Each of the church estates was run the same way as any other estate. The church representatives who ran the estate used the services of serfs as did any other feudal lord. They also used soldiers to enforce their decisions as did any other feudal lord. As the feudal lords owed their allegiance to higher feudal lords, the representative of the church who

49

ran the estate owed allegiance to a bishop or other church authority. This system included monasteries and nunneries.

Not only was the church a great landowner, but it also was the main information center of society. It was the media, the schools, and the religious training center. One of its primary messages was that the feudal system was ordained by God, so all good Christians must obey the feudal laws and traditions. Thus the serf was told to serve the lord in all he asked the serf to do, while the lord was told to follow the wishes of the higher lords and the king.

There were few written laws, though many traditional rights, because the lord made all the decisions and enforced them by might. Each feudal lord, secular and religious, had his own court where the peasants had to come for justice. Of course, they had a good chance to get justice against another peasant, but had no chance against the feudal lord himself. Some feudal laws may seem very strange to people living in contemporary capitalist society. There was, in theory, no land ownership. The serf merely was able to use his or her land as long as he or she gave services to the feudal lord—but the serf never owned the land outright. Even the feudal lord had the right to use his land only so long as he served the greater lord above him. In theory, even the king did not own his land, but could use it only as long as he served God, who was the greatest landlord, and owned all the land.

Property "belonged" to the lord because he possessed it and defended it with his knights. There were no land title documents and most lords never even considered the possibility of selling a piece of their estate.

In early feudalism, the kings were merely the strongest lords, with no legal power on another lord's estate. In later feudalism, as kings became stronger, they appointed traveling justices who represented the king and presided over a system of courts. The peasant could in theory appeal the lord's decision to the higher justice of the king or a bishop. So there were traveling judges, representing kings or bishops. But one had to give gifts to these judges to be heard. And it was very unwise to bring a case against the lord, because the lord was often close friends with the judges.

Men, Women, and Feudalism

Peasant men, whether serfs or technically free, were subordinate to the feudal lord. Women were subordinate to the feudal lord, but they were also subordinate to male serfs to some degree. Men usually served the lord in the fields, doing heavy labor such as plowing and also herding animals. Female serfs did long hours of service to the lord in domestic tasks, especially in making clothing. The labor of the serf women included shearing sheep, preparing the wool, and sewing the finished garments. They also cooked for the lord, minded his children, and cleaned his house. When they finished the day's work for the lord, they were allowed to go home and work about their houses, preparing food, minding children, cleaning, and so forth until sunset. In England, as late as the twelfth century C.E., most serfs were too poor to afford candles.

Women were not only exploited for their labor, but also for sex. Many lords and their sons had children with serf women, who had to agree to sex under coercion or threat. In some regions, the lord had the right of the first night, that is, the right of sex with a virgin bride before she could have sex with her new husband.

All marriages among the ruling class were arranged for purposes of enlarging the lord's power or allies. Many marriages were arranged when girls were just born or very young. Frequently, a teenage girl was married to an old man. Supposedly, if a girl was engaged very young, she could change her mind at age twelve. In practice, however, the pressure from her parents usually prevailed, so the marriage to the old man went ahead as planned.

Romantic love, as we know it, hardly existed in this age of arranged marriages and forced sex. When the lords went off to fight in the crusades, however, they had to leave their wives at home. Of course, the lords had sex with women along the way to Jerusalem, but what about their wives at home? At this time, there was a class of wandering minstrels who went to sing in every castle on their route. They often gave a special service to the women of the lords who had not had sex in a long time. Of course, a minstrel could never marry a lord's wife, even if her husband was killed in a battle. Thus, there were many ballads of a love that was brief and beautiful, but had to end without a happy life for the lovers ever after. In these circumstances, the notion of romantic love first appeared in literature, with a few exceptions, during the late Middle Ages.

Economic Institutions, Self-Sufficiency, and Trade

There was very little trade and there were very few merchants in the early Middle Ages. Each feudal manor was mostly self-sufficient, trading only for a few goods it could not produce. The lord who suddenly needed more food to feed his retainers simply told the peasants to give him more. Of course, if he asked the peasants for more than was traditional, that could provoke a rebellion. If a peasant wanted another chicken, the peasant could trade other goods for it on market day, which was only once in two months or more, or the peasant had to do without.

At the beginning of feudalism, most people traded next to nothing. At a fair held now and then, a peasant could bring a pig to market and trade it for a coat. Except for fairs, which were rare in early feudalism, exchange of goods was not a usual thing. There was no use of money, except by a few very rich merchants in long-distance trade. Most commodities were not produced for the market, but for the use of those who produced them or for the lord, who controlled their services.

By the mid-feudal era, however, there was a growing number of towns. Trade and towns became a big part of feudalism because they were important for a lord's needs. Therefore, large towns emerged in Italy and Flanders in the eleventh and twelfth centuries. The lords had growing demands for military and luxury goods. They needed these goods because they had to build larger military units and more ostentatious displays of power in response to the competition with other lords. The competition between lords was built into the system of multiple sovereign groups of lords, as well as problems of dominating peasants through either force or rewards.

The towns, and the merchants who were often their chief citizens, were an important part of feudalism. The towns and the merchants were perceived as helpful to the feudal lords, not as any external kind of threat. Great feudal lords often had small towns under their control. Some larger towns had certain types of independence, but they all owed allegiance to some great lord or directly to a king.

As the merchants in the towns grew stronger in the late middle ages, the towns sometimes demanded more freedom from the lords. Sometimes the towns succeeded, but not without a fight. The struggles of merchants for town rights were similar to the struggles of peasants for village rights. Both types of struggles existed, but were a normal part of feudalism and did not pose a major threat. The merchants were often in a coalition with certain lords.

The merchants also demanded and eventually got new laws that fit their needs. There was little or no law governing exchange by contract in much of the Middle Ages. Serfs did not exchange much, so they needed no contract laws. Even lords and merchants made very few transactions needing a contract. Furthermore, the lords did not want written laws, but rather wanted to maintain their own arbitrary power of judgment. Eventually, however, as the kings grew stronger relative to the lords, they granted the merchants a set of laws protecting their contracts. This change was part of the transitional struggle toward capitalism.

The merchants were not capitalists who produced goods for the market. They merely bought in the cheapest market and sold in the most expensive market. They were useful to feudalism because they helped expand the range of trading under feudalism. Merchants largely traded in luxury goods for the rich, not in the basic goods of life.

Self-Sufficient Farming and Technology

The fact that all farming by peasants on their own land was for their own subsistence, and not for the market, had many important ramifications. But why did the peasants choose to do self-sufficient farming rather than market-oriented farming? The word "choose" is misleading here. The peasants had little choice. During the early and middle feudal periods, the times were so hard that one could barely scratch out a living. Thus, there were almost no surpluses, so there was almost nothing that the peasant could choose to sell.

There was little law and order outside the manor and no established markets, only occasional fairs. Where could one safely sell goods? And, if there were a drought or other disaster, where could one safely expect to buy necessary goods? By taking the risk of not producing enough for one's family in order to produce for an uncertain market, one was courting starvation for the entire family. So, for most of the middle ages, production for the market did not exist. Subsistence farming was the rule for both peasants and lords.

In theory, the lords might have been able to produce enough for subsistence and also produce a large quantity for the market. There were, however, good reasons for not doing so. In an emergency, such as a drought, the lords wanted plenty of reserves. They did not want to be dependent on a fickle and uncertain market for the price of the goods they were selling or for the price of the goods they had to buy if they oriented their farms toward the market.

The lords had relied on self-sufficient farms for centuries. There was nothing forcing them to change their tradition and switch to commercial farming for the market. To change to commercial farming, they needed a different type of workforce, because the serfs could not be fired. For many centuries there was no incentive to try to make more profit by using their present lands more intensively. The reason was that they were able to expand into new lands.

When the lords wanted more production, there was no reason to attempt more intensive farming on existing land. If they wanted more surplus, they could usually coerce more labor services or more dues in the form of products from the serfs.

Rather than competing with other lords in an economic way, which would have been contrary to tradition, they were forced to put their resources into military-political competition with other lords. As a result of all of these ideas and institutions, there was little economic development and little innovation. There were some innovations over the centuries, such as better plows and better harnesses for animals to pull heavy loads. But there was still very little specialization of land or labor.

Change was so slow that the dominant view of the medieval period was that change never occurs and the present form of work and life was eternal. The peasant villages also had their own rigid rules about who could farm where. They subdivided the land into many small plots. Then, to ensure equality among the villagers, they often re-divided the land into different small plots. The tradition was that every peasant would have exactly the same quantity and quality of land. They carried this to the extreme that there should be equality even if people had to get tiny plots in several different areas.

On these tiny plots, new technology made little sense and was often inapplicable. The small size made some improved technology impossible, even if the peasants had the money for innovation, which they did not. As noted, the lords spent their whole surplus on military expenditures or ostentatious displays of luxuries, so they also had no extra money for investment in technological innovations.

What was the importance of the fact that peasant farming, as well as most farming by lords, remained self-sufficient and not tied to the demands of the market? If the peasant was to produce enough food to feed his or her family, then it was impossible to plant any specialized crops designed for the market. Producing the same types of things year after year, the peasant did not have the incentive or the money or the knowledge to use new technology. Because the peasant had a very limited surplus, if any, there was no extra money to accumulate more equipment or to experiment with new types of equipment.

Moreover, since the peasant was not under the compulsion of competition in the market, there was no pressure on the peasant to make costly innovations. Unlike almost everyone under our present economic system, the peasant was simply not under pressure to compete in any way. The peasant could make a technological innovation if he or she had enough surplus to do so, but was under no compulsion to do so. As shown above, the peasant also had little or no money for innovation. We have also seen that the peasant did not wish to take risks with the subsistence of the family from traditional self-sufficient farming. Moreover, tradition said the lord could not force the peasant off the land no matter how low the productivity of the peasant.

Moreover, there was a scarcity of labor in the period following the Black Death epidemic of the 1300s. The Black Death (a plague) caused a population reduction of one-quarter to one-half of the European population. The shortage of labor meant that lords wished to preserve their present peasants, not antagonize them. if the lord got rid of a peasant family, it was not easy to get new tenants, or to pay free farmers to work for low wages.

As also shown above, the lords put their own resources into military-political competition, not into competition in a mostly nonexistent market. For all of these reasons, there was little innovation, so technology continued to stagnate, or advance very slowly, during feudalism.

Remember that technology began the feudal period by going backward after the fall of the Roman Empire. After a few centuries, there was just enough stability to allow technology to equal that of Roman agriculture. Even after agricultural technology recovered, the lords could not equal the domestic conveniences of the ancient Roman elite for many more centuries in most areas.

The serfs did have more incentive than the slaves to use new technology, at least on their own land. And the lords did not object to new technology on the lord's own land if it did not cost them too much. This led to very slow technological progress during the middle and late feudal period.

But technological progress remained excruciatingly slow for many reasons. First, as mentioned above, the peasants did only subsistence farming, with no competition to force technological change.

Second, the lords also practiced subsistence farming, on a larger scale, and their first concern was to get more revenue from their peasants by squeezing more out of them by the use of force with existing technology. The lords thought this traditional way was better than taking chances with expensive technological innovations. Third, neither lords nor peasants had more than a tiny bit of cash, if any, so equipment purchases were almost impossible.

Fourth, the whole tradition of feudalism, pushed hard by the church, was that nothing ever changed and nothing should change. Most people spent their whole lives without seeing any significant change in technology. Therefore, the idea that it would never change was very believable to them.

Why Did This Picture Change?

For many centuries, the lords and peasants practiced self-sufficient farming, while the merchants practiced the art of buying cheap and selling expensive. Neither engaged in production of goods for the market. Some craftspeople practiced their craft in the lord's manor, being rewarded by subsistence goods like any other retainer. Some craftspeople in the cities worked in associations of craft workers called guilds. Each guild master employed many apprentices.

These apprentices almost all became masters in due course. Thus, the relationship was only a temporary subordination and not a permanent one as in our present society. The medieval guild was an integral part of feudalism, not an early sign of a new economic system. There were no industries, no industrial owners, and no industrial workers in the feudal period.

Then where did industrial employers and employees come from? The transition occurred in different ways in different places in Europe. The first transition came in England, so the focus here is on England. What is most fascinating is that the transformation did not occur in the cities. Moreover, the transformation was not due to the existing merchants or the craft guilds. The transformation occurred first in the English countryside. This fact seems strange, considering that capitalism is usually associated with industry in towns.

How Change Began

One catalyst for change was the Black Death and other plagues that greatly reduced the English population during the second half of the fourteenth century. The landlords faced a big problem, since there was not enough labor to provide the amount of services they relied upon for a comfortable survival of their manors. What could they do?

Most landlords in England, as noted above, first tried the traditional method of squeezing more service from the peasants. But times were very hard, so the peasants were not willing to give more time or more goods to the landlords without a fight. To give more to the landlord meant starvation for many peasant families. Rather than see their children starve, many rebelled in one form or another, including armed struggle. The landlords were forced to give up their attempt to increase the exploitation of their peasants in traditional ways.

In fact, as a result of the struggles between lords and serfs, the serfs began to fight to achieve freedom from traditional services. Not only did the lords face peasant resistance against more exploitation, but in the face of a shrinking labor supply, the lords were also forced to compete with each other to get peasants away from other lords to increase their own labor supply. To get more peasants meant they had to give more concessions than their competitors. Thus, the peasants achieved liberation from many onerous duties either through resistance or through the competition of the lords. As a result of failure to impose tighter serfdom in the late fourteenth century, lords were obliged to grant peasants full freedom from feudal dues and service. The courts upheld these rights, thereby implicitly recognizing the free status of the peasants.

The lords seemed worse off than before. But the peasants only had freedom, not land. The lords responded to the peasant struggles by changing the rules and no longer recognizing traditional peasant rights to the use of land. In the first place, the peasants had traditional rights to an area known as the commons. They could collect wood, graze animals, and get other benefits from this area. What they did on the commons provided enough extra goods and income to allow them to survive. Without it, many peasants were forced out of farming. When enclosure of commons land pushed some peasants out of farming, they became unemployed, but they did not become workers in manufacturing, because manufacturing did not yet exist.

In the transitional centuries (fifteenth, sixteenth, and seventeenth), many of the lords used the former commons area to pasture their sheep. In that period, wool became a very important industry in England. Wool became the largest single export, with British wool being considered superior to most continental wool. Thus, an important industry was born by enclosing the former commons.

At first, wool production was still mainly feudal in nature. Those lords who had sheep processed the wool for market themselves, often using serf labor. Peasants who had sheep produced the wool for market, using their family labor. In some cases, the lords or peasants who owned the sheep sold the wool to the other peasants who processed it into a form ready for sale. They then sold it to the merchants.

The merchants then sold the wool, mostly abroad. The wool merchants of England were a company with a monopoly. At first they sold almost all the wool to Holland, where it was made into cloth. For a long time, however, the merchants produced no wool themselves. It was much later that the wool merchants began to have their own cloths woven from the wool in England.

As time went on, the merchants started to put out orders to peasants in advance and then sold the resultant production. This was called the "putting-out" system. And it was a long time before a merchant or a new manufacturer gathered the former peasant weavers of wool into a factory of some sort. But that is getting way ahead of the story.

Change from Unfree Labor to Leasing

At the height of feudalism, the lords used military force to extract unfree labor from the serfs in the form of service on the lord's land and/or dues in goods or money. But in the struggles of the fourteenth and fifteenth centuries, as was noted above, the peasants won a large degree of freedom from the traditional services and payments. And the peasants were demanding even more. They wanted land with fixed rents, rather than arbitrarily changing feudal dues for the land. They wanted their children to inherit their traditional land. If they got that, they would be freeholders and effective owners.

To prevent outright peasant ownership, lords asserted their own right to ownership. They forced the peasants into renting the land with a temporary lease. Thus, the peasants were now free, but had no guarantee of land. They had to pay for the land. Furthermore, a price change was possible every time the peasant renewed the lease.

In other words, the lords claimed the traditional land of the peasants as their own and the courts upheld this right. In their fight with the peasants, this tactic of the lords proved to be far more earthshaking than they intended. The peasants won their freedom. But the lords, having law and force on their side, insisted that peasants could no longer use their own traditional land for farming. The peasants could not use the land unless they paid rent under a lease to the landlords. The lords did not mean to change the system in any basic way. They merely meant to grab any revenue they could in their fight with the peasants.

But the system did change. There was a market in land to be leased from the landlords. For the first time, the peasants had to compete to rent the land. Renting the land meant that the peasants needed cash to pay the rent on the lease. Therefore, the peasants were no longer self-sufficient and could not choose to remain in subsistence farming. The peasants had to sell enough goods in the market to make the money to pay the lease. Therefore, peasants were forced out of subsistence farming into commercial farming, that is, farming for the market. Peasants were now under the control of the market and had to follow its competitive dictates. This meant that they could not plant enough food for their families. Rather, they had to plant commercial crops that could be sold in the market. They would then have enough money to pay the lease and retain their land. The change had begun from feudal relations, maintained by tradition and force, to the monetary and market relations that characterize capitalism.

Farming changed from self-sufficient subsistence to intensive production of commercial crops. When the peasants produced only for their own families, they were under no pressure to use the latest technology. Now, however, they were competing on the market to sell their crops. Therefore, they were forced, often with enormous sacrifice, to purchase the best equipment and fertilizer. The peasants became involved in the process of technological innovation. Many of the most important inventions of this period were discovered or first applied in the countryside, not the towns. Therefore, as technology in England began to make progress, it was mainly agricultural technology.

Furthermore, since the peasants could no longer produce all of the things they needed, they focused on a few commercial crops as the only way to survive. For the first time in history, peasant families faced the need to buy many of the necessary goods at the market.

Peasants who produced mainly commercial crops no longer had time for many of the necessary crafts. Therefore, much of the craft production moved out of its traditional place in the peasant home. Where would the peasants now get all of the craft goods they needed? They had to buy them at the market. Since it was forced out of the countryside to some extent, the production of the craft goods moved to the city for the first time.

Eventually, although very slowly, a market was born for the products of industrial production. At the same time, thousands of peasants had been forced off the lord's newly enclosed lands, both the former commons and those peasant lands of those who could not afford the new leases. These peasants roamed as vagabonds all over the British countryside, looking for work, without success, for a very long time. As time went by, however, the newer industry of the towns needed workers and it utilized many of the thousands of unemployed peasants in industrial jobs. Being used to the life of a self-employed peasant, most of them found it very hard to adjust to the factory discipline.

Eventually, the competitive leasing by peasants led to cash crops and many agricultural innovations in the countryside, while buying other goods from the city. One result was increased agricultural productivity, which lowered the price of food. This meant that workers in the cities could eat and survive even at fairly low wages. Low food prices also meant that many people had income left over to buy things other than food.

In the cities, the combination of unemployed workers and relatively cheap food led to far more extensive craft production and the beginning of industry. Much earlier industry consisted of simple crafts, sometimes with a few employees, in the houses of merchants. In the countryside, much of the farming was done by families with no other employees. Although they were becoming more tied to the market, the structure of industry and agriculture was still based on family production. It took a long time for production based on an owner and many employees to become widespread.

Slowly, however, the better-off peasants began to accumulate more land. They started to improve their methods of production to compete on the market. Some families also increased their animals from one per family, as in the feudal times, to many animals. They began to specialize in certain crops and in certain animals. All of this specialization and trade meant further increase in production.

The richer farmers began to employ landless peasants on their farms. Production was growing faster than the number of farmers. They were thus able to feed the growing population, ending the supply shortage crisis of the late feudal period. Since the richest peasants now had their own land by lease, owned their own equipment, and employed others to work for them, they fitted the definition of a capitalist entrepreneur in agriculture.

The English Revolution of the Seventeenth Century

Although there were still people called lords in the countryside, much of feudalism had disappeared by the time of the revolution that ended the remnants of feudalism in seventeenth-century England. Tenants leased their land and owed no feudal services. Lords were now landlords who received rents from a commercial, capitalist relationship with the tenants. If one says that the English Revolution got rid of the remnants of feudalism, what remnants are being discussed? There were still some very important remnants of the political structure coming from feudalism, plus some very important economic aspects.

First, the British crown and court had vast powers that were used to enrich themselves in order to lead a very luxurious life with vast spending on palaces and such. Thus, the power of the king and court remained a serious economic issue. Second, in addition to the vast waste of the court, the king also imposed all kinds of minute regulations on business and industry, which the crafts and the new industries found very irksome.

Third, high church officials also had vast landholdings and other powers, which were used to enrich themselves and the church. Thus, the power of the church remained a very real issue. Fourth, the king sold monopolies to certain merchants. The stranglehold of these monopolies, such as the monopoly of trade with the East Indies, was preventing a flourishing of capitalism in several important areas.

Altogether, these political-economic remnants of feudalism were seen as obstacles and burdens upon those trying to make a living through the market. Eventually, there was a revolution in England in the mid-seventeenth century that ended the remnants of feudalism and established a state friendly to market-based industrial development.

It would be very wrong, however, to think of the leaders of this revolution as typical industrial manufacturers since very few of those existed. One of the most important groups in the revolutionary process was the former peasants, who now became commercial farmers. The second group was the merchants, who lived and died by market exchange. These merchants very seldom produced goods; they merely bought and sold them.

A third group in the English revolution were those who owned small craftshops, some still organized in medieval guilds. In feudal times, almost all the apprentices eventually became masters, when they had demonstrated enough skill. The guilds, however, were changing. Some masters became richer and many apprentices failed to become masters. Thus, as demand grew for their products, the guilds slowly became more like modern market-oriented manufacturing enterprises.

The commercial farmers, the merchants, and the craft masters were called "bourgeoisie," named after the burghers who led the German towns. But they were still a far cry from our modern industrialists. The revolution of the town bourgeoisie and the rural bourgeoisie led to a new governmental and a new legal framework for the economy. The new economic relations plus the new legal and political framework was called capitalism.

Yet the English revolution that legalized capitalism was not fought under the banner of making the world safe for capitalism. The English revolution of the mid-seventeenth century was not only fought by a pre-capitalist bourgeoisie and farmers, but it was fought under the banner of religion. The various political parties in the revolution were all marching under various religious banners, which masked the economic issues.

In addition to the religious issues between Catholics and various sects of Protestants, there was also a stated political issue between the Parliament and the king. The climax of the revolution was the beheading of the king. But underneath the religious and political issues, a basic economic change occurred. The remnants of feudalism were destroyed and the stage was set for the emergence of industrial capitalism.

To better understand the true nature of the English revolution, let us go back and recall briefly the sequence of events that led to this revolution. Remember that the story began with the struggle between the peasants and the lords under a feudal system, which reshaped both of these classes and made them bitter antagonists. It was discussed above that in the crisis situation where both sides felt they were fighting for survival, the peasants won freedom from feudal services, but the lords won the right to enclose the commons and charge rents for the traditional peasant lands. This turned out to be a major change in economic institutions. The new economic institutions in the countryside led to profit maximization and technological innovation in agriculture. The new rural relations led to commercial crops in the countryside and the slow growth of industry in its earliest forms in the cities.

The change in the relative power of different classes led to further conflict over peasant rights—and conflict over the power of the lords versus the merchants, craftspeople, and store owners. These conflicts resulted in revolution. The revolution set the basis for industrial capitalism, which grew very slowly for some centuries. Big merchants in long-distance trade and big financiers who financed that trade came long before large-scale industrial capitalism was established. Eventually, however, the modern capitalist scene did emerge.

After capitalism was established to a considerable extent in England, British overseas activities helped greatly to expand it further. These overseas activities were called "patriotic" by the British, but they included piracy against Spanish treasure ships, massive raids on Africa for slaves to be sold in the Americas, and establishment of colonies by military force all over the world. England had an enormous empire and all kinds of loot came from overseas to England, much of it used to build English industry.

The English intentionally kept most of these colonies largely agricultural and used them as raw material producers, while selling manufactured goods to them at high prices. Thus, the surplus coming from many other countries through the use of piracy, slavery, and colonialism helped to build English industry. That enormous treasure, however, could not have built industry unless England was already largely capitalist. Notice that Spain also received vast treasure from its colonies, but it could not build much industry because it still had largely feudal institutions.

Four Features of Capitalism

To understand the rest of this book, it is vital to understand exactly what is meant by capitalism. It may be defined in terms of its four basic features.

First, what are the relations and institutions comprising the capitalist economic system? Capitalism is an economic system in which a small group of people (called capitalists) owns the natural resources, factories, and equipment of industry and agriculture. Most of the population are employees who receive wages and salaries by working for the capitalist employers. The capitalist employers produce and expand production only as long as there is a profitable market for their goods. Production is for profit. Therefore, production declines if the expected profit declines. These are the basic principles of the economic institution of capitalism.

Second, what technology and other economic forces have been used by capitalism? The economic forces of capitalism grew quickly, including rapid improvement of technology, rapid growth of factories and equipment, and rapid growth of population. These forces grew throughout the transitional fifteenth, sixteenth, and seventeenth centuries. Then technology, factories, equipment, and population had explosive growth in the late eighteenth and the nineteenth centuries. This crucial change was called the industrial revolution (discussed later in the chapter).

Third, what are the social and political institutions of capitalism? In the period after the English Revolution of 1648, the British government eliminated all feudal restrictions. The government managed the economy in the interests of the merchants. As power slowly changed in the transitional centuries from trade to industry, the government economic management slowly changed from following the interests of the merchants to the interests of the industrialists, though that shift was not fully accomplished until the beginning of the nineteenth century.

There was a whole new system of schools to train both skilled workers and professional workers as well as elite managers and executives. The religious system stopped supporting kings and feudal nobility and now began to tout the virtues of capitalism and the capitalist leaders of trade and industry.

The family no longer produced what was necessary for survival, but bought its goods at the market and sold its labor at the market. This changed the family from working together, usually under the dominance of the father, to dependence on the market and awareness of the monetary importance of marriage and divorce.

Fourth, what is the ideology of capitalism? The emergence of the capitalist institutions was accompanied by a great change in ideology. People no longer assumed that nothing could ever change, but came to

Table 4.2

Four Features of Capitalist Society

Technology	Industrial revolution
Economic institutions	Employees work; employers get profit
Social institutions	Democratic forms, but wealth dominates all institutions
Ideology	Market is always right, so employers and employees get what they deserve. Continued racism and sexism

expect rapid change in technology, either welcoming or dreading it under various circumstances. The status of women changed from being property to being free to work or starve. Most women were still dependent on a man, so there was a long ideological fight to view women as equals of men.

Under capitalism, there are no more slaves or serfs, so racism is no longer an excuse for that type of domination and unfree labor. Yet, under capitalism, there were still subordinate ethnic groups, such as the Irish in the late nineteenth century in the United States, and subordinate racial groups, such as African-Americans throughout the twentieth century. These oppressed minorities were mostly employed at the lowest wages and assumed to be inferior by many people in the majority group. So racism persists as a part of ideology under capitalism.

These four main features of capitalism are summarized in Table 4.2.

The Industrial Revolution

The economic, political, and legal framework of British capitalism, which reached its full bloom in the late eighteenth century, paved the way for the industrial revolution. In Britain the industrial revolution took place in the last part of the eighteenth century and in the nineteenth century. This industrial revolution was composed of both technological changes and further institutional changes.

In 1750, a person could not get from Rome to London any faster than in the days of the Roman Empire, using relays of fast horses in both cases. The same relays of fast horses were still the best way to get a message from Rome to London. But by the second half of the nineteenth century, there were railroad lines that could take passengers and freight rapidly from Rome to London. Moreover, the telegraph meant that a message could travel instantaneously from Rome to London. Thus, transportation and communication were both changed in truly revolutionary ways.

Moreover, in 1750, most power for work was supplied by people or animals, just as it had been in the Roman Empire. By the second half of the nineteenth century, steam engines were used in industry, railroad engines were driven by steam, oil, and eventually electricity.

At night in 1750, people still had to use candles for light or else they had to retire. In the last half of the nineteenth century, there was lighting by kerosene lamps and then electric lighting. The new methods of lighting meant that people could pursue whatever activities they wished all night long.

The increased use of power encouraged coal production to increase by leaps and bounds, while production of iron and steel also increased at an amazing speed. This cheap power and great production capacity meant that vast quantities of consumer goods could be produced very cheaply for the first time. Altogether, the output of British manufacturing doubled from 1750 to 1800.

Industry needed people for its expansion. People moved from the rural areas to the cities, first pushed out by landlords who enclosed the land to produce wool for commerce, but later attracted to the cities by the new factory jobs. Britain thus changed from a rural, agricultural country to a mainly urban, industrial country. For example, the manufacturing town of Manchester had only 17,000 people in 1760, but by 1850 it had 400,000 people.

All of these changes that constituted the industrial revolution could not have occurred without the institutions of capitalism. It was the capitalist motives of landlords that convinced them to enclose their estates. These enclosures produced a homeless and unemployed class of workers available for industry. It was the capitalist pressures on farming that raised productivity and supplied more food at lower prices to the cities. With the new labor supply and a greater demand for manufactured goods, the crafts eventually changed through a very long process into manufacturing enterprises owned by capitalists. The factory system started to produce revolutionary changes in technology only after these institutional foundations had been laid.

The industrial revolution, which shifted the majority of production from agriculture to industry, resulted in a class of industrial capitalists. Earlier capitalists had been involved in trade and finance. It was only after the industrial revolution that there were a significant number of rich manufacturers and vast numbers of employees who worked for wages in manufacturing.

In England the revolution against feudalism occurred in the mid-seventeenth century, but the industrial revolution did not really begin until the end of the eighteenth century. The industrial revolution was made possible by the capitalist structure of industry, including private ownership and competition. Emergence of capitalism also required a capitalist-friendly government, as well as a set of laws that defined capitalist relations. The new technology did not drop out of the sky, but emerged from an environment that encouraged it.

Suggested Readings

There has been a lengthy debate with heated exchanges on exactly how feudalism ended in Western Europe and how capitalism began. The debate focused on England because it led the way to capitalism. The whole complex history of the debate is clearly explained in Ellen Meiksins Wood, *The Origins of Capitalism* (2002). Wood also adds her own interesting contribution. The pioneering writer, who set off the debate, was Maurice Dobb, whose contribution may be seen in the excellent collection of essays edited by Hilton, *The Transition from Feudalism to Capitalism* (1976).

For about the last three decades, however, the debate has centered on the outstanding work of Robert Brenner, whose work is also the best single source for these issues. Brenner's insightful work, along with the work of his critics, can be seen in the book edited by T.H. Aston and C.H.E. Philpin, *The Brenner Debate* (1985), including two lengthy contributions by Brenner himself. The writings on the Brenner thesis and the earlier works on the transition from feudalism to capitalism, however, are difficult reading. The reader is therefore advised to start with the brief and far more readable survey by Ellen Wood, mentioned above.

A very enjoyable book that presents the lives of six actual medieval people from documents is Eileen Power, *Medieval People* (2000). The fascinating story of how law changed as the institutions changed is told in clear, but not fun, prose in Tigar and Levy, *Law and the Rise of Capitalism* (1977).

– 5 –

From Pre-Capitalism to Capitalism in the United States, 1776–1865

Chapter 4 revealed that capitalist institutions first came into being in England's countryside and then spread to the urban areas of England. After that, they spread to Western Europe and then to the rest of the world. The initial rise of capitalism in England was due to the internal evolution of feudalism. The spread to Western Europe was partly by internal evolution of each country, but partly by diffusion from England. The European powers spread capitalism by fire and sword to the rest of the world, whose independent evolution was cut off in mid-stream. The Europeans set up a system to extract wealth from the colonies, but allowed little development of the colonies.

Pre-Capitalist Institutions in the United States, 1776–1840

At the time of the American Revolution in 1776, the future United States was a British colony. It was very underdeveloped because of British restrictions, such as the restriction on importing new technology in most fields. It was largely rural, agricultural, poor, and dependent on English trade for vital goods.

At that time, capitalist institutions did not exist in the United States to any large degree. The South still had slavery, which operated differently from the rest of the country. Since slavery is very important to the story of the development of the United States as a whole, the development of the South and its relations with the rest of the country will be discussed in detail in the next chapter.

In the North and West, there were millions of farmers, each of whom owned their own land and employed no one but their own family members. In 1810, 81 percent of the U.S. labor force was in farming. These farmers were not part of capitalism. In fact, they were neither capitalists nor workers, but part of a type of economic system that might be called independent. An independent type of production system means that the farmers were neither an exploiting elite nor a subordinate group that was being exploited. Their farms were mostly self-sufficient, producing their own food, clothing, and shelter.

Gradually, throughout the nineteenth century, the farmers became less self-sufficient and more tied to the market, both in buying vital goods and in selling their product for cash. As they became tied to the market, they had to compete by using better and more expensive machinery. They found they were paying monopoly prices to a few large farm equipment producers, paying the giant railroad corporations monopoly prices to ship their products, and selling at relatively low prices to large wholesalers. As their costs rose and their prices were limited, they went into debt to the banks. Then slowly throughout the nineteenth and twentieth centuries, farmers went bankrupt, left agriculture, and became employees in manufacturing and service industries.

From 81 percent of the labor force in 1810, farmers fell to 63 percent of the population in 1840. The disappearance of small farms and the rise of a few giant ones continued steadily from 1840 until the present time. By the year 2000, the number of farmers fell to less than 2 percent of the population. A large portion of that 2 percent was no longer independent farmers, but agricultural workers.

In the East Coast cities, after the American Revolution there were merchants and craftspeople. There were, however, very few manufacturing owners or manufacturing employees. The craft shops were small, usually with one or two apprentices, who eventually became masters.

Craftspeople—such as blacksmiths, silversmiths, cabinet-makers, and candle-makers—did not produce a steady stream of goods. They stopped production whenever they worried about not being able to sell all that they could produce. Instead, they worked only for special orders in most cases. Crafts eventually became market-oriented, turning out a steady stream and expanding their production, but it was a very slow evolution.

Merchants bought and sold commodities, but they did not produce them. Only slowly did some merchants start to order specific amounts from craftspeople or from farmers. Eventually, after a long time, the merchants started their own production. By the early 1840s, there were only the beginnings of manufacturing, with a few hundred employees in the biggest factories.

Most foreign trade was with England. The U.S. economy was clearly subordinate to England and shipped lumber and agricultural goods, while buying manufactured goods. This pattern of trade was similar to that of many underdeveloped countries today. During the War of 1812 against England, some manufacturing businesses started to produce things previously imported from England. But England retained its domination over the U.S. trade throughout the first half of the nineteenth century.

There were just a few banks, law firms, and insurance companies. The most important banks in the world were in London. American banks remained subservient to English finance until long after the Civil War. For most of the nineteenth century, even the U.S. government borrowed money from London banks and tended to be subservient to their wishes in financial matters.

Transportation and communication slowly improved but news, people, and merchandise still moved at a snail's pace. So most industry remained local until the 1840s, when national transportation and communication began to improve.

At this time, the corporate form of doing business emerged. A corporation is defined as a business in which all of the assets are owned by people who buy shares of its stock. By law, investors could lose their investment if the share price falls to nothing, but creditors have no right to pursue the investors beyond the assets of the corporation. Thus, the corporation is said to have limited liability. Noncorporate businesses, owned by individuals or partners, are liable to creditors, not only for the assets of the business, but for all of the assets of the owners as well. Limited liability means that corporate investors are vulnerable to creditors only for the money they invest, not for their other assets. Thus, the corporate form allows a large group of investors to work together, with liability limited to their investments.

Yet, because most businesses were very small at that time, only a few businesses made use of the corporate form. After the Civil War, however, more and more businesses adopted the corporate form in order to limit their liability. Although the corporate form is still used by a minority of all businesses today, it represents close to 90 percent of total output.

National income expanded and grew 30 percent from 1810 to 1840. With the growth of crafts and merchandising, towns grew. Farms produced more goods per farm; so fewer farms were needed to satisfy the market. Therefore, the number of farmers declined while towns grew. The urban population increased from 6 percent of the population in 1810 to 11 percent in 1840. Urbanization continued to increase throughout the century. Thus, the urban population produced 35 percent of GDP (gross domestic product) by 1890, which increased to 46 percent by 1910.

Beginnings of American Capitalism, 1840–1860

Railroads grew rapidly in the eastern United States from 1840 to 1860. Building, supplying, and operating the railroads was the largest single industry and helped start many fortunes as well as many financial empires. The railroads were helped by large government giveaways. It is estimated that these giveaways amounted to 158,293,000 acres, a land area greater than many whole countries. The government also helped canal and telegraph systems. With the help of the earliest telegraph and the railroads, some of the most important industries of the nineteenth century, including the oil industry, began in this period. But they were only beginnings because railroads and telegraph lines covered only a small area of the country.

At the beginning of 1840, only 10 percent of all the labor force was in manufacturing. There were few enterprises with more than 200 workers and none with more than 500. The railways were the first large industrial firms, but even they were still relatively small throughout this period.

In fact, large, nationwide enterprises were impossible in this period because of the slowness of transport and communication. It was impossible to have a national firm when there was no communication or transportation to California other than a wagon train or a horse. Ships had to go all the way around the tip of South America to bring heavy loads to the West coast of the United States. Thus, building a transcontinental system of railroads and telegraph was an essential prerequisite for large-scale industry.

Only the first minor beginnings of the railroads and telegraph emerged in this period, mostly serving the East Coast. Total railroad mileage was only 2,000 miles in 1840, but it had risen to 47,000 miles by 1860. The United States had some industry and was ready for a big push on the eve of the Civil War. The fact that Northern industrialists saw the South as an obstacle to countrywide industrialization was one reason for the war.

The national product began to rise consistently in this period as an internal product of the new capitalist system. The earliest beginning of a system with a small elite of owners and bosses, but many low-paid employees, meant the beginnings of increased inequality by the end of this period. By 1860, the top 10 percent of wealth holders owned 75 percent of all the wealth. The economic structure looked like a pyramid with a few wealthy people at the top and an enormous number of people at the bottom, with no wealth and just enough income to survive.

In addition to a material basis, industrialization required the proper ideological climate. There had been no long history of feudalism in the United States. Therefore the ideology of the 1840s became one of unbridled capitalism. The dominant view was that everyone should make their fortune any way possible and there were unlimited possibilities. The California Gold Rush started in this period and men fought over every pretty pebble in the stream. Some people got rich overnight, but many faced years of misery for nothing. There were no income taxes, no regulations of business, and no safety net of unemployment compensation or welfare. This was perceived as the perfect basis for building capitalist industry, once slavery was ended.

In the 1850s and 1860s when railroads needed vast sums, investment banks became important. Railroads were 60 percent of all stock issues. Banks became very close partners with railroad corporations and with various other corporations to whom they loaned money. In this period, corporations started having bankers on their boards of directors, leading to increased control of bankers over corporations.

The Status of Women

This chapter has been almost purely on economics up to this point, but economic development cannot be understood without considering the political institutions, social institutions, and ideas of society that influence it every single day. The story of ideas begins here with women's rights because the status and treatment of women in a society is important in itself, but it is also important for its reflection of society and for its impact on society. A society that mistreats and discriminates against women is a long way from overall democracy and decency. In the early days of the United States, discrimination against women has to be seen in the context of enslavement of African-Americans, the extermination of many Native Americans, and laws preventing the poor and property-less from voting. Overall there was extreme snobbery by the elite to-ward all their "inferiors."

In addition to Native-American women who were here already, women came to the United States as free immigrants, as slaves, or as indentured servants. Usually, an indentured servant was someone who agreed to pay for his or her passage to America by serving a master for seven years. Leaving aside the slave women (discussed in the next chapter), what was the status of women after the American Revolution?

Status of Women from 1776 to 1840

Early U.S. law about women was the same as British common law, which gave the husband all the rights, while women had none. Specifically, wives had no right to hold property, even their own dowry. The husband owned and managed everything. Wives had no right to keep their own wages. Wives had no control of children. Women had to give up custody of their children in case of a divorce. Wives had no right to sue in court. Wives had no right to testify in court, nor could women serve on juries. Women could not vote.

Over 99 percent of women worked all day every day. Women on the farm, who made up over 80 percent of all American women, planted, tended, and harvested crops. When they were not doing agricultural work, women made clothes, prepared food, cared for health needs, took care of children, and repaired houses. Men hunted. Men fought Native Americans to steal the land from them. Men began the farm by chopping down all the trees on their land. Men also built extensions on houses.

Women had higher status on the frontier than on the east coast. Why was that the case? On the frontier, women were scarce, their work was absolutely necessary to the farm, and they obviously worked equally hard as the men, serving just as vital a role.

During the American Revolution, the only man to speak for women's rights was Tom Paine, but he was known to be a troublemaker. Most towns did not employ women as teachers, and those that did, required

73

them to resign when they had children. There was no education for most women. A few rich women attended female seminaries, where they were taught how to sew, sing, speak French, and act like a "lady." Some women produced textiles, but not in factories. They worked at home and sold their products to merchants.

Status of Women From 1840 to 1860

By 1850, there were some women in textile factories. They worked thirteen to sixteen hours a day and their wages were one-quarter to one-seventh of men's wages. A few tried to build unions, but it was very difficult. Furthermore, in the 1840s no women had any property rights, but this started to change in the North by the 1850s. In a campaign that had some early success in the northeastern states, but took decades to be successful all over the country, women's right to hold property independently from their husbands was finally won. Some women were aided by their rich fathers, who were annoyed that their daughters' husbands controlled their dowries.

Some revolutionary ideas also emerged from the American and French revolutions about liberty and equality for everyone before the law. If "everyone" is equal before the law, why should women not be treated equally? Later, some women fought in the movement for the abolition of slavery. But the question of abolishing slavery for black men also raised the question of abolishing the subordination of women. Not only were many women abolitionists, but they did some of the most difficult jobs. For example, the African-American woman abolitionist, Harriet Tubman, was a conductor on the Underground Railroad, which meant that she helped many slaves to freedom under very dangerous conditions.

The church and much public opinion said that it was not feminine to work in a political movement, help the Underground Railroad, or speak in public. Women, however, learned much about activism by working in the abolitionist movement. Some male abolitionists wanted them to help very quietly and "stay in their place." For example, at the 1840 World Abolitionist Meeting in London, women were kept in the gallery and were not allowed on the convention floor.

Since the abolitionist movement taught many women how to run a movement, while many abolitionists rejected the equality of women, it was one factor leading toward a separate women's movement. In 1848 in Seneca Falls, New York, women met for the first time as a separate movement. They wrote a declaration in favor of equal rights for women, including the rights to keep their own wages, to keep their own property, and to keep their children.

There was fear, however, of something so revolutionary as the vote for women. It was only after a very long debate that they voted for a demand that women should have the right to vote. All of the demands of women were met at first with ridicule. The big city newspapers attacked the women's movement, especially the demand to vote, as unfeminine and silly. One response of women was local organization. For example, women took control of many local newspapers.

Racism

In the entire period from the Revolutionary War (begun in 1776) to the Civil War (begun in 1861), Native Americans were held to be dangerous savages and were driven out of their lands or exterminated in large numbers, amounting to genocide. Most African-Americans remained in slavery and were considered to be property, not humans, as discussed in detail in the next chapter.

Labor Relations and Unions

Before the Civil War, the U.S. economy was still dominated by rural and agricultural production. In the cities were small craft businesses. There were few large concentrations of workers in one factory. Consequently, unions were weak and usually short-lived. Nonunion employees, who made up most of the labor force, were oppressed in ways that seem hardly believable today. Remember that capitalism in the nineteenth century remained virtually unregulated and employers were free to mistreat employees. Since most employees were nonunion, they continued to have poor working conditions, very low wages, and very long hours of work.

Environmental Issues

Since there was little industry until the 1840s, there was little industrial pollution. There was, however, continual chopping down of forests in all regions. There was exhaustion of the land in the South (as will be discussed in the next chapter). Some animal species, such as the buffalo on the Great Plains, were reduced from vast herds almost to extinction when guns were used for wholesale killing. Killing the buffalo was part of a deliberate attempt by interest groups wanting land or precious minerals to eliminate Native Americans from the Great Plains.

U.S. Law and Economic Development

Laws reflect and are influenced by the institutions and group relationships of a given society. On the one hand, laws change with each transformation of society and group relationships. On the other hand, laws influence economic institutions and relationships of different groups, locking them into place until changed. For example, in order to keep slaves subordinate, the Southern states passed laws making it a crime to teach a slave to read and write, with the death penalty as a punishment. Thus, the ruling group in a society controls the laws according to interests. Of course, the laws of the South before the Civil War, such as the law against slaves learning to read and write, not only reflected Southern slavery, but also helped to preserve the institution of slavery. The object of the Southern laws was to freeze into place the existing slave institutions.

The laws change in a fundamental way only after institutions change. Once the Civil War ended slavery, the law changed with the passing of new Amendments to the U.S. Constitution. How has this process of interaction of law and institutions developed in the United States?

The Law from 1776 to 1840

The first period of U.S. law corresponded to the period of a mostly pre-capitalist economy before the market institutions of capitalism were developed in the United States. That period lasted from the founding of the British colonies in the present borders of the United States until roughly the 1840s. In that period, besides slavery in the South, there were millions of independent farmers on small farms, who were neither capitalist employers nor employees.

How did the law reflect the transition from the pre-capitalist stage of the U.S. economy to the later stage of actual capitalism? In the Western

United States, the early laws reflected the needs of agriculture with iso-lated farms and small communities. In these small farm communities, tradition played a big role in a society that appeared to be unchanging. When the economy changed to an expanding industry with rapidly chang-ing technology, the law had to change. Those groups that ruled the gov-ernment no longer saw land and farming as most important, but rather favored the needs of industry. What was rational for a backwoods soci-ety is not rational for a modern industrial society.

For example, under modern industrial capitalism, people think of con-tracts as inviolate and assume that things will be sold at the price agreed in the contract, no matter how much one party could be hurt by it. On the contrary, in the early period of pre-capitalist relationships, what counted to courts was a "just price" or fair price by community standards. This was especially true in the so-called equity courts, where people could appeal a decision. This notion of a just price made sense for a small com-munity where everyone knew each other and where "profiteering" from one's neighbors was abhorrent and was denounced in church. What counted in later contract law in a complex industrial society was simply the market price as set by supply and demand, whether it was fair or just or not. Often, the formal legal terminology remained the same, but talk about what was "just" slowly changed to talk about the market price by 1840.

The Law from 1840 to 1865

Although industrial capitalism was still weak in the 1840s and 1850s, the entire period from the 1840s to the 1920s was the era of mostly unregu-lated industrial capitalism. In this period, the law recognized contracts as sacred. Moreover, property law was revised to meet the needs of the in-dustrialists as opposed to the farmers. For example, with respect to water rights, polluting a river was a terrible thing from the viewpoint of its use for farming. But water pollution was seen as secondary to production when the representatives of the industrialists wrote the laws. When in-dustrialists came to power, labor law consisted of nothing but the right of the employer to do as he or she pleased. It was a period of unregulated capitalism, in which private enterprise was completely dominant.

As the next chapter explains, the end of slavery also contributed to changes in the law. Slavery became illegal and male ex-slaves were given the right to vote.

Colonialism and Economic Development

The United States was a colony of England until the Revolutionary War. During the colonial period, over 80 percent of the people worked in agriculture. Thus, it is not surprising that most American exports were agricultural products, including a lot of lumber. Also some products from mining were sent abroad, but there was very little industry, only small craft shops.

England tried to keep a monopoly of trade and exclude other European powers. In return for American agricultural and mining products, England sent finished manufactured products to the United States. This meant that America stayed dependent on England and did not develop its own industry. Moreover, England did everything it could to keep its American colonies agricultural and extractive, rather than manufacturing. England prohibited import of new machines into the American colonies, thus forcing the colonies to remain agricultural.

This was the traditional pattern for almost all the colonies controlled by the European powers. Agricultural and extracted materials were produced by relatively cheap labor in the colonies. When the cheap raw materials came to England, they were changed by crafts and manufacture into finished goods, worth far more than the raw materials. Some of them were then shipped back to the American colonies to be sold at a high profit. The American colonies provided to England cheap food, cheap raw materials, and a market for more expensive finished goods. Thus, industrial, trade, and military domination brought a flow of profit from the American colonies to England. This pattern was repeated in all of the other European colonies.

The colonists accurately felt that England was extracting profit and taxes from them, while holding back their economic development. This was one of the major causes of the Revolutionary War. England tried to reconquer the United States in 1812, but did not succeed. Nevertheless, the economic power of England and economic weakness of the United States maintained the same economic pattern. Until the Civil War, the United States exported mainly agricultural and raw materials to England, while England was the main source of finished, manufactured goods for the American market.

Since the pattern of production and trade remained similar to the colonial pattern, the United States was a neocolony of England. For the

United States, being "neocolonial" meant that it had formal independence and no occupying troops, but its economic relationship to England remained the same as the colonial one. It was only very slowly as
U.S. manufacturing increased, starting especially in the 1840s, that some
degree of economic independence was slowly achieved.

Suggested Reading

An outstanding book on the economic aspects of U.S. history—and the
source of much data in this chapter—is Richard DuBoff, *Accumulation
and Power: An Economic History of the United States* (1989).

The social aspects of U.S. history are covered excellently in Howard
Zinn, *A People's History of the United States* (1999). The history of
women and sexist discrimination is covered in a powerful book by Barbara Sinclair Deckard, *The Women's Movement* (1983). The story of the
fight for women's right to vote is told in a wonderfully exciting style by
Eleanor Flexner in *Century of Struggle: The Women's Rights Movement
in the United States* (1975). This is the classic book on which much of
the later work on women's history has been founded.

The book by Michael Reich, *Racial Inequality, Economic Theory,
and Class Conflict* (1980), is a very thorough history and an insightful
theory of racial discrimination. Since Reich's book is more difficult than
the other books listed here, which were chosen to be easily readable as
well as excellent, a noneconomist should only read the first chapter plus
the introductions and conclusions of each chapter.

The fascinating story of the financing and building of the first transcontinental railroad is told in beautiful prose in Stephen Ambrose,
Nothing Like It in the World (2001). The history of the rise of the oil
monopoly and its unscrupulous tactics is told in a biography of
Rockefeller by Ron Chernow, *Titan: Biography of John D. Rockefeller*
(1999). The history of the rise of finance is told in interesting and well-
written prose in Ron Chernow, *House of Morgan: An American Banking
Dynasty and the Rise of Modern Finance* (1998). The history of law and
U.S. institutions is given in Anthony Chase, *The American Legal System: The Evolution of the American Legal System* (1997). This is a very
clear book if you skip the footnotes. It is fun to read if you are a lawyer
or historian, but more difficult if you lack the background.

A book on the amazing history of the labor movement that is riveting and interesting to read for anyone is Richard O. Boyer and Herbert Morais, *Labor's Untold Story* (1970). A very detailed, but very easy to read history of the labor movement is Philip Foner's many volumes, which cover the period from the earliest colonial times to the 1920s. (ten volumes, 1947 to 1994). Finally, the whole evolution of environmental problems is presented in a short, beautifully written, and fascinating book by John Bellamy Foster, *The Vulnerable Planet: A Short Economic History of the Environment* (1984).

– 6 –

Slavery in the United States, 1776–1865

There were many similarities and differences between ancient Roman slavery and the system of slavery that existed in the Old South of the United States before the Civil War. The main features of both societies were similar. First, both had predominantly slave economic institutions, which produced most of the output. Second, in both cases the political, religious, and military power was held by the master class. Third, in both cases, the ideology that supported slavery was based in part on racism. Fourth, both had a mostly stagnant technology, relying on heavy, but crude, agricultural equipment.

On the other hand, the two slave societies came into existence by different paths. They evolved into somewhat different social forms, though retaining the same basic institutions. And they disappeared for somewhat different reasons.

Features of U.S. Slavery

Most of Southern agriculture was divided into large plantations. On each plantation, there was a magnificent mansion for the master and small, ramshackle shacks for the slaves. The master and his friends often sat on the veranda drinking mint juleps, while the slaves did hard, agricultural labor or tedious domestic labor from sunrise until after sunset. The master had all kinds of good food to eat, while the slaves were never given enough for an adequate diet. The master class had beautiful clothing, while the slaves had scraps to wear.

Slaves worked under supervisors who were often cruel and brutal. The slaves were whipped for tiny mistakes or for not working fast enough. In the fields, most slaves picked cotton, a backbreaking job. In the mansion, slaves cooked the meals, cleaned the house, made the clothing, and performed other endless tasks. Everything produced by the slaves belonged to the master class.

In addition to extremely hard work and beatings, the slaves received less food, clothing, and shelter than was needed for long-run survival, so their life expectancy was much shorter than that of the masters. The slave owners faced a trade-off in calculating how to maximize their profits. If the master gives little food, bad clothing, and very poor shelter to the slaves, then the slaves die very quickly. When a slave dies very quickly, then the master loses a valuable piece of capital. Therefore, the master had to give enough necessities to the slaves so they would stay alive as long as possible. On the other hand, to make profits in the short run, the slave owners wanted to give the slaves as little as possible in food, clothing, and shelter. The temptation to give the slaves less than minimum sustenance was always there, especially when the plantation owner had financial problems. The end result was that the slaves usually lived a relatively short life while working very hard, with a life expectancy that was far lower than that of the masters.

Slavery was so dominant that even members of the elite who objected to it in principle, such as Thomas Jefferson, owned slaves. There were, however, other classes in the South. There was a fairly large number of free, white farmers, who farmed on the worst land, produced small crops, and were often in debt. In the cities, there were craftspeople of all varieties, including small independent workers, as well as some larger shops with masters and apprentices. There were merchants, with businesses ranging from small to very large, who were often middlemen for cotton sales. The merchants also imported manufactured goods from the North or from Europe, since very little was manufactured in the South.

Slavery encouraged certain kinds of social and political institutions. After the Revolutionary War, the South was part of the United States, so it had political democracy in theory. It was, however, a "democracy" in which the slaves were not allowed to participate. Women were not allowed to vote, either in the North or the South

Most power in every state in the South was held by male slave owners, with very limited representation by the free farmers, craftspeople, or even the merchants. The state governments, under the control of slave owners, passed severe laws to protect slavery. It was perfectly legal to beat slaves or to sell their children separately from families. It was a crime punishable by death for a slave to learn to read and write. Any slave revolts were punishable by death. Any attempts to escape were also severely punished.

There was a largely private education system, but it was mostly open only to white, male students. Slaves were prohibited from reading and writing because it was thought that it would be harder to control them if they were educated. Most of the churches were run by and for whites only. The white churches provided much of the social life and a great deal of information or misinformation to their members. The churches were the center of white life before the Civil War and played a major role in defending and perpetuating the existing system.

But there were also underground African-American churches. The African-American churches were the center of the social, musical, educational, and political activity of the African-American population. These churches were centers of revolt, as well as spiritual and social balm for their members.

Every place where slavery has existed, there also has been racism. Those who made vast profits by capturing or buying slaves in Africa claimed that the slaves were little better than animals. Those who sold the slaves at a high profit in the South said that they were very useful animals. Slave owners also held them to be inferior beings, so they were justified in keeping them as slaves, making them work very hard all day long, and giving them very little to eat, bad clothing, and insufficient shelter. The preachers of the white churches agreed that they were inferior. The preachers said it was the duty of white Christians to keep the slaves, provide them minimum provisions, and help them learn to be Christians so their souls would be saved. The slaves could be beaten in this world to teach them to live proper Christian lives, so they would go to heaven in the next world. Thus, racism and religion cooperated to support slavery with a rhetoric of saving the souls of inferior creatures.

The relation between economics and racism can be seen most clearly in the Southern reaction to President Lincoln's Emancipation Proclamation, which set the slaves free. The Southern politicians and journalists unanimously said that Lincoln was "stealing" their property. The slaves were not human beings, but property. As livestock—counted in the same category as cows and horses—the slaves were valued at three billion dollars. Therefore, Lincoln was robbing the South of three billion dollars of their private property. Many in the North agreed with this racist view of the slaves as property and denounced Lincoln as a robber.

In addition to racism, certain family values were an important part of the Southern ideology. The family was considered to be vital to the Southern culture. The family of the white master, however, was viewed and treated very differently than the family of an African-American slave. Within white families, all power was held by the father or husband. Women were placed on an ideological pedestal as the finest product of the Southern culture. But it was an isolated pedestal. The woman of the master class was not allowed to mingle with other men, not allowed to wander freely about a town, not allowed to get an education beyond sewing and perhaps French. Reading—except for the bible—and any further education was discouraged for women. Women played no role in public life or politics. Women could not be doctors or lawyers or even teachers until after the Civil War.

Women were expected to run the master's mansion by telling the slaves what to do, but the male master could always change his orders concerning the house or the children. If there was a divorce—which was rare, but sometimes granted at the request of the husband—women had no rights to money (even their dowry), no rights to property, and no rights to children! It was rare that women of the master class did any work outside the house. In the South, as in the North, if women had income, it belonged to their fathers or, if they were married, their husbands.

The rights of slave families were not recognized by the masters. As noted earlier, children could be and often were sold separately from their parents. Even Benjamin Franklin once advertised for sale a woman slave and her child, but said that they could be sold to separate masters. Some plantations essentially raised slaves by encouraging their slaves to have children and later selling them. Slave women could be used for sexual purposes by the male master or his sons. If the slave woman had her master's child, the child was often sold, thus getting rid of a problem while making more profit. Even Thomas Jefferson was rumored to have had children by his slave mistress, which he never acknowledged.

Yet if a woman of the master class had sex with a slave, the slave was killed and the woman could be divorced, beaten, or even killed without any legal consequences. Why was there a double standard between men and women with respect to sex? The justification was that it was necessary to know who was the legitimate child of a master male. Only the legitimate child could inherit property. Otherwise, the system of private property in land and slaves would—it was claimed—fall into chaos. Therefore, the severest punishment was meted out to women, while it did not matter what the men did.

Ideology in the South was thus characterized by support for strict class divisions, racist discrimination against slaves, and sexist discrimination against women of all classes. The sexism, however, had different forms depending on the class of the woman. All of this ideology was sugar coated by a pervasive religion that claimed that class division between masters and slaves, superiority of whites over African-Americans, and sexist superiority of men over women, was all dictated by an omnipotent God who loved everyone.

Slavery and Economic Progress in the Old South

One way in which slavery in the Old South differed from slavery in Ancient Rome was that Rome was surrounded by barbarian tribes, but the South was surrounded by capitalism in the North and free farmers who were becoming more and more commercialized in the West. Roman masters paid little attention to technology because they lived in Rome, far from their plantations, and technology was considered part of work, which was beneath them. Southern slave owners, however, tried to run their plantations in an efficient way and make profits. Thus, they were part of the international capitalist market and, to a certain extent, ran their plantations as capitalist enterprises.

Although Southern plantations tried to be efficient profit makers, they were very different from capitalist enterprises. Production was done by slaves, so there was no free labor market. Unlike capitalist enterprises, their assets consisted mainly of slaves who were bought and sold, unlike free workers. Those economists, who see the Southern plantations as part of the market, have argued that they were quite efficient and made good profits.

Slave holders were in fact intent on maximum profit, making them part of the capitalist marketplace with capitalist motives. They showed their desire for profits and ability to ignore the agony of people in many ways. For example, they sold children when that was the way to make maximum profit. The children were often sold without their parents. Moreover, the children were sold even if their father was the slave owner. So the slave owners strove for efficiency and profits.

Slavery was usually profitable. The slaves produced varying degrees of surplus, which was sold by the masters for a profit. In the late eighteenth century, after the Revolutionary War, the profit was fairly low and some talked of voluntarily ending slavery. Slave owners like Jefferson, who wrote the Declaration of Independence, were troubled by the contradiction between slavery and the high ideals of the Declaration. The Declaration said that "all men are created equal" and that all men have the right to "life, liberty and the pursuit of happiness." Thus, Jefferson owned slaves, but fought in the legislature to end slavery.

In the nineteenth century, the cotton gin made slavery more profitable, so slave owners stopped any talk of voluntarily ending slavery. Instead, they fought against abolition of slavery tooth and nail. As the Civil War began in 1861, the South was not in economic decline or stagnation. In fact, the South experienced rapid economic growth for fifteen years before the war. This explains why the Southern ruling class was willing to risk war to keep slavery.

At first glance, it appears that Southern agriculture was doing even better than Northern agriculture. The average value of a Southern farm was 34,000 dollars, while an average Northern farm was valued at only 4,000 dollars. But averages can be very deceiving. It is true that the wealth of the South was concentrated in the slave plantations.

A majority of all Southern farmers, however, were not slave owners. The majority were free, but were backward and poor compared to Northern farmers. The average farm belonging to free Southern farmers was worth less than 2,000 dollars. Therefore, even though the average for a Southern farm was 34,000 dollars, the majority were worth far less than the Northern farms. Agricultural wealth in the South was highly concentrated. The slave owners were rich men with large plantations, while free farmers were poor with small farms. In acreage, slave plantations were five and a half times as large as free Southern farms.

Slavery caused three problems for the South. First, most Southern agriculture consisted of small, nonslave farms. But the wealth of the slave owners allowed them to dominate the South, even though they were a minority. They kept the best land for themselves while the free farmers had much worse land. Thus the productivity on the lands of the free Southern farmers was far below that of the slave plantations and far below that of Northern farmers.

A second problem caused by slavery was that industry did not develop in the South. It is inconceivable to run a complex factory with slaves. Slaves would break complex machinery because any rational person would want to work as little as possible for a slave master. If a machine is broken, there can be no more work until it is repaired, so a slave could rest until then. Broken machines could also be used as weapons because they are both sharp and heavy.

During the first half of the nineteenth century, the North in the United States developed extensive industry. By the time of the Civil War there were projects in the North for a cross-continental railroad., large suspension bridges, and a transatlantic telegraph cable. But the South remained mostly agricultural with little industry and few railroads.

Third, and fortunately for the future of the United States, slavery weakened the Southern army. It had no industrial base, so it was soon short of supplies. Moreover, the slaves would not fight for the South. The slaves were much more likely to use any weapons against the Southern armies. In fact, many escaped to the North and became Union soldiers. The slaves going north were told by friends to "follow the drinkin' gourd," that is, the big dipper and the North Star. Furthermore, a large number of Southern troops were required to be on guard at all times against slave revolts. So the South had a shortage of soldiers.

Conflicts over Slavery

The Civil War did not result directly from the existence of slavery in the South, but from the attempt to expand slavery into the West. Why did the slave owners wish to expand into the West? As part of the capitalist market system, the slave owners put a heavy emphasis on producing a cash crop for profit. Therefore, they did not plant a diversified crop, but rather planted cotton year after year. This practice tended to deplete the land. Depletion of the land was one of the main reasons for the policy of expansionism.

There was still a certain amount of land available in the South, but it cost money. The land in the West was free, so it drew Southerners and Northerners alike. Even within the South, the plantations moved west to the more fertile land, increasing the productivity compared to the older regions.

Another reason why Southern slave owners found the western lands so attractive was that they could easily move most of their capital. Their most important capital was the slaves and they were completely mobile. Thus, even in regions with scarce labor supply, the slave owners had their own labor supply.

Finally, Southern state governments encouraged migration to the West because of the desire for more slave states. Thousands of free Northerners migrated to the West, so the Southern politicians worried over the need to maintain the balance between the number of slave states and free states.

The ancient Roman slave owners expanded easily into the European areas of France and Germany against barbarian tribes, who had inferior weapons and technology. The Southern slave owners, however, faced a very different situation. There were large numbers of independent farmers in the West. All of these farmers possessed weapons and were hunters who knew how to use their weapons. They did not want the competition of slavery in their midst. They did not like slavery, feared it, and sometimes attacked its morals.

There was one conflict after another between the free farmers and the slave owners in the West. A series of compromises were made by which slavery was restricted below a certain latitude, but escaped slaves were to be returned to the South. Compromises included explicit laws with regard to the Northwest Territory in 1787 and the Missouri Compromise of 1820. Eventually the intense struggle over the West could no longer be compromised. The war that broke out resulted in long years of bloody fighting, but it finally put an end to slavery.

In the Civil War, the South faced not only the farmers of the West and many former slaves fighting for the North, but also the Northeast farmers, workers, and industrialists. In the North, there was growing industrial production, which was largely lacking in the South. Northern industrial workers resented any competing goods made by the South, since they were produced by cheap slave labor. So Northern workers tended to support the abolition of slavery.

It was not only Northern workers, but also Northern industrialists who opposed slavery. On the subject of slavery, the Northern industrialists sounded like revolutionaries, claiming it was their religious scruples against slavery. But in addition to religion there were good economic reasons for opposing the slave owners. First of all, the fact that slavery threatened to expand into the West was deeply feared by Northern industry. As their businesses grew, the Northern capitalists expanded them into the West.

Since the slave owners wanted to expand into the West and the Northern industrialists also wanted to expand into the West, there came an inevitable clash between these two giants. The clash over who was to expand was not limited to the West. The slave owners also had a negative impact directly on the North through their control of most of Congress, the presidency, and the Supreme Court. The issues on which they clashed with the North were many. One important issue was the fugitive slave laws. These laws specified that escaped slaves living in the North should be returned by force to the South. The slave owners saw these laws as simply a return of their property, while the abolitionists saw these laws as the taking by force of free men and women into the morally abominable situation of slavery.

The other big issue was the tariff laws. The Northern industrialists wanted high tariffs on manufactured goods in order to protect their industries. Southern plantation owners wanted low tariffs on manufactured goods so that they could buy them cheaply. Moreover, the Northern industrialists wanted to expand their industries into the South, but there was no welcome in the South for industries with huge numbers of free workers. So Northern owners were frustrated in their desire to expand into the South.

In the political arena, the issue of slavery became more and more the focal point of all elections at the national and state levels. Northern white voters remained racist, but largely opposed slavery as bad for the country.

White women's groups in the North made alliances to abolish slavery with white and African-American abolitionist groups. In fact, the women's groups disappeared and merely became part of a united abolitionist movement. Women often played a leading role, especially as "conductors" or guides in the dangerous work of the Underground Railroad, leading slaves all the way out of the South to safety in Canada. The most dangerous work was often done by a small group of courageous African–American women.

At first, women were not allowed to speak in public for the abolitionists, but they eventually started to play more public roles. It was explicitly agreed in the abolitionist movement by the time of the Civil War that the movement should not only fight to end slavery, but should also fight for equality between both whites and African-Americans and between men and women.

Since slavery was eventually prohibited in all the Northern states, why did the slaves have to go to Canada for complete safety? This involves the legal struggle over slavery. One of the reasons that the Northern industrialists did not like the slave owners is that the two interest groups fought for dominance, not only in all the elected political bodies, but also in the Supreme Court. For a long time, the slave owners were dominant politically on the national scene through the Democratic Party. They also dominated the Supreme Court. In the pre-Civil War Dred Scott case, named after an escaped slave, the Supreme Court of the United States declared that slavery was not only legal in the South, but the slaves were property of their owners. As property, the Constitution supported the right of the slave owners to hunt down the slaves in any state of the United States and to bring them back South in chains.

After many years of fighting for the abolition of slavery in various political forums, the Republican Party was formed with the abolition of slavery as one of its goals. The Republicans received much financial support from the Northern industrialists, becoming not only the party of abolition, but also the party representing industry owners' interests. Eventually, in coalition with the Western farmers and the free workers of the North, the Republican Party elected its first president, Abraham Lincoln.

Much of the ideological battle was fought out in religious terms. The white preachers and politicians of the South almost all declared that slavery was a divinely ordained policy by which good Christians tamed the slaves, took care of the slaves, and brought them to Christianity. More and more, however, the Northern preachers and politicians declared that slavery was a work of the devil, an evil that had to be ended. The Baptists in the North were one of the strong voices against slavery. Some of the Northern industrialists, such as John D. Rockefeller, were Baptists and spoke out very strongly against the evil of slavery.

With Lincoln's election, there was an antislavery president in the White House, an antislavery Republican Congress, and an ideological climate in the North, fueled by religious views, against slavery. There was also an emerging antislavery literature. The antislavery novel, *Uncle Tom's Cabin*, became famous. It looked like the nation would inevitably move toward the abolition of slavery by constitutional and peaceful means. Therefore, the South rebelled and started the Civil War to maintain slavery. They spoke of the right of each state to decide its own economic system, but they meant their right to keep slaves.

The Civil War was the bloodiest war fought on American soil, lasting from 1861 to 1865. The South began with better-trained soldiers and generals and plenty of munitions. But the North had much greater industrial power. Therefore, as the war dragged on, the North eventually had to win by its superior arms.

After the war, during the period called Reconstruction, the South was occupied by federal troops and forced to give democratic rights to all. African-Americans were even elected to the U.S. Senate. Three Amendments to the U.S. Constitution were passed: to end slavery (Thirteenth), to give equal civil rights to former slaves (Fourteenth), and give the former slaves the right to vote (Fifteenth). The next chapter will show that the freed slaves remained in a subordinate situation economically, and that it took them almost a hundred years to get in practice the legal rights granted to them in theory by the Fourteenth and Fifteenth Amendments.

Conclusions

The conditions leading to the end of U.S. slavery were similar to those of Ancient Rome in that slavery held back most agricultural production and because industrial production was practically impossible under slavery. The situation was also similar in the desire of the slave holders for new lands and more slaves. But U.S. slavery was very different from the ancient type because it was part of the capitalist market, so it ran its plantations to maximize profit. It was also different because it had to deal with independent farmers in the West, industrialists and free workers in the North, and escaped slaves in the Union army. The inevitable clash, as slave owners, industrialists, and free farmers all tried to expand their holdings in the West, led to a war that ended slavery.

The end of the Roman Empire and the end of Southern slavery were similar in the sense that deep structural tensions in the political-economic system of each led to conflict among groups and classes that eventually ended slavery. The fall of U.S. slavery, however, did not lead to feudalism, nor did it lead to centuries of stagnation. Instead, it led to sharecropping, which appears to be a cross between feudalism and capitalism. This existed for many decades before the capitalist economic system finally conquered and integrated the South (sharecropping and Reconstruction are discussed in the next chapter).

These differences between Roman and Southern evolutions show that the same type of economic system can proceed in very different ways in different areas. Such different results occurred because the surrounding circumstances were different, and the systems that were quite similar in basic structure had different paths of development. Thus, each path differs a great deal and no specific path is the inevitable result of evolution in all places.

Suggested Readings

A pioneering book on Southern slavery that is well-written and good reading is Eugene Genovese, *Roll, Jordan, Roll: The World the Slaves Made* (1976). A more scholarly book by Genovese is *The Political Economy of Slavery: Studies in the Economy and Society of the Slave South* (1989).

A book (not recommended) that tried to argue that slavery was an efficient system and not so inhumane as usually portrayed was Robert Fogel and Sydney Engerman, *Time on the Cross* (1989). That book caused a firestorm of criticisms of its basic ideas. One excellent evaluation of the issues of the operation and fall of slavery—a very clear and readable book—is Roger Ransom, *Conflict and Compromise: The Political Economy of Slavery, Emancipation, and the Civil War* (1989).

– 7 –

Rise of Corporate Capitalism in the United States, 1865–1900

After the Civil War ended slavery in 1865, capitalism became the dominant system throughout the United States. Northern capitalists, not the former slave owners, controlled Congress, the presidency, and the Supreme Court.

The U.S. Industrial Revolution

Between 1865 and 1900, the United States changed from a relatively backward, rural, agricultural country to an urban, industrialized country with some very large businesses in the corporate form of enterprise. U.S. firms made major industrial innovations. Industry expanded in every geographical area, though far more slowly in the South than in the North.

The number of miles of railway jumped from 47,000 in 1860 to 237,000 in 1900. Both railroads and telegraph lines were extended all the way across the United States from East to West.

The expansion was driven by the investment of private capital, aided by extensive government subsidies. Gross private investment rose from less than 15 billion dollars between 1849 and 1858 to 28 billion dollars between 1889 and 1898. Production in the earlier period had been on a very small scale, often in the home, and much of it was in rural areas. Now production was in greater units, shifted from homes to factories, and from the countryside to cities.

Finally, there was a change from agriculture to industry. In the period from 1859 to 1899, agricultural production fell from 56 percent to 38 percent of gross national product. At the same time, manufacturing rose from 32 percent to 53 percent of gross national product. These changes mark the end of underdeveloped capitalism and the emergence of a new, major capitalist power.

The First Transcontinental Railroad

The first transcontinental railroad was begun in 1869, with a telegraph line right next to it. After the railroad was finished, goods and people could cross the United States in a week. This achievement was in stark contrast to the six months to a year it took to cross the country by wagon or around the southern tip of South America by ship. It was possible to go a much shorter distance by boat to Panama and cross to the Pacific over the narrow waist of Panama, but it was through disease-ridden jungles, where the death toll was high.

The fact that the train could provide a relatively pleasant trip in one week from coast to coast was an incredible change. In addition, the telegraph meant that messages could be sent instantaneously from coast to coast. Thus, the stage was set for a large number of nationwide firms.

The first transcontinental railroad extended the existing railroad from Omaha to San Francisco. Its construction is a fascinating story. During the Civil War, Abraham Lincoln strongly endorsed the idea of a transcontinental railroad and helped push it through Congress. The idea was to have a transport system that would make it easier to move goods, people, and soldiers. At the same time, the telegraph would be extended along the same line for rapid communication.

It was a daunting feat, since it meant covering thousands of miles by rails where there was often no water, no wood or rock for building, hostile people, lengthy desert terrain, and very high mountains. Its accomplishment in only about seven years was amazing and had major positive consequences on the U.S. economy and on the unification of culture, not to mention on military unity.

Congress and the president agreed it could not be done without government aid, but they believed that there could be no government ownership or control because of possible corruption. The result was that a small group of railroad financiers received immense amounts of low-cost government bonds and immense amounts of land, which exceeded the size of France.

These fortunes were not enough for the financiers, who proceeded to underpay or not pay the employees, robbed the railroad corporations themselves through other corporations, and robbed even more money from the government. One corporation set up by the financiers was the Credit Mobilier, which robbed both the railway corporation and the government of millions of dollars. When the whole scheme was exposed, it resulted in the biggest scandal of the nineteenth century. Until the exposure, these financiers all became fabulously rich and most of them managed to remain fabulously rich even after the exposure.

Much of the financiers' money came from paying the workers miserable wages for backbreaking work. The eastern part of the transcontinental railroad, called the Union Pacific, used thousands of Irish-American immigrants, who were paid low wages and were treated with prejudice and contempt.

The western part of the railroad was called the Central Pacific and employed many thousands of Chinese-American immigrants, who faced even more prejudice than the Irish and were paid even lower wages. On the Central Pacific, white men were paid three dollars a day, while Chinese-Americans only received one dollar a day.

The low wages had to compensate for extremely hard work from morning to night, with many workers getting hurt and many killed. For example, in the Sierra Nevada, the Chinese workers were lowered down the side of a cliff with a straight side and a very long drop, Then they had to drill a hole, set dynamite, and yell to be pulled up quickly. Many were killed in the process. The Chinese employees were thought to be docile. Finally, however, the conditions became so bad that even they went on strike.

The Chinese had worked six days a week from sunrise to sunset so they demanded a few less hours a week. They wanted an increase from thirty-five dollars a month to forty dollars a month, at least for the most dangerous jobs. They also wanted the supervisors to stop beating them, a demand which gives a chilling picture of the work conditions. In reply, the railroad stopped their food supply and starved them into submission. After terrible suffering, they had to agree to the same old salary, dangerous work, long hours, and beatings.

While this situation was more dramatic than most industrial processes, it symbolized the usual process of capitalist production at that time. Employees, from manual workers to engineers, were paid the lowest sum that the market allowed corporations to pay. Every employee had to earn profits for the company or else he or she was fired immediately.

The average employee, without a union, had no power. So the average employee worked part of the day to produce a product equal to his or her own wages, which were about equal to subsistence at a low level. Part of the day, however, was used by the employee to produce a profit for the corporation.

This economic oppression of the average employee was made much worse when prejudice was added to the picture. The existence of racial or ethnic prejudice caused public opinion to turn against the immigrants. Therefore, the immigrants had even less bargaining power than the average employee. In short, although the average employee was oppressed economically by having to produce a profit for the corporation, minority employees were twice as oppressed, while minority women employees were three times as oppressed. Although many things have changed, it will be shown that this basic pressure on employees to produce profit for employers remains in all countries with capitalist institutions.

Rise of Monopoly

This period not only saw the emergence and rapid expansion of industry under capitalist institutions, it also saw the change in the form of capitalism from individual entrepreneurs to corporations and the rise of monopoly power.

Most large firms decided to use the corporate form, which comprised a majority of manufacturing output by 1902. As noted earlier, a corporation is defined as an enterprise that is owned by many investors, each owning a share of its assets. This form allowed a large number of investors to put capital into an enterprise. Moreover, by law, creditors may sue the corporation, but investors have no personal liability for corporate debts.

Larger size meant more concentration of production and sales in a few firms. By 1902, just one or two firms did more than half of the production in seventy-eight U.S. industries. These giant firms had monopoly power, which means that they could raise prices by controlling supply. The one hundred largest firms had one-half of all manufacturing assets (see DuBoff, 1989).

What caused this change from small, often rural, and competitive firms to giant firms with monopoly power? First, the new technology in transportation and communication allowed the creation of nationwide firms. Second, new technology meant cheaper production with larger-scale firms. Not only were the costs cut by using better machinery, but the large size also meant that groups of workers could specialize in a particular area. Third, larger size enhanced a firm's ability to borrow money at lower rates. Fourth, giant firms could wield more power over government in any deals negotiated with government. Large size also gave firms more power to obtain government subsidies.

Finally, it was not just size that counted but monopoly power in an area of industry, which allowed higher prices and higher profits. For example, Standard Oil either destroyed its competitors—often by artificially low prices or by control of oil pipelines or railroads—or merged with them. Once it had enough power, it raised prices and made enormous fortunes for John D. Rockefeller and his associates.

Legal developments also propelled monopoly. At first, competing firms used informal agreements on price, then formal agreements on price, then trust agreements. A trust agreement set up a trust corporation that owned the stock of several firms. The trust then set the price for all the firms. But legislation, such as the Sherman Antitrust Act of 1890, eventually made these methods of price-fixing illegal.

One large loophole was left in the antitrust laws as interpreted by the courts. The law allowed a single firm to set its prices as it wished. The law also allowed firms to merge with each other into one firm. Many firms chose to merge into one giant firm. Then the new giant firm used its monopoly power to set prices.

In the period from 1895 to 1905, mergers between firms proceeded in a frenzy of combination and reached a new peak. In one industry after another, large numbers of competitors combined into one firm. In the oil industry, Standard Oil owned 95 percent of refineries at one time. United States Steel controlled 85 percent of steel production. The courts tended to punish certain anticompetitive business practices, but did nothing to prevent control of the market by sheer size.

Banking Corporations

Bankers came to be part of some corporate boards from 1840 to 1860, as was discussed in Chapter 5. After the Civil War, corporations needed more and more money to run larger-scale enterprises; so more bankers joined corporate boards. Banks also became very close partners with, and had much influence over, governments to whom they loaned money. For example, even the federal government borrowed money from banks to pay for wars. The U.S. government used banks to penetrate new foreign areas, such as China, by offering loans. The banks used government to protect them from prosecution of their acts both in the United States and abroad.

In the state governments, U.S. banks bought legislators. For example, when Maryland stopped interest payments on its debt, bankers bought "worthless" bonds. Then the banks bribed legislators to reinstate the bonds. In addition, the bank–government coalition financed the railroads and the canals.

From 1865 to 1900 was the period of the so-called robber barons. These included John D. Rockefeller in oil, J.P. Morgan in banking, Cyrus Vanderbilt in railroads, and Andrew Carnegie in steel. The motto of the robber barons was that anything goes; all is fair in love, war, and business.

Each of the robber barons worked closely with a big bank or a group of banks. In the early twentieth century, there were only six big banking groups. Each banking group controlled many corporations and worked with one of the robber barons. Thus, the J.P. Morgan banks helped create the monopoly called United States Steel. The Morgan banks also helped create a world shipping trust.

Under the robber barons and the bank groups, the railroads gave preferences to big customers, such as oil firms. The preferred prices were usually given when both firms were owned by the same group. Thus, Rockefeller was able to ship oil much more cheaply than his competitors.

The robber barons and their bankers reacted violently against unions. In the steel strike of 1892 in the town of Homestead, Pennsylvania, and in the railroad strike of 1894, the strikes were crushed when the robber barons convinced the government to use police and soldiers against the strikers.

Women After the Civil War

The Civil War and the rise of corporate capitalism had an immense effect on society. This chapter examines those changes, beginning with the changed role of women.

In 1865, most women were still living and working on farms, but were slowly moving into cities and industry. Most women were uneducated and almost all the schools were private schools for men only. There was a long fight for free, public education for both boys and girls. The campaign for free education for both sexes was at first accused of being "communist." There was also the notion that women should have a segregated education, separate from men. Eventually, schools were set up that were free and coeducational.

For the first time, teaching became respectable for women, and women began to take over primary school teaching from men. But because of discrimination against women, the salary of primary school teachers dropped relative to other professions once women entered the field. Women teachers had to be unmarried in most places and were fired if they got married. Women were not admitted to most universities and there were few women's colleges. Even as late as 1960, when I interviewed for a job at Princeton University, I was told that one of the best features of Princeton was that it had no women as students—and certainly no women faculty.

A few rich women did not work except to direct servants. Rich women were not supposed to do anything but look decorative, so they wore corsets that did not allow much movement and sometimes caused fainting. Most women were not rich and worked on the farm or in factories in addition to their work in the home. Women in the factories received much lower wages than men.

There was resistance to women entering all professions except prostitution. The reason was that women were considered inferior to men. Therefore the only profession open to many women who needed money was prostitution. As an example of obstacles to women, in 1872 Illinois prohibited women from becoming lawyers. The Supreme Court, filled with conservatives representing industrialists or landowners, upheld this law.

By 1890, women still made up only 17 percent of the paid labor force. Most unions discriminated against women, but the short-lived Knights of Labor invited them to join and they did so in large numbers.

In the 1890s a few women joined the American Federation of Labor (AFL), but received little support. The head of the AFL, Samuel Gompers, was anti-women, anti-African-American, and anti-Asian. Middle-class women worked hard in reform organizations, including the Women's

Christian Temperance Union, which supported many reforms besides temperance.

One problem for the women's movement after the Civil War came when the Thirteenth, Fourteenth, and Fifteenth Amendments to the U.S. Constitution were passed. These amendments gave civil rights and the right to vote to African-American men. Women, however, were not included in these amendments. Therefore, women—including, of course, former slave women—did not get the right to vote. Women, who had worked so hard in the abolitionist movement in solidarity with white and African-American men, were infuriated. They formed their own movement to fight for equal rights for women and for their right to vote. The women's movement for a long time tended to consist of liberal, middle-class, white women, having little or nothing to do with African-Americans.

Women had been left out of the Fourteenth and Fifteenth Amendments as a tactical move to get them passed in spite of prejudice. At this point, many women leaders not only split from their former friends in the abolitionist movement, but some of the women's leaders used racism as an argument for votes for women, claiming that the right to vote for white women could offset the "ignorant" votes of the former slaves. It was not until the 1960s that the women's movement and the African-American movement got back into close alliance as a result of new battles.

It required a long, hard fight from 1848 to 1920 to get the vote for women. In that period, the women's movement eventually forgot all other issues and concentrated only on the right to vote. Oddly, because it has been mainly a rural and conservative state, the first to give women the right to vote was the territory of Wyoming in 1869. The vote was given to encourage women to move to the territory. When Wyoming became a state in 1890, it became the first state whose constitution gave women the right to vote.

Sharecropping and Racism Against African-Americans

After the Civil War, the freed slaves received no land, so land ownership was still concentrated in a small class of former slave owners. This new landlord class did not think in terms of employing free workers to farm their large lands. The landowners did not have the heavy equipment or technology for large-scale farming and they no longer had the extremely cheap labor. What suited their relatively limited resources was to lease out their land to a class of subordinate farmers. The sharecroppers consisted mainly of former slaves and poor whites. The former slaves did not want to work on their masters' plantations, but wanted their own land and independence.

As a result, the landlords leased their land to poor whites and African-Americans. Although the slaves had been given their freedom, they were given no land and no money, so they were in a very poor bargaining position. They needed money to lease the land, money for equipment, and money for food until the crop was harvested. In return for the land, the sharecropper had to share half of his or her crop with the landlord.

Usually, when half the crop was given to the landlord, the remaining half was far from enough to pay for food for the farm family for a year, fertilizer, equipment, and seeds for the year. So they had to renew the lease on bad terms once again, usually about 50 percent of the crop. They also had to borrow money during the year in order to survive until the harvest, either from their landlord or from a moneylender. Therefore, as the system continued, the sharecroppers became deeper in debt each year. Just as in feudalism, they owed a payment in goods to the landlord. In sharecropping, however, many also owed money for repayment and a high interest to the moneylenders. The system was better than slavery or serfdom, but resembled them in that the sharecropper was clearly subordinate to the landlord and the moneylenders. The subordination was economic, legal, social, and political.

The economic subordination, as explained already, consisted of having no land but what they leased, paying half their crop for the lease, and heavy debts. The legal subordination consisted of the fact that the law not only held sharecropping and high rates of interest for loans to be legal, but also held that it was illegal to leave the state without paying all one's debts. If a sharecropper was caught trying to leave the state while owing money, he or she could be imprisoned. Moreover, the courts held that it was perfectly legal to use the prisoners in chain gangs, in which people were chained together, to go to various government work projects. The state even sent out prisoners in chains to do jobs for private businesses for which the state was paid. Thus, the result for many was the same as slave labor.

The sharecroppers clung to the lowest rung of society. They seldom received any education. They had no participation in any community decision making and they certainly were not invited to white churches.

Most important, during the entire period of sharecropping, from the Civil War to World War II, there was an all-pervasive racism. This racist prejudice and discrimination began under slavery, but it continued under sharecropping. Racism continued because it was very useful to the ruling elite, particularly the landlords, merchants, and moneylenders, since it reinforced their economic and political power.

The story of political power and its relation to racism is amazing and unpleasant. The Thirteenth Amendment to the Constitution ended slavery, the Fourteenth gave civil rights to everyone, and the Fifteenth gave the right to vote to black males. With these three amendments, and with the protection of federal soldiers, the former slaves participated in the democratic process after the Civil War. They voted, elected candidates, and participated in the then-radical Republican Party. But in 1876, there was a close and contested presidential election between the Democrat, Samuel J. Tilden, and the Republican, Rutherford B. Hayes. A compromise was reached behind the scenes of power by which the Republicans got the presidency, but the Democrats got the South. Federal troops were withdrawn.

Immediately, the South was terrorized by the illegal Ku Klux Klan, who tortured, murdered, and raped African-Americans. Eventually, the number of African-Americans able to vote or participate in politics dwindled away to a tiny few. The terrorism against the African-Americans in the South was carried out by various gangs and organizations, but it was helped by the police and supported by the white elite.

Then in the 1880s and 1890s, poor whites and poor African-Americans got together in the Populist Party and started to make big gains in the South. Feeling threatened, the ruling elite deliberately increased the amount of racist propaganda to split the races apart in the Populist Party. Laws were also passed to segregate every public place, though segregation had not legally existed after the Civil War. Laws were also passed to force voters to pay a poll tax, read and explain the Constitution, and to create other obstacles to voting. It was said that these laws would prevent African-Americans from voting so that whites would have the political power. But a great many poor and illiterate whites were also prevented from voting. By this means, the landlords, moneylenders, and merchants kept their power over the sharecroppers.

One result of this political-economic system was the stagnation of technology. Sharecropping held back technological progress as well as further investment of capital in agriculture for many decades until after World War II. If the sharecropper was foolish enough to invest in better equipment and technology to produce a larger crop, then the next year the percentage going to the landlord was raised. If the sharecropper refused to pay, the family was forced off the land. Of course, usually the sharecropper had no opportunity to invest in improving the land or equipment because the sharecropper did not have idle cash, but mounting debts. Wise tenants worried about the current crop, not about long-run development.

The landlord continued to own the land, so one might expect that the landlord would be interested in long-term improvements. But the landlord only got half the benefit from improved productivity, so landlords in this situation had much less incentive to invest in improvements than did those involved in ordinary capitalist enterprises. To be enticing, the investment had to improve the output by at least twice its cost.

Finally, since the sharecropper was deeply in debt, and since the contract was for only one year, the sharecropper had no margin for experimentation. Therefore, they stuck to production of cotton. In addition to harming the land, limiting themselves to cotton production meant that much of the new technology that became available had no application to their farms.

Racism Against Other Minorities

In the American Southwest, Mexican-Americans faced racial discrimination of many kinds. They were one of the largest minority groups and faced some of the worst discrimination.

Asian-Americans faced intense discrimination, with frequent campaigns against them in California. Even white labor attacked Asian-Americans on the grounds that they took jobs from whites. During World War II, in an atmosphere of hysteria, all Jews faced discrimination in education, where they were not admitted to some medical schools, not allowed in any major law firm, excluded from elite society, and were harmed in their businesses. During the Civil War, General Ulysses S. Grant refused to allow Jewish soldiers in his part of the Union army. From the Civil War until World War II, the J.P. Morgan bank never admitted a Jewish partner, even though some Jews ran their own banks.

In the ideological conflict, all of these minorities were labeled with false and cruel stereotypes. Such stereotypes drastically narrowed job opportunities. Stereotypes are prejudices that prevent people from seeing reality and maintain a certain image of a group regardless of reality. For example, it was assumed that African-Americans were only good for manual labor. When the federal occupation of the South allowed real elections, however, a large number of African-Americans were elected to various offices, and some served with distinction in the U.S. Congress.

In addition to these minorities, the white majority included a very high percentage of immigrants, who often made up as much as 40 percent of the population in many big cities. Each group of immigrants was treated with discrimination that was similar in result but different in degree. For example, the Irish were said to be loud and stupid. When one subtracted all of the minorities, all of the immigrants, and all of the women, the supposed superior white, male, long-time citizens were a small minority. That small minority of white men voted and controlled almost all political power in the period from the Civil War until 1900.

Labor Unions

After the Civil War, U.S. capitalism expanded rapidly into the South and the West, industry became large scale, and enterprises with large numbers of employees became commonplace. At the same time, working and living conditions were miserable. For example, in New York City in the 1860s, thousands of preadolescent girls and boys worked from 6:00 A.M. until midnight and were paid only three dollars a week. These conditions led to the spread of local unions, national unions composed of many local unions, and national federations composed of many national unions.

The Knights of Labor was a militant federation that was founded in 1869. The Knights of Labor expanded rapidly because of a major depression in 1873, combined with much police brutality toward strikers. After one strike in which police killed twenty men, women, and children, the *New York Tribune* applauded the police for attacking the strikers: "These brutal creatures can understand no other reasoning than that of force and enough of it to be remembered among them for generations" (quoted in Boyer and Morais 1970: 69). Anyone could join the

Knights, so the middle-class small business and professionals joined. Then the character of its leadership changed so dramatically that it turned to the advocacy of currency reform and opposition to all strikes, which led to a rapid decline in membership after 1890.

The American Federation of Labor (AFL) was formed in the 1880s. At first it was quite militant and socialist-oriented. The preface to its first constitution stated: "A struggle is going on in the nations of the world between the oppressors and oppressed of all countries, a struggle between capital and labor which must grow in intensity from year to year and work disastrous results to the toiling millions of all nations if not combined for mutual protection and benefit" (quoted in Boyer and Morais 1970: 90). But the AFL soon gave up the struggle between capital and labor. It became a "business union," which meant that it tried to win incremental wage increases, it paid no attention to larger issues, it had highly paid leaders with no militant qualities, and it tried hard to compromise with businesses.

The biggest and bloodiest strikes of this period were fought by unions that were independent of the AFL. For example, the American Railway Union struck the railroads in 1894, but was defeated with violence when the U.S. Army came in to move the trains, using the excuse of "protecting the mail."

Environment

While industry grew rapidly, there were very few environmental laws to restrain practices that harmed the environment. Since the side effects of business that harmed the environment did not lower profits, they were ignored by corporations. The land was harmed by mining and oil drilling with no worry about pollution. The tightly integrated ecology of plants and animals was harmed by cutting down forests and by killing whole species. The air was polluted by vast numbers of smoke-belching factories. Steel towns like Pittsburgh became very unhealthy places to live. The lakes and rivers were contaminated by waste.

There was only a small environmental movement. Advocates argued in favor of national parks against considerable resistance from businesses that wanted to use the areas to make profits. John Muir spent his whole life working for the environment and started the modern environmental movement with his founding of the Sierra Club in 1892.

Government and Economic Development

Chapter 6 discussed the fact that the U.S. government was generally dominated by the Southern slave owners until the election of Abraham Lincoln in 1860. We saw that the South then seceded from the United States and was defeated in a long and bloody war.

The influence of Southern slave owners on the national government completely disappeared after the Civil War. In the South, however, the influence of the new class of landlords and moneylenders continued to be supreme in that region. African-American sharecroppers and other poor farmers had almost no influence in the South after 1876, when the federal troops withdrew from the South.

The federal government was strongly influenced by business interests, who spent money to pay lobbyists, bribe legislators, and even bribe members of the executive branch. Of course, many of the bribes were more subtle than direct exchange of money for a favor, consisting of campaign contributions. Only rarely, as in the farmers' protest votes of the populist period of the 1890s, did farmers and workers have some influence.

As a result, in this period government helped business as much as it could and often boasted about it. One senator was said to have given a speech to rich industrialists in which he said: you give us the money to get elected and we give you the laws and subsidies you need. Even when popular pressure forced the passage of the Sherman Antitrust Act (an antimonopoly law) in 1890, it was filled with so many loopholes that it had little effect.

Government was also used to attack anyone with thoughts that were considered dangerous. Thus, college professors who advocated Darwin's theory of evolution were fired by many colleges in the late nineteenth century. Any college professor who was critical of business could also be fired.

The United States and Colonialism

Before the Civil War, the U.S. economy was much weaker than that of the British, so it remained in a neocolonial relation to England. The term "neocolonial" means a pattern where the stronger country sells mostly finished goods to the weaker country, while the weaker country sells only raw materials and agricultural goods to the stronger country. It also means that the stronger country invests in the weaker one, while receiving amounts of profit and interest that are larger than the annual new investment.

England established the largest colonial empire because it reached the stage of industrial capitalism first, so it had the greatest economic strength. As each European power became an industrial capitalist nation, each tried to catch up with the British in the extent of their colonies. None of the other countries ever succeeded in surpassing the size of the British empire, though they fought wars to accomplish that.

After the Civil War, U.S. industry grew rapidly. As a result, the relationship with England began to change. Eventually, the American economy began to compare in strength to the British and the two were on a more equal basis. For example, before the Civil War, the American economy slavishly followed every boom and bust of the British economy with a short time lag. After the Civil War, the American and British economies still moved together, but they each played the leader at different times.

As the U.S. economy became stronger, it followed the European example by trying to get its own colonies. It expanded to the Pacific through a war with Mexico in the 1840s. It was, however, too late to get many colonies by the time America was strong enough to do so. During the Spanish-American War of 1898, the United States defeated Spain, making Cuba independent of Spain. The peace treaty, however, gave the United States many extraordinary rights in Cuba, so it now resembled an American colony. The U.S. army also took over the Spanish colony of the Philippines against fierce Filipino resistance. Puerto Rico remained a U.S. colony. Alaska and Hawaii were occupied by the United States in this period, but were eventually incorporated into the United States.

The United States had to settle in the peace treaty with Spain for the Philippines, part of Panama, Puerto Rico, and a base in Cuba. When the Latin American countries gained their freedom from Spain and Portugal, the United States immediately began to gain influence in Latin America. In what is called the Monroe doctrine, the United States told the European powers to keep their hands off Latin America. The United States slowly came to dominate the region's politics. U.S. corporations moved in to dominate their economies in most cases.

Suggested Reading

Several of the best suggested readings for this chapter are the same as for Chapter 5, including DuBoff, Deckard, Flexner, Reich, Zinn, Ambrose, Chernow, Foster, Philip Foner, and Boyer and Morais.

By far the best book to start reading on the sharecropping period is Roger Ransom and Richard Sutch, *One Kind of Freedom: The Economic Consequences of Emancipation* (1977). A book that is powerful and wonderful to read on the peculiar twists in the politics of racism in the South after the Civil War is by C. Vann Woodward, *The Strange Career of Jim Crow* (1974). An excellent general history of the reconstruction period is Eric Foner, *Reconstruction* (1988).

− 8 −

Growth and Depression in the United States, 1900-1940

In the early twentieth century, as the economy grew, so did the power of corporations. Corporate income was 53 percent of all business income in 1929 and the percentage has continued to rise slowly ever since. Corporate savings—in the form of retained earnings and allowances for depreciation—became the most important form of saving. The ratio of corporate saving (earnings they did not pay out to stockholders) to all private income rose to 5 percent in the 1920s and has continued to trend upward ever since.

As corporate power grew, reformers tried to regulate their power, but that was very difficult. For example, In the early 1900s, Congress investigated trusts, but did little to change the situation. To reply to Congress, J.P. Morgan and his friends bought news organizations and newspapers, which were used to attack the congressional investigators.

Corporations were profitable and unregulated, with few taxes, so corporations got larger. The second great merger wave lasted from 1916 to 1929. The first merger wave had been mostly mergers with competitors on the same level, so they were called horizontal mergers. This form of merger, however, was now made illegal by congressional action and court interpretation. The second wave of mergers was smergers of firms along the upward production path, from the raw materials to the factory to the wholesale and retail sales places, so they were called vertical mergers.

Growth of national product was slowed by a financial panic in 1907, but then took off strongly after World War I gave production a boost due to military demands. The 1920s showed rapid economic growth, interrupted by short recessions. Especially important was growth in railway equipment, electricity, and automobiles.

The rapid growth in the 1920s included some ominous trends. One basic problem was increasing inequality. The United States was rapidly becoming a country with a small percentage of rich people and a very large percentage of poor people. There was persistent poverty of 15 percent or more. The problem of inequality was not only a human problem for those whose lives were ruined by it, but it was also a problem for the entire economy. Inequality harms the entire economy because the small income of the majority of the population—including the so-called middle class—meant a small consumer demand for most products.

Growing monopoly was described above, which meant high prices and smaller amounts of output. This trend made every downturn worse because the large firms kept their prices high to maintain profits, while millions of small firms were forced to set low prices, trying to compete with the giants. Thousands of small firms went bankrupt in every downturn. Finally, the 1920s witnessed a huge growth in consumer and corporate debt, which made the economy very vulnerable to catastrophe in the case of a recession.

Earlier periods had also seen instability. In spite of overall rapid economic growth, there were major depressions in the 1870s and the 1890s. In these depressions, the economy appeared to be running backward. Production fell. and vast numbers of people became unemployed. As income dropped, demand for goods dropped precipitously. People thought each depression would never end.

On the other hand, a long period of prosperity always gave rise to the notion that prosperity would last forever. This was true before the 1873 and 1893 depressions and was especially true in the 1920s. In 1929, on the eve of the Great Depression, many economists believed depressions were a thing of the past. (Investors and economists had the same unreal hopes in the 1990s, when it was thought that the boom in the economy and the bubble in the stock market would go on forever.)

After a depression begins, the extreme optimism turns to extreme pessimism. But the optimism and pessimism each come after the economy has changed direction, so the psychology of investors obviously is not the initial cause of the downturn or the upturn.

The Great Depression

The Great Depression was shocking. After so much optimism, it was very deep and very long, with 1938 production still below that of 1929. Human misery could be measured by the fact that official data said that one of every four workers was unemployed. Yet official data on unemployment underestimate unemployment because of several systematic errors, such as counting someone as employed if they work even one hour a week. In addition to manual workers, a large percentage of engineers and professionals of all types were unemployed. There was no unemployment compensation, so unemployed workers starved, stole, went to private charities, or called on soup kitchens to meet their material needs.

Not only did many corporations go bankrupt, but many banks also closed their doors. There was no insurance on bank accounts, so millions lost their savings when banks failed. There was almost no regulation of business, so a number of business empires built on smoke and mirrors completely collapsed. Each of these aspects reinforced the others and made the depression worse. It lasted for ten years, with a brief recovery followed by another decline in 1938.

The Great Depression forever changed American politics. Before the Great Depression, labor laws were antiunion, minimum wage laws were held to be unconstitutional, and business was largely unregulated. All of this changed.

Before the Great Depression, the Republican party ruled the country as the acknowledged representative of big business. When the Depression started, the Republicans were in power, so the Democrats claimed they could cure the depression. The Democrats overnight came to be considered the party of the lower-middle and middle-income groups, who constituted the majority of the population. The Democrats appealed to the majority interests in their propaganda, and to some extent, in their extensive reforms. They did not cure the depression, but they did accomplish many other things for ordinary people by what was called the New Deal. These reforms could only have emerged from the political upheaval caused by a great catastrophe.

Banks and the stock market were regulated by the New Deal legislation. Unemployment compensation was started. Social Security for retirees was initiated. Laws were passed to set minimum wages and maximum hours. Labor unions were recognized and made legal, with mandatory elections by the employees to determine their representatives.

Regulating the Banks

It should be noted that throughout the nineteenth century the United States had no central bank. There were monetary panics every ten years or so. A few large bankers sometimes stepped in to restore monetary stability, sometimes successfully, but often not. During the monetary panic of 1907, J.P. Morgan used his immense wealth and banking power to help restore stability to the banks and the stock market, while getting richer himself by the maneuvers.

After 1907, there were calls for a central bank, which finally led to the creation of the Federal Reserve in 1913. But the Federal Reserve had only limited powers to aid banks in distress and to manipulate the interest rate. Moreover, the Federal Reserve was and still is, by law, a curious combination of bankers and public interests. The central board is appointed by the president, with bankers' influence. The governing board of each of the regional Federal Reserve banks is mostly appointed by bankers. The New York Federal Reserve, the most important one, was completely dominated by J.P. Morgan for many years. It was not until the 1930s that there were strong regulations put on the banks and the stock market, as a result of the Great Depression.

The U.S. economy had changed in the 1930s from unregulated capitalism to regulated capitalism. In other words, the United States changed from fend-for-yourself capitalism to a mixed economy, with government providing a social safety net to the elderly, the unemployed, and the infirm.

Status of Women

Because it was believed that women were weaker and had to be protected, some protective laws for workers were passed exclusively for women. Some were very good laws, such as maximum hour laws, which the unions argued should be applied to men as well as women. For a long time, the Supreme Court, which was dominated by conservative representatives of the employers, decided that minimum wage and maximum hour laws were unconstitutional. They argued that such laws were unconstitutional because they violated private property. The court, however, made exceptions for women workers. The court ruled that because women were weaker than men, both maximum hours and minimum wage laws were constitutional when applied to women only.

Some "protective" laws, however, prohibited women from getting certain higher-paying jobs, so they protected men from the competition of women. An example was a law in many states that women could not be bartenders. The argument was that bartending tended to degrade women. Yet women were allowed to be the lower-paid bar girls, a job that frequently led to degradation.

Quite a few women joined the Socialist Party between 1900 and 1912, when the party grew rapidly to about 10 percent of the American electorate. While there was some prejudice against women even in the Socialist Party, at least this party firmly supported women's right to vote. Therefore, there was some alliance between the growing women's movement and the growing socialist movement with many people belonging to both.

One area of the country that never supported the constitutional amendment to give women the right to vote was the South. The South combined prejudice against African-Americans with prejudice against women. Both prejudices had their ideological source in the institutions of slavery, but carried over into the still mainly rural and poor South until the 1960s. Southern white, elite men wanted to keep power in their hands, without sharing it with African-Americans, women, or any low-income persons. The Southern elite claimed to put women on a pedestal, but it was a lonely pedestal. Women of the ruling elite were isolated from society at home, separated from politics, and usually denied much education.

For decades the women's movement in the United States proceeded very quietly and respectably so as not to antagonize men, but they achieved little. Then in the short period from 1914 to 1920, by taking advantage of the need for women to support World War I, some women practiced very militant tactics. They often landed in jail, but in 1920 women did gain the right to vote by the Nineteenth Amendment to the Constitution.

Because of tight control by high income, white males, no states in the deep South ratified the amendment until long after it was passed. (In 1984, Mississippi was the last state to ratify the amendment.) Outside the South, women's right to vote was also opposed vehemently by the liquor industry, because the industry was afraid that women would vote against liquor, as many did during the prohibition era. Opposition to women's right to vote also came from the Catholic Church, which felt that women in public positions would violate the "proper" subordinate place of women. Women's right to vote was strongly opposed by big city bosses, who felt they had men under their control, but that women added an uncertain factor.

Finally, much of big business opposed women's right to vote because prejudice was profitable. Prejudice allowed business to keep paying women very low wages, which produced higher profits. By maintaining sexist prejudice among male employees, corporations were able to pit men against women in bargaining and strikes. The corporate objective was to divide the two groups and thus continue to rule over wage bargaining.

The women's movement had over two million active members by the time the Nineteenth Amendment was passed in 1920, but by 1924 there was almost no movement. Why? Mostly because the coalition was built around one issue, the right to vote, so it fell apart when that issue was won. Although the women's movement declined, the number of women voting rose slowly, so politicians began to fear the wrath of women.

The Great Depression hurt both men and women employees with falling wages and massive unemployment. As men worried about their own jobs, some men said women did not need to work, so they should be fired before men and get lower wages than men if they did work. In reality, most women had to work—and still do—just to keep their families out of poverty. Many husbands of married women have wages too low to support a family, while single women need the wages just to support themselves.

As more families moved to the cities, women became more integrated in society outside the home. In 1890, women were only 18 percent of the paid labor force. By 1940, they were 25 percent of the paid labor force, though most continued to work many unpaid hours at home. In 1890, women had only 17 percent of all bachelor's degrees, but that rose to 41 percent in 1940.

Unions

In the early 1900s, the Western Federation of Miners struck against miserable conditions in the Colorado mines owned by Rockefeller. But Rockefeller had great influence in the state government. The union was defeated by the state militia, who used machine guns on some miners' camps, killing men, women, and children.

In 1912 there was a strike by women and children against long hours, low pay, and notoriously bad working conditions in the textile mills of Lawrence, Massachusetts. The strike turned into a long, hard battle. The women strikers sang the song, "Bread and Roses," asking for both higher wages and respect. Although they lost, they did make the miserable working conditions known to most of the country in a series of sympathetic protests, covered by the media.

During the Great Depression wages fell by one-third, while one of every four workers was unemployed. The American Federation of Labor (AFL) did nothing to help the unemployed and it even opposed unemployment compensation as an un-American proposal. Again, independent unions led some militant strikes. One example was the strike of the International Longshoreman's Association on the West Coast in 1934. When the union first tried to bargain with the employers, the employers simply fired all the union leaders. Eventually, about 35,000 maritime workers were out on strike.

The center of the strike was the Embarcadero at the port of San Francisco. On July 3, 1934, the police decided to break the mass picket lines to allow scabs (replacement workers) to work. One reporter wrote: "The police opened fire with revolvers and riot guns. Clouds of tear gas swept the picket lines and sent the men choking in defeat. . . . Squads of police who looked like Martian monsters in their special helmets and gas masks led the way, flinging gas bombs ahead of them" (quoted in Boyer and Morais 1970: 285). But this was only the beginning. The pickets returned on July 5 (known as Bloody Thursday), and they were joined by many young people from high schools and colleges, as well as by hundreds of other union members. The police charged, using vomiting gas, revolvers with live ammunition, and riot guns. Hundreds were badly wounded, and two workers were killed.

The pickets finally were driven away, and the employers thought they had won. But many union locals, as well as the county Labor Council, called for a general strike. In spite of a telegram from the president of the AFL forbidding any strike, the workers of San Francisco launched a general strike to support the maritime workers and in protest against the killings by the police. The general strike was amazingly successful: "The paralysis was effective beyond all expectation. To all intents and purposes industry was at a complete standstill. The great factories were empty and deserted. No streetcars were running. Virtually all stores were closed. The giant apparatus of commerce was a lifeless, helpless hulk" (newspaper report, quoted in Boyer and Morais 1970: 287).

During the general strike, labor allowed emergency food and medical supplies into the city, but nothing else. Thousands of troops moved into the city, but there was no violence; workers simply refused to go to work. The general strike lasted until July 19, when the local AFL officials, refusing to hold a roll-call vote of the central labor council, announced that a majority of the council had called off the strike. The employers, worried about another strike, raised the wages of the maritime workers to ninety-five cents an hour.

Then, in 1935, John L. Lewis, head of the United Mine Workers, led an exodus of the most militant unions out of the AFL to form a new federation, the Congress of Industrial Organizations (CIO). The CIO engaged in many strikes, used many socialists and communists as organizers, fought the employers tooth and nail, and spread very rapidly. The CIO supported President Franklin Roosevelt and the New Deal, which legalized unions (forcing elections when enough workers petitioned). Because of labor militancy and a supportive government, union membership grew from 11 percent of all employees in 1930 to 32 percent in 1950.

Environment

In this period, there were very few government regulations, and little was done to preserve the environment. One exception on the environment was President Teddy Roosevelt. In the early 1900s, Teddy Roosevelt became the first oresident to make the environment a top priority and created the National Park System. In the 1930s, President Franklin Roosevelt used unemployed workers on many conservation projects. Nevertheless, until the 1960s the growing capitalist manufacturing met few environmental regulations.

Racism

The period of sharecropping in the South lasted from the Civil War until World War II. The previous chapter showed how this institution plus other Southern social and political institutions held back Southern eco-

116

nomic growth in the last half of the nineteenth century. These obstacles continued to hold back the Southern economy all the way to World War II. From 1900 to 1929, while growth in the North was rapid, growth in the South lagged far behind, particularly in its lack of industrialization. From 1929 to World War II the depression hit the South very hard, so economic conditions for sharecroppers were abysmal.

The group that was hurt worst by the depression was African-Americans because most were still sharecroppers in the South until World War II. They could not shift into industry because there was little industry in the South, and no jobs in Northern industry were open during the Great Depression. They were also handicapped because there were strong legal barriers preventing African-Americans from voting in the South, which meant that they could not turn to the political system for help.

African-Americans did try to organize themselves in various organizations for political and economic defense, but it was very difficult for sharecroppers to organize. They lived on isolated farms, far from each other. That isolation made organizing very different from organizing a manufacturing plant with large numbers of workers. Another obstacle to organizing was that African-Americans were often illiterate or had very little education because the Southern schools were all segregated, with little or no resources going to African-American schools. Moreover, sharecroppers had no equipment for quick communication, no vehicles for quick transportation, and no money for political purposes.

Not only was there racism against African-Americans in the South, but there was racism against Mexican-Americans in the American southwest. This racism began after the conquest of the southwest by the United States in its war against Mexico. Mexican-Americans were pushed out of their farms by various legal means and most became low-paid workers in agriculture. In the period from 1900 to 1940, many Mexican-Americans went to the cities, but they still found low-paid jobs and were treated as second-class citizens.

Racism in the United States in this period was not only affected by U.S. institutions and economic conditions, but by ideologies and movements around the world. Racism in the 1930s became a global phenomena because racism in one country reinforced racism in all the others.

On the world stage , the worst racism was against Jews. In the 1930s and during World War II, fascist Germany put all Jews in concentration camps, tortured them, and killed millions in the largest genocide of the twentieth century. Fascism spread to some groups in the United States that tried to prevent Jewish participation in well-paid careers in the economy.

In the United States, the business elite were just as prejudiced against Jews as the least-educated white, male workers. Some of the elite actively encouraged prejudice. For example, both Henry Ford and J.P. Morgan were violently anti-Jewish and certainly never considered African-, Mexican-, or Asian-Americans as anything but inferiors who should be their servants. Henry Ford edited a newsletter that often praised Adolph Hitler and was filled with anti-Jewish prejudice. Thus, fascist sentiments caused additional prejudice in the U.S. labor market until World War II drastically changed the situation.

Fascism

While the American government became more liberal and tolerant in the 1930s, Germany, Italy, and Japan became fascist. Fascism included one-party dictatorship, blood-thirsty intolerance, and extreme reactionary actions against workers. To understand U.S. history after 1930, it is necessary to detour and take a look at fascism.

Fascism in Italy and Germany in the 1930s took the pattern of entanglement and cooperation between business and government to an extreme. The heads of the fascist (Nazi) party in Germany became heads of many large corporations. These corporations were guaranteed to get all of the government business.

In addition to its merger of business and government, fascism also had a practice and ideology of racism and sexism. Women were told to stay in their place, which was in "the kitchen, the church, and [with] children" according to Adolph Hitler.

Anti-Jewish views were a principal feature of German fascism. At first, Jews were harassed, then herded into concentration camps, and eventually six million were killed. Hitler used anti-Jewish ideology to gain power by blaming all of Germany's troubles on the Jews. Hitler's standard speech to German workers claimed that their troubles were all due to the Jewish bankers, who controlled finance and ruined the economy. Yet, Hitler's standard speech to the German bankers claimed that all of the labor organizers were Jews, who were causing all of the problems for German bankers.

It is very revealing that U.S. business leaders were very friendly toward fascism in Germany, Italy, and Japan. For example, Henry Ford wrote favorably about Hitler and the institutions of German fascism. J.P. Morgan's bank worked with the Italian fascist leader, Benito Mussolini, giving him loans, advice, and assisting him with propaganda to improve his public relations. The J.P. Morgan Company also had close ties with militarist Japan and provided it with many loans. When Japan invaded Manchuria, an act of unprovoked aggression, the top J.P. Morgan partner secretly wrote a news release defending Japan. The Japanese government changed a few words, and then released the statement as its own to the U.S. media.

Colonialism

U.S. corporations moved into Latin America in the nineteenth century and have been there ever since. In some cases, the U.S. military aided these corporate efforts. In Nicaragua throughout most of the 1912–33 period, for instance, the Marines helped U.S. corporations and the U.S. government to collect debts, to manage Nicaragua's tariff collections, and to quell left-wing rebellion. The pattern of production and trade between the United States and Latin America conformed with the classic picture of neocolonial countries.

The pattern of production and trade was reinforced by the pattern of investment. The U.S. corporations invested in the agricultural and mining sectors of Latin America, with emphasis on extraction of oil and other raw material exports. Areas of interest to U.S. corporations included copper in Chile; oil in Venezuela; and cotton, bananas, and coffee throughout much of Central America. There was very little investment in manufacturing. U.S.-owned agricultural and extractive corporations generated financial profits, which flowed in the form of money back to the United States. Some of the food and raw materials produced were purchased by the parent corporations at low prices to be shipped to the United States and made into high-priced finished goods. Many of these finished goods were sent back to Latin America, where they generated more profit by being sold at high prices. Again, this pattern of investment characterized all of the colonizing powers in the late nineteenth and early twentieth centuries.

Why were the colonizing powers, including the United States, so eager to gain colonies? First, their conquering armies looted all the gold and silver owned by the natives. Then they made huge profits in agriculture, mining, and oil extraction with cheap labor. When these treasures and profits were returned to the colonizing country, they helped the process of accumulating capital for industry.

It has often been pointed out that it takes more money to conquer and hold a colony than can be extracted from it. Thus, most people in the colonizing country do not gain from colonization, but actually lose, due to the expense of maintaining armies and the loss of the lives of their soldiers. But those corporations that control the colony's economy and trade usually make extremely high profits. This was true in the nineteenth century and remains true today. For example, colonizing India cost England greatly in money and lives, but some British companies made fabulous fortunes there. Thus, the colonies helped capitalist corporations to grow faster and to create more economic advancement in the colonizing country, while the outward flow of profits held back the growth of the colonial economies.

Italy, Germany, and Japan came relatively late to industrialization, and therefore lacked the power to gain a large empire at the time when Britain and France had already created theirs. In this period, many wars were fought to subordinate other countries and make them colonies. But there were also wars between the imperialist countries, which were always rivals for new territory. German economic power was increasing, and by 1914, the German economy had surpassed the British economy. Therefore, Germany resented and envied England's large empire. Thus, one reason for World War I was the clash of these two rivals. England desired to maintain the status quo and its large empire, while Germany was seeking a large new empire in keeping with its new economic power.

Economic Institutions and War

Let us remember from earlier chapters the nature of war in different historical periods. In the prehistoric communal period, there were occasional individual fights over hunting grounds, but no sustained warfare because there was no wealth to fight about. In the ancient empires built on slavery, there were wars to take the wealth of cities, to conquer new land for plantations, and to take more slaves. In the feudal period, lords fought over who controlled various villages of serfs, both for wealth and for military power.

In the period of capitalism, the underlying mechanism for war has been the expansionist drive of corporations and their governments to take over colonies, or later, neocolonies. Colonies and neocolonies are sources of markets, cheap labor, cheap raw materials, and profitable investments. From 1776 to 1940, there were wars between colonizing countries and weaker countries, in which the object was to take over the weak country as a colony. But there were also wars, such as World War I, that were between rivals for empire.

Suggested Reading

Several of the best sources and suggested readings for this chapter are the same as they were for Chapter 7, including DuBoff on economic history, Deckard on gender discrimination, Flexner on the women's suffrage struggle, Reich on the history of racism, Foster on environment, and Philip Foner, as well as Boyer and Morais on unions.

– 9 –

Development of the United States Under Global Capitalism, 1940–2004

Global capitalism is the latest stage of capitalism, in which capitalist institutions dominate the entire world and global corporations are found in every country. The focus of this chapter is on the development of the United States and its relationship to global capitalism.

U.S. Evolution from Power to Superpower

U.S. participation in World War II lasted from 1941 to 1945. During that war, many entire cities were destroyed and tens of millions of people were killed. The economies of most of the world were devastated. The U.S. economy, however, recovered from the Great Depression and rose at a very fast pace during World War II.

By 1950, the U.S. economy was producing 80 percent of all world manufacturing production. As other nations' economies recovered slowly, they needed financing and goods from the United States, both for consumer survival and industrial revival. The United States was the world's greatest economic and military power.

The closest contender was the Soviet Union, whose economy had been badly hurt by the war. The Soviet Union lost perhaps a third of housing and industry to the German invasion. Moreover, during the war with Germany, it had twenty million deaths. There was an economic and ideological conflict, known as the Cold War, between the U.S. bloc and the Soviet bloc. The Cold War lasted from 1945 until the overthrow of the Soviet Union in 1991 (discussed in Chapter 12). The Soviet demise left the United States as the sole superpower.

The Long Boom in America from 1945 to 1970

To fully understand how the United States became the sole superpower, this chapter begins with a look at the great U.S. boom of 1945–to 1970. Some American capitalists became fabulously rich during a long upward trend from the end of World War II to the crises of the early 1970s. In that period, the United States had short recessions and long, strong expansions. Real wages rose from year to year. Profits rose in most years. The U.S. economy dominated trade because other countries had been destroyed in the war. Thus, money flowed into the U.S. economy.

American exports were very profitable in this period. Therefore, the percentage of production going to exports kept growing. Moreover, U.S. corporations made large, very profitable, investments abroad. The U.S. government and U.S. banks made vast loans abroad, so many other countries were in debt to them.

The brightest people from all over the world immigrated to the United States to make their fortune. This drain of the best brains to America from the rest of the world accelerated technological progress. The U.S. economy alone had money for a large amount of research, so its technology led all others. The average unemployment rate was relatively low. In short, the period from 1945 to 1970 was a long-run boom, a golden age.

The Long Stagnation in America from 1970 to 1990

There was, however, a long-run stagnation, lasting from about 1970 to 1990, with weaker booms and longer, deeper recessions. As compared with the average for 1945 to 1970, the growth rate of gross domestic product fell, while the rate of unemployment rose. The average amount of annual net investment also declined. Real weekly wages reached a peak in 1973 and then fell during the rest of that period.

For those who like precise data, from 1947 to 1970 the U.S. gross domestic product grew 3.7 percent per year. By contrast, the period from 1970 to 1990 witnessed only a 2.5 percent growth of gross domestic product per year. While fixed investment grew 3.5 percent a year in the earlier period (1947–70), it grew only 2.8 percent per year in the later period (1970–90).

Why did the great boom of the 1950s and 1960s turn into the great stagnation of the 1970s and 1980s? As usual, there were many reasons, but a few are probably most important. First, the rest of the world rose from devastation to become strong again, so the corporations of Japan and many European countries began to compete effectively and successfully. As foreign competitors grabbed away U.S. markets, the U.S. share of global industry fell.

Second, the boom of the early post–World War II years was helped by pent-up U.S. demand in savings that could not be spent in the war years. After the war, this demand was unleashed and gave a strong initial push, which eventually petered out. Third, the United States started out with a technological advantage, but other capitalist countries caught up.

Boom and Bust in America from 1990 to 2004

In the 1990s, American technology spurted ahead and the American economy had an unusually long expansion. It out-competed all of its rivals in many areas and again looked like a superpower.

The boom, however, was not as spectacular as it looked at first glance. The American economy grew rapidly only for four or five years in the late 1990s. Real wages also hardly rose before 1995, then they did make significant gains for a few years in the late 1990s. Since the stock market grew very rapidly in the 1990s, profits greatly outstripped wages for the entire period. The fact that profits and stock market prices grew far more rapidly than wages and salaries meant that income distribution became more unequal.

Even in the 1990s, the U.S. economy was not anywhere near as dominant as it had been in the 1950s. The European Union was still catching up to the U.S. economy. After the end of the Soviet Union in 1991, the U.S. military became the only super military power. American military spending has run far ahead of the American economy. Thus, the U.S. economy slipped in the economic race, but the U.S. military remained dominant at a growing cost.

Some economists predicted the boom of the 1990s could go on forever.

In the early 2000s, however, there was a recession. In addition, the stock market bubble burst, providing three years of market decline. The recession created large unemployment and lower real wages. Thus, real wages were stagnant and actually fell in the thirty years between 1973 and 2003.

The U.S. recession and stock market decline influenced the rest of the world and there ensued recession and stock declines all over the world. The fact of global capitalism caused both boom and bust to be transmitted around the entire world instantly.

Emergence of Global Capitalism, 1970–2004

What is "global capitalism"? Most countries are predominately capitalist or moving that way as fast as possible, though some are at a less developed stage while others are in an advanced stage of capitalism. The term "globalization" refers to the process by which the world is moving toward a fully global capitalism.

Beyond this simple definition of the global economy and globalization, the new global economy has several important features in finance, trade, and colonial relations discussed in later sections. One obvious feature was the new technology that emerged in this period. The economy of the entire world is held together in a tighter and tighter network by thousands of economic strings.

Why has the world become such a tight, closely knit economic unit even while individual nations persist and remain important? Communication and transportation have been improving for centuries. Since the information revolution of the 1990s, however, global communication has become instantaneous, while people and goods can be transported around the world in hours rather than months. In the time it takes to make a few keystrokes, billions of dollars can be moved from one continent to another.

Although some of the changes in the global economic network began hundreds of years ago, many changes accelerated in the early 1970s. Thus, the stage of global capitalism may be dated to around 1970.

More important than communication and transportation improvements, the institutions of capitalism—and its ideology—have spread to every nook and cranny of the world. While some aspects of global capitalism began to emerge clearly in the 1970s and 1980s, full global capitalism did not become a reality until the 1990s. Only after the Soviet

Union, China, and Eastern Europe turned toward capitalism did it dominate most of the world.

One indicator of the magnitude of global capitalism is the fact that by the year 2000, the total movement of money across borders every day amounted to 1.5 trillion dollars. Another indicator of the growth of global capitalism in this period is the fact that in 1982 the flow of direct investment across borders amounted to 57 billion dollars for the whole global economy. By 2000, the flow of direct investment across borders amounted to 1,271 billion dollars. This was an incredible increase of over twenty times. (These data and the entire international financial scene are found in Burton and Nesiba, 2004.)

America from Surplus to Deficit in Global Trade, 1970–2004

Earlier sections examined the domestic changes in the United States beginning around 1970 and the ensuing long stagnation. In addition to the domestic changes in the early 1970s, there were also important changes in the U.S. international sectors of trade, finance, and investment. The story begins with changes in trade.

From 1870 to 1970, the U.S. economy sold more goods and services abroad than it bought. Therefore, money flowed into the United States. Thus, until 1970, the United States had a trade surplus and an inflow of money, called a favorable balance of trade.

After 1970, for the first time in a century, the United States was buying more goods abroad than it sold. Because the United States moved from having a trade surplus to a trade deficit, money was flowing out on net rather than in. Since 1970, the unfavorable trade balance and trade deficit have been seen every year and have been growing greater over time.

The U.S. trade deficit has become very important as trade has become a bigger part of the U.S. economy. In fact, the ratio of U.S. exports to gross domestic product was only 5 percent in 1950–54. But then it began to rise and was an average of 11 percent in 1980–84. Clearly, the U.S. economy had became more dependent on international trade by the end of the 1980s The trend to more dependency on trade continued throughout the 1990s and early twenty-first century.

Some of the U.S. trade deficit is due to the great amount of military goods and services bought abroad. Some is due to competition from the growth of technology and industry in Europe and Asia.

The deficit has been increased by new free trade areas in Europe and Asia that exclude the United States. A free trade area means an area with low or nonexistent tariffs and other barriers to trade. The free trade area of the United States includes only Canada and Mexico. The European Union has now established a free trade zone in all of Europe, leaving the United States outside. Moreover, eastern Asia now has its own free trade area covering China, Japan, and all of Southeast Asia, which also leaves the United States outside. South America is also moving toward a free trade area for all of its countries that will exclude the United States. Thus, the most favorable trading conditions for the United States are now limited to a small area of the globe.

America from Creditor to Debtor, 1970–2004

The changes in international trade affected the international financial position of the United States. After 1970, instead of money flowing into the United States because of a trade surplus, money started flowing out of the United States because of a trade deficit. A country must find some way to pay for its trade deficit. In order to pay for a trade deficit, a country must pay out cash or go into debt.

Thus, from World War II until 1970 the United States was a creditor nation to whom other countries owed money. After 1970, the United States has become a net debtor, owing money to other countries. This means that U.S. companies go into debt each year because they buy far more goods from foreigners than foreigners buy from U.S. companies.

The United States is now the largest debtor among all nations. In addition to private debt, the American government has been spending vast sums abroad for military purposes, including for bases in many countries as well as wars. For this reason, in recent decades the U.S. Treasury has had to borrow money abroad. For the first time in a hundred years, foreigners now own more of the U.S. national debt than Americans own of foreign debt. So the United States is again a net debtor as it was in its early days when it was a neo-colony of England.

Not only is debt to foreign countries a sign of weakness, but it also puts the United States in some economic danger. For example, the Chinese government owns quite a bit of the U.S. national debt. If China should decide to shift its bondholding rapidly from the United States to the European Union, it would disrupt the U.S. economy to some extent.

There were also changes about this time in U.S. international invest-ment. From 1914 until recently, American corporations have invested more abroad than foreigners have here.

Since the 1970s, however, the amount of foreign investment in the United States has been growing rapidly in size. By 2003, total foreign investment in the United States was 2.3 trillion dollars more than U.S. investment abroad (National Bureau of Economic Research, 2004). While the United States remains the largest single investor, Japan and Europe have been gaining since the 1970s. The United States still has immense foreign investments, but it has become relatively weaker economically compared with Europe and Japan. In other words, in the economic race the United States is still the largest single economy, but Europe and Asia have been closing the gap.

Furthermore, American investment abroad has become far more im-portant to the U.S. economy. Thus, U.S. investment abroad was 7 percent of all U.S. investment in 1929, but rose to 30 percent by 1987. The United States, however, remains the world's only military superpower.

American Governmental Power and Its Limits Under Global Capitalism

Throughout American history, government spending was very low in peacetime. For example, the federal government spent only 1 percent of gross domestic product in 1929. In wartime, however, the amount going to government spending rose drastically. For example, govern-ment spending rose to 40 percent of gross domestic product during World War II.

After World War II, military spending was at first reduced. But then there was the Cold War, and money was used for propaganda, economic pressure, and some military adventures against the Soviet Union. Both sides used the Cold War as a rationalization for increased military spend-ing. The percentage of military spending in the United States continued to increase until the end of the Cold War in 1991. The percentage of military spending then fell for a time. Under the second President Bush, however, it rose again, partly to pay for the invasion and occupation of Afghanistan and Iraq.

A few conservatives argue in general that the government should spend nothing on anything, but most conservatives qualify that preference by several major exceptions. The argument that government should do nothing, or as little as possible, is based on the proposition that the private economy will use all resources better than the government. The broad statement by conservatives that the government should be relatively tiny is completely reversed by the major "exceptions" they admit to that policy. What are these exceptions?

The most important single exception is military spending. Military spending is said to be good because it protects private property. Conservatives fight to spend huge amounts on war because it will protect the property of their country. Wars bring very high profits for corporations in military production. These corporations give financial support to conservative parties.

Conservatives similarly argue for expenditure on police and prisons because these institutions also defend private property. Finally, many conservatives, but not all, argue for subsidies to various types of businesses, including agriculture and shipbuilding (to transport vital materials for war).

Conservatives are split on using government for social purposes, with libertarian conservatives opposing any such use. For example, many conservatives, such as President George W. Bush, advocate using the police and courts to prohibit women's right to abortion. Bush and other conservatives would also use the legal enforcement system to spy on the political actions of people who advocate policies contrary to theirs. One example is the conservative attempt in 2005 to extend the so-called Patriot Act, which reduces the safeguards against government spying on people. In the 1950s, conservatives spent large amounts of government money spying on millions of citizens.

Most liberals, though not all, have argued against high military spending except in time of war. Liberals argue that it is more important to spend money on universal education, universal health care, free national parks, and other social necessities. Their announced standard is not what is good for private property, but what is good for all the people. Thus, one vital political issue is: in which categories should the government spend money?

Since the election of a more conservative government in 2000, there has been a strong tendency to spend more on military equipment but less on social services, unemployment compensation, and other assistance to common people. Military contractors support conservative governments because the average profit rate on military spending is much higher than it is on nonmilitary manufacturing.

The reason for higher profits in military spending is that there is often no free bidding, but rather a process run by insider connections with an integral relation between the military industry and the generals in charge of procurement. In fact, every corporate military contractor employs former generals at high salaries, who discuss procurement with their former subordinates, These former subordinates also expect to become high-paid employees of the military corporations. This has often resulted in spectacular, well-publicized cases of corruption, such as the military paying 5,000 dollars for a toilet seat The important point here is not the expensive toilet seats, but the fact that most military goods are bought at higher prices than the market would allow. This point is proven by the extraordinarily high profits on military equipment. Profit rates for the average of all military goods have often been two or three times the profits on civilian goods. This point is well-documented all the way back to World War II and the period following it (see, for example, Sherman, 1968).

The other question often debated is the total of government spending versus taxes. The past thirty years have often witnessed extremely large deficits. A deficit means that government spends more than it takes in taxes and fees. People often assume that deficits are bad because they know that debts by individuals are bad. If I spend well over my income, I go bankrupt. Governments do not go bankrupt because they can always issue more money. Governments can pay off any debt that is owed to their own citizens. Of course, paying off a debt by issuing new money tends to be inflationary. If a country owes money abroad, then creditors abroad want real assets, not inflated paper money.

Government deficits are not necessarily good or bad; it depends on the situation. Deficit spending means government spending beyond the amount of its revenue because such spending will create a deficit. In a depression, deficit spending by the government tends to stimulate the economy. For example, the large military spending by President Franklin Roosevelt during World War II brought the economy out of the Great Depression.

On the other hand, deficit spending adds to the national debt. The bad effect of a big unpaid government debt is that interest must be paid on it. Interest payments come from the average taxpayer. But interest payments go to the relatively few rich bondholders. Only a few rich Americans hold significant amounts of government bonds. Therefore, the flow of money from the average taxpayer to the very rich bondholder causes an increase of inequality in the United States.

Moreover, in recent years foreigners have purchased a growing share of our outstanding government debt. So now average taxpayers make interest payments not only to wealthy people here at home, but also to rich people abroad.

Quite a different problem results from deficit spending if the economy is already at full employment and the government stimulates it further. This overstimulation has happened only in wartime. During each U.S. war, the government has spent more than its tax revenues. The result has been a pressure toward inflation in each war. Sometimes, price controls have prevented actual inflation, but the inflationary pressure has always caused problems eventually. Poor and middle-class people always get hurt worst by inflation because the rich own stocks, whose value rises with inflation.

Deregulation of the American economy began under President Jimmy Carter in the late 1970s and accelerated under President Ronald Reagan in the 1980s. For instance, the Airline Deregulation Act was passed in 1978, removing regulation from many aspects of the airline industry. This deregulation caused many questionable practices to change from illegal to legal status.

The trend toward deregulation has continued. Especially important has been the removal of many of the safeguards against speculative financial empires put in place by the New Deal during the Great Depression. For example, it is now easy for a single bank to spread all over the United States. The bank may spread from one state to many states either by internal growth or by acquisition of other banks. The concentration of incredible amounts of wealth in a few major banks has steadily increased.

There has been a large reduction in the regulation of the stock market and of corporations, which has resulted in many scandals involving billions of dollars each. In addition to making it easier for corporate leaders and stock brokers to get away with outright crime, the deregulation of industry and finance has made the economy more vulnerable to instability.

The recovery from the 2001 recession was very unusual. The strange recovery spotlighted the lack of government control. For two years, unemployment remained high and almost no new jobs were created. In most recoveries, there is rapid increase in employment very soon after the expansion begins. In this case, there was the usual rapid technological improvement, which tends to reduce the number of workers needed. Technological improvement, however, usually does not prevent rapid net job creation. There was also a strenuous attempt at speed-up by most corporations. Speed-up of the labor process means more output could be produced by fewer workers. Speed-up is normal in expansions, but it was more pronounced in this case than in most expansions. Still, it was not enough by itself to account for the tiny growth of jobs.

The unusual factor was that a great many jobs were sent overseas to other countries with lower wages. Newer technology has allowed workers in places such as India and China to do work for U.S. corporations, that was previously done in American factories. Thus, the entire world population has become the reserve supply of labor for U.S. corporations, rather than just the U.S. population as in earlier recoveries.

Colonialism to Neocolonialism, 1945–2004

Under colonialism, as shown in the preceding two chapters, European capitalist countries took over much of the world, including North and South America, Africa, and Asia, except for Japan. Colonialism was described as forceful occupation of another country, extraction of its treasures, and extraction of continuing profits. The previous chapter showed that the imperial country invested mostly in the raw materials of the colonial country. The imperial country held back colonial industry and limited the colonial exports to agricultural and raw material commodities. Finally, the imperial country sold finished goods to the colonial country at a high profit. This period of colonial occupation and exploitation lasted until the end of World War II.

During World War II (1939–45), the colonial peoples heard much about freedom and equality from the antifascist coalition that won the war. So when the war was over, the colonial peoples each asked for their independence. When it was not granted, they each eventually revolted and took independence at gunpoint. The freeing of the colonies began in 1945 and was mostly over by about 1970.

When a colony became legally free, however, it often remained dominated, both economically and politically, by the major capitalist powers. Moreover, the economic pattern often remained the same for a long time. These neocolonial countries are formally free, but are in fact dominated by others and have the same old economic pattern. Their natural resources are owned by foreign corporations. The foreign corporations export food and cheap raw materials, and import expensive finished goods. That was the portrait of a neocolonial country around 1970, including most of the world's population.

While those features are still true of many neocolonial countries, what has changed in a large number of them is that global corporations have now built and own a large amount of industry in these countries. The foreign corporations make use of the cheap labor supply. This has greatly increased the flow of profits out of those countries.

It is also vital to understand that in the global economy, global corporations are strong in every country. By sheer economic power the global corporations are able to coerce the neocolonial countries to adopt political and economic policies that are favorable to the global corporations, though they are often very unfavorable to the neocolonial country.

Only in a few cases is economic power in itself insufficient to coerce neocolonial countries to follow the policies that are most profitable to the global corporations. In those few cases, the imperial countries support the global corporations by military force.

For example, the United States has military bases in many neocolonial countries, but seldom has to resort to military force to keep profits flowing smoothly from the neocolonial countries to the United States. In a few cases, such as Iraq, the United States is unable to change policies it does not approve by economic coercion alone. Then it may be forced to launch an invasion and act as a colonial occupier with large expenses in money and in killed and wounded American soldiers.

In terms of costs and benefits, the expenses of the U.S. occupation of Iraq are born by the American taxpayer and by the American soldier. Most soldiers come from poor families and join the army because it is the only job available to them. On the other hand, U.S. corporations make large profits from occupied countries, such as Iraq. For example, there is the lucrative work done by the Halliburton Corporation, which received a very profitable contract in secret with no other bidders allowed. There are also the oil companies who want Iraq's oil. This is the usual pattern of all colonial and neocolonial wars and occupations. the common people bear the costs, while the global corporations reap large profits.

Although they benefit either way, global corporations prefer peaceful domination to the expense and inconvenience of using military force. To use force or not to use force is a question of the bottom line or profit. Once they decide on their interests, the global corporations influence imperial governments to follow their policies.

The U.S. economist John Kenneth Galbraith wrote: "Corporate power is the driving force of U.S. foreign policy—and the slaughter in Iraq" (Galbraith, 2004). Normally, capitalist governments aid corporations to penetrate a country peacefully, while holding military force in reserve as a threat. So the most successful capitalist empire would make the rest of the world its neocolony, not its colony. The military occupation of Afghanistan in 2002 and Iraq in 2003 were anomalies, showing an ineffective foreign policy.

One cause of the underdevelopment of the neocolonial countries is that the flow of profits and interest out of these countries is greater than the flow of investment into them. For example, for many decades U.S. corporations have invested only about half as much each year in Latin America as they have extracted in profits from their accumulated investments. The outflow of profits and interest will hold back the development of the neocolonial countries. Thus, the American empire, covering the globe, is mainly neocolonial and does not rely on military occupation. It rather relies on the vast economic strength of the world's only superpower. The problem is that American economic strength is declining relative to the rest of the world.

International Governmental Organizations, 1945–2004

American power is not only exerted by armies, but to some degree through domination of some international organizations. These organizations have become more important in the period of global capitalism. After World War II, the United Nations was formed to stop wars. It has complete power in the world on paper, but its decisions require agreement of the five permanent members of the Security Council. Therefore, the United Nations is actually helpless without their agreement.

Many of the subsidiary organizations of the United Nations are important, such as UNICEF, which is a fund to help children. There is also the International Labor Organization, which attempts to improve the conditions of labor. Outside the United Nations are the World Bank and the International Monetary Fund (IMF), designed to support monetary systems when they are in trouble and to provide financial help for development to underdeveloped countries.

At a conference led by the United States and England, the IMF was formed at Bretton Woods in New Hampshire in 1944. It was designed by the great liberal economist John Maynard Keynes to be the lender of last resort to prevent recessions and monetary panics. Considered at first to be too liberal by global bankers, it very slowly became a conservative organization, making countries safe for the interests of global banks. In the 1980s especially, the IMF changed its ideology from the concept that the market has problems and we solve them to the concept that the market is perfect, just force everyone into the market. (This process is described in detail in Stiglitz, 2002.)

On the contrary, the World Bank was designed to help economic development. At first, the World Bank was considered to be a conservative policeman oppressing the Third World. It became more liberal, however, during the Clinton administration.

Joseph Stiglitz, who was head of the Council of Economic Advisers under President Clinton, and was later president of the World Bank, says he discovered that in international organizations, "especially at the IMF . . . decisions were made on the basis of . . . ideology and bad economics, dogma that sometimes seemed to be thinly veiled special interests" (Stiglitz, 2002: xiii). So the harmful conditions imposed on a country by the IMF were designed to help those outside groups that wished to invest in that country, not the people of that country.

Globalization has been leading, under pressure from the global corporation, toward completely free movement of international trade and capital flow. There is, however, no freedom of labor to move across international borders. Even if the new free trade treaties were good ones, there is no world government to enforce laws such as safety, minimum wages, or antimonopoly regulations.

The World Bank is supposed to help the biggest problem: world poverty. The extent of world poverty may be seen in the fact that 1.2 billion people live on less than one dollar a day. The World Bank and the IMF, however, have accomplished very little. "One reason for failure of globalization to help people has been that policies of international organizations have been set by commercial and financial interests and mindsets" (Stiglitz, 2002: 224). This is not a conspiracy, but happens naturally, because they are international institutions dominated by governments that are dominated by global corporations.

The International Monetary Fund does give emergency help to countries in financial trouble and some of its projects have been constructive. It demands, however, that these countries accept conditions, referred to as Structural Adjustment Policies that harm their development. The first condition is to reduce the neocolonial government's services to its people. This condition is required to save money and reduce international debt. These cuts in services have included health care, fuel and food subsidies, and even anti-AIDS money. The reductions in services hurt people directly, but they also hurt the neocolonial economy because they remove the stimulus from that government spending.

The second condition imposed by the IMF for any loan is that the borrower must privatize many state agencies. A change from public to private ownership often leads to enormous disruption. It also leads to more profits for a few corporations, but less services for most people.

The third IMF condition for any loan is complete freedom for capital to flow in and out of the borrower country. Huge flows of capital, however, can easily disrupt an economy and have often done so. Many critics argue that these three conditions of the IMF—and at times also of the World Bank—mean that such international agencies cause more harm than good.

Critics of Globalization

At the beginning of the twenty-first century, there were many critics of globalization. Some fought to stop globalization, but what does that mean? How can anyone stop better communications, better transportation, or building new plants around the world? And why stop these improvements in technology and ability to move or communicate? People resisting globalization in this sense were trying to do the impossible for no good reason.

Even if most critics accept technological improvement, they still see quite different problems in globalization. The globalization process has meant that giant corporations have exercised economic control, and to varying degrees political control, around the world. Global corporations have lowered wages in the United States and Europe by outsourcing jobs to areas of cheap labor.

The global corporations, however, have attempted to keep the wages of the poor, underdeveloped countries as low as possible. In other words, they have extracted enormous profits from the global industrial revolution. Yet they have kept employees in all countries from sharing much in the higher production. Moreover, there have also been disastrous environmental effects in some areas.

A very different kind of resistance to globalization has arisen from these problems. Organizers have attempted to build a movement dedicated to stopping environmental destruction, fighting for democratic rights in each country, and getting a share of the global gains for employees in all countries. One interesting support for this movement has come from trade union organizations that have turned some of their attention from national organizing to international organizing.

War and Global Capitalism

To understand how global capitalism has changed war, a very brief description of the past evolution of war is necessary. Wars are shaped by human relationships, so they reflect certain types of political and economic institutions. This book has shown how institutions shape wars. Chapter 2 found that early communal societies had only skirmishes over hunting grounds. Chapter 3 emphasized that slave societies warred for land and slaves. Chapter 4 revealed that feudal lords warred over land and serfs.

American wars have changed as American society has changed. The Revolutionary War was a war of liberation of the United States from British colonialism. The War of 1812 was a war in which the United States defended itself against British attempts to once again make the United States its colony. The war against Mexico (1846–48) was naked aggression to take over Mexican lands in order to extend U.S. slavery to the new Western lands (the slave owners were in control of the U.S. government at that time). The American Civil War was the crucial and bloody event deciding whether slavery or capitalism would rule the United States.

After the Civil War, the rapidly industrializing capitalist country pursued the usual motivations of corporate capitalist countries toward war. In 1898 the United States fought a rival imperial country, Spain. Spain was much weaker and was easily defeated, allowing the United States to take control of its colonies of Puerto Rico, Cuba, and the Philippines. In Cuba, the United States dominated by treaty, but did not occupy except at Guantanomo. America conquered the Philippines only after a long, bloody colonial war against the native people.

World War I involved the United States, England, and France against Germany and Austria. The result changed which country owned which colonies. The war also changed the power relationships of different countries in Europe.

World War II was the fight of the fascist, capitalist powers (Germany, Italy, and Japan) versus the Soviet Union and the liberal, capitalist powers (America, England, and France) over who would control the world. It was the bloodiest war in human history by several magnitudes and ended with American atomic bombs destroying Hiroshima and Nagasaki. One good result of World War II was that fascism, a system of dictatorship, racism, and sexism, was destroyed. A second good result was that an international organization, the United Nations, was formed in 1946 to end wars.

One bad result was the emergence of the Soviet Union and the United States as rival superpowers. The two powers had opposed ideologies, completely different economic systems, and opposing global interests. During the forty-five-year Cold War, there were also two "hot" wars in Korea and Vietnam. Vietnam was not just a clash of the two giants, but also involved the attempt of the Vietnamese people to free themselves from the colonial domination of France and then the United States.

Since capitalism matured in the nineteenth century, all of the large capitalist powers have fought colonial wars to extend their colonial holdings. The capitalist powers fought to defend their colonies against rivals. Finally, the capitalist powers fought to hold the colonies against the colonial peoples who launched wars of liberation to end their colonial oppression. It was shown in this book that the motivation for colonialism changed from land and slaves or serfs to extremely profitable investment and control of trade under capitalism. This background for wars changed to a considerable degree when the colonies achieved formal independence between 1945 and 1970.

As shown in this chapter, under global capitalism, the end of colonialism has brought a new system of neocolonialism in which advanced capitalist countries dominate weaker capitalist countries through investment, unequal trade, and threat of military power. Usually, no war is necessary. But the wars against Afghanistan and Iraq show that the rulers of imperial countries sometimes feel it is necessary to use force to establish neocolonial control against native peoples or rivals.

In addition to the basic system of neocolonialism, however, there are impulses toward war from the military, from military equipment producers, and from particular corporations, such as the profiteering of the Halliburton corporation. If the world is lucky, neocolonial dominance will continue to be mostly determined by peaceful economic coercion rather than war.

Summary of Stages in the Development of U.S. Capitalism

It is clear that U.S. capitalist institutions have changed and evolved. The story to this point has shown roughly three stages in American capitalism. The first stage was industrial capitalism from about 1840 to about 1870, with unregulated companies owned and run by individuals. The second stage was corporate capitalism, from roughly 1870 to 1970. It had corporations instead of individuals running industry. It had giant firms. And it had highly concentrated ownership, with just three or four large firms in each industry, a hundred giant firms owning most of all U.S. industry, and only one percent of individuals owning most stock. The third stage is global capitalism, of which the United States is only one part, but an important part.

These three stages are summarized in Table 9.1

Conclusion

This chapter has very briefly sketched the main lines of the transition of the United States from a relatively isolated country as late as 1940 to a global superpower. The United States now has vital connections to every aspect of the global economy, military bases throughout the world, economic domination of many countries, and outright occupation of some countries. Globalization, or global capitalism, may be defined as the domination of the world economy by a small number of

Table 9.1

Three Stages of U.S. Capitalism

	U.S. industrial capitalism	U.S. corporate capitalism	U.S. in era of global capitalism
Social institutions	Democracy, but excludes women and slaves	Democracy with no women until 1920s, few blacks until 1950s	Democratic forms, but wealth rules politics, media, all institutions
Economic institutions	Individual capitalist enterprises	Corporate form, monopoly power	Global corporations with great monopoly power
Technology	Industrial revolution	Continued rapid improvement, except in depressions	Information revolution, but also depressions
Ideology	Automatic progress, no regulation	Market is usually right, but some regulation after 1929	Market always right, people get what they deserve; reduce regulation

very large corporations; technology that makes the world a small place; and conservative policies. The conservative policies are imposed by the giant corporations, by the governments influenced by those corporations, and by the international organizations controlled by those corporations. The next two chapters will spell out the consequences of this regime for the American population.

In more general terms, one conclusion is that the era of global capitalism is here, but the basic system is still capitalism, and individual nations still exist and have some influence. The United States is a military and economic superpower. The United States is the only global superpower, but its economic strength is rising slower than that of Europe and Asia, so it is less dominant than it was in the 1960s.

Suggested Readings

Once again, an excellent source on U.S. economic history is DuBoff (1989) and an excellent source on social history is Zinn (1999). The fascinating story of the clash of conflicting economic policies, their role in globalization, and the meaning of globalization for the world, is told superbly by Robert Pollin (2004). An outstanding, comprehensive book on this period is by Samuel Rosenberg, *American Economic Development Since 1945: Growth, Decline and Rejuvenation* (2003).

International organizations are explained and criticized in clear prose by an insider in Joseph Stiglitz, *Globalization and Its Discontents* (2002). An interesting collection on imperialism is contained in the entire issue of *Monthly Review,* "Prisons and Executions: The US Model" (July–August), 2003. The new Asian trade organization is described in Evelyn Iritani, "New Trade Pact Could Cut Clout of U.S. in Asia" (2004).

– 10 –

Inequality in the United States Under Global Capitalism

This chapter focuses on the various aspects of inequality in the age of global capitalism, beginning with inequality between countries. Then it looks at the United States to consider inequality of income and wealth among individuals, inequality between genders, and inequality by race. In each of these aspects of inequality, there is shown to be drastic change in the stage of global capitalism, yet the basic problems remain because the basic system remains.

Inequality Between Countries

There are two worlds under global capitalism. One world consists of a small number of rich, dominant countries. Another world consists of the many poor, neocolonial countries. Neocolonial countries are not occupied by foreign troops, but their economies are dominated by outside corporations. Because of that domination, profit and interest flow out of the poor countries to the rich ones.

Not only are the neocolonial countries much poorer than the dominant countries, but the gap has been growing for centuries. In 1750, both the countries that are now dominant and the countries that are now neocolonial had 180–190 dollars of income per person a year (in 1960 U.S. dollars). By 1930, annual income in the colonial and neocolonial countries per person was still at 180–190 dollars, but people in the dominant countries had 780 dollars a year (in 1960 U.S. dollars). These trends have continued to the present day.

What are the exact mechanisms by which wealth flows from the neocolonial countries to the dominant countries under global capitalism? With some exceptions, domination does not involve military occupation. No one is made into a slave or a serf by the usual definitions. Unlike early colonialism, no physical treasure of precious metals is taken away from the population.

Rather, the neocolonial countries produce minerals and agricultural goods, some of it under the control of foreign corporations. These goods are sold to the dominant countries, often at very low prices. These basic goods are transformed by manufacturing in the dominant countries into finished goods. These finished goods are sold at a very nice profit. Thus, the process involves investment that brings a flow of profits to the dominant country from raw materials produced in the neocolonial country. There is also trade in which the neocolonial country sells cheap raw materials while the dominant country sells relatively expensive finished goods, providing more profit for the dominant country. Some finished goods are produced in the neocolonial country, but by plants owned by the corporations of the dominant country, Finally, there is finance that takes money from the neocolonial country by means of the interest on loans from the dominant country. The most obvious example of this process is Latin America. Every year, Latin America sends profits to the United States about twice as large as the yearly investment of U.S. corporations in Latin America. This leads some Latin Americans to say that their countries are subsidizing U.S. growth.

Inequality Between Individuals

The distribution of wealth in the United Sates is shaped like a pyramid. At the bottom are a huge number of individuals, while there are only a tiny number at the top. Bottom and top here refer only to wealth, nothing else. For example, if a man has low intelligence, but has inherited a vast fortune, then he is at the top,

The Propertyless. At the bottom of the pyramid are four of every ten Americans who have almost no net property or wealth. This entire 40 percent of the people have only one-half of one percent of all the wealth (net of debts). In other words, their debts are about equal to all of their small personal and real property. They must spend all of their small income and can save nothing. They are mostly unemployed or low-paid manual manufacturing workers or low-paid service workers, such as poorly paid waitresses. They produce profit and wealth for others.

The Poor. Among those who have no property are the poor. At the bottom of the bottom are one-fifth of all Americans who have no wealth, but have lots of debts. Their debts equal 7,100 dollars on average. (All data sources for this section are explained in Suggested Readings; all data in this section are for 1998.) Many of the poor are unemployed or receive minimum wages—or even below minimum wages. They have poor clothing, poor food, and terrible housing.

The Medium-Paid Employees. The middle group, mostly medium paid employees, is defined to be the fifth of the people in the middle of the wealth distribution, that is, from the 40th percentile to the 60th percentile of wealth. This middle group has an average wealth of $45,000 (including their net ownership in automobiles and homes). Altogether, the middle 20 percent of Americans have only 4.4 percent of all the wealth. They are mostly medium-paid workers or low-paid professionals, such as teachers or nurses. They create wealth for others, but obviously get little of it.

The Upper-Middle Employees. The next fifth of people—from the 60th percentile to the 80th percentile of wealth—are employees who are paid better than the average. Their average wealth was 116,800 dollars (including net ownership in automobiles and homes). This fifth of the people had 10.7 percent of the wealth in 1998. Their wealth rose more till 2000, then fell rapidly in the next three years. Most of them had most of their small savings in the stock market, so many lost a significant amount of savings when the market crashed. This group consists of higher-paid workers: many professional workers with medium incomes in their areas; and well-paid service workers, such as plumbers. They keep some wealth for themselves. But most of what they produced becomes wealth for others.

The richest fifth of the population had 85.4 percent of all the wealth in 1998. This fifth covers such a wide range that it is better to consider it two different groups. The top one percent are the rich. The other 19 percent of Americans in the top 20 percent are mostly professional and managers.

The Professional Managerial Class. These highly paid employees comprise 19 percent of the population, but they have 45.3 percent of the wealth. Their wealth covers a wide range. They vary from people with some possessions to people with significant wealth. They include well-paid professional workers, successful owners of small businesses, and medium-paid managers. They have good incomes and put away some savings each year in bonds or stocks, so they did very well in the late 1990s and poorly in the dismal years from 2000 through 2002. The wealth they created went to them in some part, but some also went to corporations. They were very well off by average standards, but were not rich, so even these well-off Americans often feel remarkably insecure because of systemic instability. The recession of 2001 took jobs away from many of them.

The Rich. The top one percent are the rich. That one percent held 40.1 percent of all the U.S. wealth by themselves. Their wealth ranged from 2,419,000 dollars at the bottom to over a hundred billion at the top. Much of their wealth is in the form of ownership of businesses, corporate stock, and municipal and other government bonds. They include the highest-paid managers and corporate executive officers, who are paid millions every year. Much of their income is really profits, but is called salary so that it is a corporate expense and can be deducted from corporate taxes. The rich, therefore, are those who own much of the economy and receive much of the income from it. Since most of their wealth comes from ownership of capital, they are often called the capitalist class.

One aspect of the concentration of wealth is that most gains in the stock market go to a small number of people. For example, from 1989 to 1997 the bottom 90 percent of people (grouped by wealth) got 14.1 percent of the stock market gains, while the top 10 percent got 85.9 percent. In fact, the top one percent of wealth holders got 42.5 percent of the gains all by themselves.

At the other end of the spectrum were those who lived by wages. The average weekly wage in 1973 was 502 dollars. By 1998, the average weekly wage had dropped to 442 dollars. (These figures were after removing inflation, that is, in 1997 dollars.) While workers' wages declined, aggregate U.S. production actually rose by 32.8 percent in the same period, and the incomes of the rich rose, as shown above. Therefore, there was a shift in income away from the average worker toward the rich and super-rich.

While ordinary production-line workers suffered in this period from declining real wage rates, corporate chief executive officers (CEOs) did very well. The salaries of CEOs rose from 41 times the average wage in 1960 to 326 times the average wage in 1997, and to 500 times the average wage in 2002. The one thing that ordinary workers were able to increase was their debt. The debt of the average household rose from 29.5 percent of personal income in 1949 to 84.8 percent of personal income in 1997.

Not only is there inequality in America, but this richest of all countries also has a large amount of outright poverty. In 2003, 13 percent of the U.S. population lived in poverty according to official government data (for a brief summary and sources, see Gosselin, "Poor and Uninsured Americans Increase for Third Straight Year," 2004: 1).

It is worth stressing that people in the richest one percent—from millionaires to billionaires—make most of their income from property ownership, mainly from ownership of corporations. The only apparent exception is the salary of CEOs, but these enormous salaries are actually corporate profits for the most part. This is so because corporations give them artificially high incomes, which are a tax deduction for the corporation. Corporations also give CEOs the option to buy stock at very favorable prices.

On the other hand, the income of the bottom 90 percent comes primarily from wages and salaries, plus tiny amounts of government handouts for things such as unemployment compensation. The bottom 90 percent, however, get only negligible amounts of property income. So the great fortunes come from corporate profits, while the low incomes belong to those who work at low-paid tasks all day, often with two jobs.

What is the source of corporate profits? If one examines what the income of the average employee can buy, it is clearly far below the amount of product that they produce. Thus, the average employee produces a surplus above their wages. This surplus is what constitutes corporate profits. Picture how much profit General Motors would make if they had no workers. The answer is zero.

Moreover, being a rational corporation, General Motors only hires men and women if they expect to make a profit from them. If it does not look profitable to use all of the employees that they have, they immediately fire those they think will not produce profits for the corporation. Thus, it is doubly clear that every employee produces a profit for the corporation as long as they work there. Multiply the number of employees by the surplus that each employee produces each day and you have the daily profit—no mystery! Actually, it is more precise to say that the surplus is produced by all the employees working together since modern labor is not done by isolated individuals.

It does not matter whether an employee's wage is high or low. Employees must produce a profit for the corporation or they are fired. It is clear if one looks at women in a sweatshop producing high-priced clothing for extremely low wages that this process produces a surplus that becomes a high rate of profit.

But a woman working as a computer engineer for IBM at 100,000 dollars a year (a long way above the average wage) also produces a surplus for the company. If she does not produce far more product than the 100,000 dollars she is paid, she will be fired. It is quite common that this computer engineer is paid 100,000 dollars, but produces a product worth 200,000 dollars a year, thus producing a surplus of 100,000 dollars a year for IBM. So the computer engineer and the sweatshop worker have something in common that neither would suspect, They both make profit for a corporation. Of course, one has a comfortable life and one has a miserable life, so their views will be very different.

For this reason, there may be conflicts over the amount of wages and the quality of working conditions at any wage level. There have been bitter strikes by women producing clothing for a tiny wage under terrible conditions. But there are also conflicts by highly paid computer engineers against a corporation. There have also been struggles by highly compensated professional athletes against owners of sports franchises.

The end result is always determined by the comparative power of the employees and the employers, expressed in conflicts under given economic conditions of supply and demand. For example, if millions of workers are unemployed, then it is possible for a corporation to cut the wages of those who are employed because of the implicit competition for jobs by the unemployed. So the wages of employees are determined by their power and courage under given economic conditions, not by some impersonal and implacable economic principle.

Inequality Through Sexist Discrimination

Up to this point, the focus has been on the economic institutions of capitalism, but these institutions are part of a tangled web with the social institutions. Social institutions include the system of discrimination against women and against minorities. The economic institutions help explain the social institutions, while the social institutions help explain the economic ones.

After World War II, men immediately took some jobs from women. Then, however, the entire economy rose for many years. Starting in the late 1940s, there were large increases in the number of women working for wages. There were also considerable increases in women's wages. Finally, there was a 40 percent rise of women as members of unions. Because of the change in their work situation, many women had a change in their consciousness and came to recognize that they were not incompetent, but really were qualified workers who could make an important contribution.

There was, however, no improvement in child care; so many women went to work without having many child-care options. Conservatives still assumed that all women were staying at home, so there was no need for child care.

Then in the 1950s, the Cold War brought repression of unions, with no more gains by women. Moreover, current media views and "expert" views by male psychologists became much more conservative. Some claimed that women only worked for wages out of penis envy, that they did not need the money, and that they could and should have stayed home. The media and the school system spread this view. In reality most women worked because they were forced to do so. Many women workers were single and were often single mothers. Many other women worked for wages because their husbands' wages were below the poverty line.

Women's wages were only 65 percent of men's wages in 1950. After twenty years of struggle for higher wages, the wages of women actually fell by 1970 to only 59 percent of men's wages. Why did this decline occur? On the one hand, many new women came into the labor market with no experience in union organization. On the other hand, there was an onslaught of sexist ideology and discrimination against women. As a result, almost all of the new women employees were kept out of high-paying occupations and were forced into low-paying ones, such as nursing. Those low-paid occupations were seen as the proper place for women. Even within those occupations men received higher wages than women. Thus, women received lower wages partly because they were pushed into the lowest-paying occupations, but also because they were paid the lowest salaries within those occupations.

By 1970, women workers were far more segregated by occupation than any group of minority workers. Even in areas such as teaching that were considered "women's work," the top jobs went to men. For example, 55 percent of all school principals in 1928 were women, but the percentage steadily fell. In 1968, only 22 percent of all principals were women.

Men in the 1960s still held all of the top jobs in corporations, in government (where there were very few women at any level), in the media, and even in trade unions. Because of all the discrimination in wages and in promotions, women began to organize political organizations of their own.

In the 1960s, women participated in large numbers and very actively in the face of danger in the Civil Rights movement, the anti–Vietnam War movement, the trade unions, and various left-wing political movements. Even within those movements, which were dedicated to equality, women met discrimination. Although male union leaders and male leaders of left-wing student and youth organizations talked about equality for women, most did not practice it. So women encountered discrimination even in the organizations that were supposed to fight for equality. Nevertheless, by participating in these movements and organizations, women learned a great deal about how to organize and fight for their rights. As a result, by the end of the 1960s, many women formed their own organizations and started a powerful women's movement.

There were many points of view in the women's movement. Liberal women believed that a few reforms could end discrimination. Some radical feminists believed that the problem of bias was inherent in all men. Therefore, they believed that women must fight for power against all men. Socialist feminists believed that the problem was caused to some degree by the institutions of capitalism. Therefore, the big corporations were the most dangerous opponents of women. Women argued that society had to be changed so that the big corporations were run democratically and not by capitalists.

What were the issues faced by the founders of the modern women's movement in the 1960s? The media image of most women was sexist in that women were often portrayed as empty-headed sexual objects. No professional women were portrayed. The media—all owned by huge corporations—tried by advertising and by the viewpoint presented in dramas to get women to spend more money on expensive consumer goods. Women were encouraged to buy expensive items such as fur coats, as well as every other conceivable item for personal beauty and home decoration without regard to cost.

In 1963, a law was finally passed that said women must have equal pay for equal work. Wage and salary discrimination was prohibited. But the law was not enforced because the enforcing agencies were themselves sexists and because the corporations used all of their power against enforcing the law. Women were not promoted as often as men. Not only big business but also the universities resisted equal treatment for women as staff members, faculty, and in sports.

Because of all of these problems, women fought for a new amendment to the U.S. Constitution called the Equal Rights Amendment, which would give every person equal rights regardless of gender. Big businesses opposed it because of the fear that they would have to raise the pay of all women workers who were paid less than men for performing the same job. Since this practice accounted for a significant percentage of all corporate profits, corporations fought hard against it and used a great deal of money in that fight (see Deckard, 1983). The Equal Rights Amendment finally passed Congress. Then, however, many state legislators, who initially supported it, had to bow to the business interests that gave them large contributions Thus, the Equal Rights Amendment failed to be ratified by the requisite number of states.

In addition to the economic issues, the social issues for women included the right to choose abortion, to have affordable child care, and to see that the laws against rape were strictly enforced. Although the Equal Rights Amendment was defeated, the women's movement grew strong enough that most of these economic and social issues were slowly won after intense battles. These battles continue today, with conservatives trying to reduce or eliminate these rights.

At the beginning of the twentieth century, only a small percentage of women had paid jobs outside the house. By the beginning of the twenty-first century, however, the usual road for most women was paid employment. Against many obstacles, women are now a very large part of the labor market and an increasing percentage of union members. Also overcoming many obstacles, women went from a small percentage of all those earning bachelor's degrees at universities to a majority, though they still lag far behind in the number of PhDs in most fields. Women's salaries rose relative to those of men. Women now have more high-paying jobs as doctors, lawyers, and college professors. There has even been a major increase in the number of women holding elected office.

What has been the impact of the global economy on women? Instant communication has improved the ties of women to other women around the world, so it has helped strengthen the international women's movement. Better knowledge of other countries has also given impetus to the women's movement in those countries with extreme discrimination because of the contrast with news about other countries.

At the same time, however, the movement of jobs to areas of cheap labor outside the United States and other advanced capitalist countries has badly hurt women in the advanced countries. In these less developed countries, however, the increase of manufacturing jobs has not greatly raised the extremely low wages, because corporations have done all in their power to keep wages as low as possible. Moreover, the work conditions are not good. In these less developed countries, corporations have tried to change the way of life of women in order to make these women come exactly on time, work at high intensity for long hours, and never go on strike. The situation is complex and different in each country.

Inequality Through Racist Discrimination

One of the most shameful episodes in American history occurred during World War II. Japanese-Americans on the West Coast were put into concentration camps as enemy aliens. This extreme discrimination applied even to those Japanese-Americans who had been here for generations.

The effect of the war on African-Americans was far different. It was only during World War II that a great many African-American sharecroppers moved out of agriculture into the war production industries or into the army. After the war, more Northern capital moved into the South, so there was some employment in manufacturing in the cities. Only then did sharecropping finally die away and the South become fully capitalist. The process of industrializing the South, however, was slow and took decades. The Old South still witnessed lynching, segregation, and resistance to change in the 1950s.

But African-Americans changed from a mostly rural group of people to the most urbanized people in the United States. This migration led to changes in the political equation. Living in the cities meant that African-Americans could organize the civil rights movement to fight for changes in the South. The fact that millions of African-Americans lived in Northern cities meant that politicians had to consider their political clout. African-Americans in the South could not vote, but they became an important voting bloc in Northern cities. Because of this power and the whole civil rights movement, in the 1960s the civil rights laws were passed. These laws helped further change the South. Finally, the South became formally democratic and capitalist like the rest of the country.

Employers, however, can benefit from a certain degree of racial prejudice among their employees. If white employees are prejudiced against African-American employees, then it is impossible to build a strong union or a sense of solidarity among the workforce. Any strike activity supported by one group may be opposed by the other group. During many strikes in the South, one minority group was actually used to break the strike of another.

As a result, the South continued to have the fewest unions and the lowest wages in the nation. But the same divisions among employees existed to a lesser degree in the North. Therefore, prejudice also reduced wages of both whites and minorities in the North, though to a lesser degree than in the South.

While both whites and minorities were hurt by these racial and ethnic divisions, the lowest wages still went to minorities. Moreover, minorities were the first fired and the last hired. So minorities continued to have low wages and high unemployment rates. Economic discrimination is still a major cause of inequality.

It is true that the laws have made overt discrimination illegal, so that battle has been won. But informal discrimination, which is difficult to prove, continues. Thus, African-Americans and Latino-Americans still have lower wages, higher unemployment rates, less access to housing and home mortgages, poorer schools in segregated neighborhoods, and less access to health care. A large amount of data are available on discrimination, but some of the most dramatic are on differences in the median wealth of various groups. In 2002 African–American median wealth was only 6,000 dollars; while Latino–American median wealth was 8,000 dollars. The minorities had far less wealth than the white majority; white median wealth was 88,000 dollars. All of the detailed studies support these basic points, so discrimination continues in the United States. (See the studies cited in the Suggested Readings in this chapter.)

What has been the impact of globalization on racial discrimination? Improvement of communications and movement of people around the world looking for jobs has meant that all ethnic and racial groups have come to know more about each other, which tends to decrease prejudice.

Global corporations, however, have increased the level of competition among workers of different groups and countries. As a result of the increased competition for jobs, many groups have blamed job loss on other groups, which has tended to increase prejudice. That has certainly been the trend in the United States, where white male workers now tend to vote for conservatives, viewing all liberals as the friends of minorities who are taking their jobs away from them. At the height of the New Deal in the 1930s, white male workers were the strongest support for the left wing of the Democratic Party. Now, a majority of them vote for conservative Republicans.

The author witnessed one form of this tendency at a university. In the late 1960s when jobs were plentiful and universities were radicalized by opposition to the Vietnam War, white male assistant professors took the lead in militant action favoring Affirmative Action for women and minorities. Any other position was considered barbaric. But a few years later in the early 1970s, when the number of jobs at universities was reduced or in danger, many white male assistant professors led the opposition to any affirmative action as a special treatment for women and minorities. The reason that assistant professors are affected so strongly by job competition and instability is that they do not yet have tenure. Tenure is the strong job security that an assistant professor can sometimes win by hard work, but the achievement is difficult and uncertain. Thus the instability and competition of global capitalism has tended to increase prejudice. This example is within the academy, but it is true of every area where there is job competition.

Repression and Inequality

The Cold War of the 1950s led to repression in both the Soviet Union and the United States. In the name of patriotism, Soviet hardliners attacked all reformers and other opponents as agents or supporters of the United States. With this excuse, the hardliners caused large numbers of Soviet citizens to lose their jobs or be sent to prison. Repression was worst until the death of Stalin in 1953. During Stalin's era, there were many political executions, but after his death, there were no more clearly political executions and only a few questionable cases. There was continued repression as long as the Cold War lasted.

In the name of patriotism, hardline American conservatives used repression against all reformers and almost anyone guilty of being militant in favor of peace or equality. Many Americans lost their jobs and some went to prison for advocating peace with the Soviet Union or changes in the U.S. economic system designed to increase equality. In the midst of the hysteria throughout the government and the media, there were even two people (Ethel and Julius Rosenberg) who were executed for handing military secrets to an enemy, even though no one in American history had ever been executed for this crime in peacetime. The severest repression was in the 1950s, but some continued throughout the Cold War.

Much of the organized witch-hunting in America was done by the Un-American Activities Committee of the U.S. House of Representatives and by the Internal Security Committee of the U.S. Senate, chaired by Senator Joseph McCarthy. Because of his activities, the whole repressive behavior of this period is called McCarthyism.

Although defense of inequality was always the underlying reason, espionage or "subversion," that is, advocating the overthrow of the government, was almost always the official charge. The attempt to defend inequality is shown most clearly in the fact that a large majority of the attacks centered on trade unions, which are the strongest defenders of equality and critics of inequality in America (as shown in the next section). There were also attacks on college professors who had unpopular and antiestablishment views, Hollywood stars who opposed the Korean war, and "subversives" in the U.S. Army.

One cannot grasp the witch-hunting atmosphere of the 1950s without examples in every area of American life. But limited space allows examples from only one area, so let us examine the repression in the U.S. Army.

In 1953, Senator McCarthy investigated subversion within the U.S. Army and tried to show that the Army leadership was "soft on communism." A week after the Army–McCarthy hearings started to be broadcast on national television, the Army passed a new regulation requiring an anticommunist oath of all soldiers. The oath said that "I am not and never have been a member of the Communist Party." The same oath also required the soldier to say that he had not been a member of any of five hundred other organizations that the government claimed were sympathetic to communism! There was never any evidence offered in a court to show that any of the other five hundred organizations had ever violated any law.

In the army, individual soldiers who refused to sign were investigated, given hearings, and then given discharges called undesirable. I was drafted at that time and was told to sign the oath. I had just graduated law school, where I had been taught that such oaths violated my right of free speech guaranteed in the First Amendment to the Constitution. On the form, it said that you may claim your constitutional right not to sign the oath; you could just put an X in that the box for that alternative. After a few minutes of fright and cowardice, I put an X in the box to say that I claimed my constitutional right not to sign the oath.

After many months in the army, I was suddenly given a list of 21 extraordinary charges. Every charge against me took the form: "An informant says that Private Sherman . . ." The army never put any of these informers on the witness stand. Therefore, they could not be cross-examined, so I could not prove that they told many lies. Even their names were secret, so the army merely alleged what they had said.

The army claimed that they could discharge anyone at their convenience if they were not fully satisfied with them. Thus, the army charges were not criminal, but were a strange mixture of rumors of unpopular ideas. In effect, I was asked to prove that I had never uttered a single word against the army or any criticism of the government that might be considered disloyal. One cannot prove such a general negative statement.

The first specific charge was that I had refused to sign the anticommunist oath, even though the army agreed that this was my constitutional right. Another charge was that I had refused to sign the oath a second time when they invited me, as a law graduate, to join the Judge Advocate General Department. This oath had far more detailed questions than the ordinary oath. The question that struck me as most fascinating in the second oath was: "Has your mother-in-law ever been a member of the Communist Party?"

Another charge alleged that I had been a delegate to the convention of the Independent Progressive Party in New York City. I had never been in New York in my life and that party was a California party that never met in New York! I was not allowed to question the informant who made this false statement.

Another charge was that I had a letter in the student newspaper at the University of California, Los Angeles advocating an antiwar demonstration. Still another charge alleged that I wrote a letter to a Chicago labor newspaper advocating proportional representation in the election of Chicago aldermen. My article showed that the Republicans had taken a large percentage of the vote, but had only elected a few aldermen. So I concluded that proportional representation would be a much fairer electoral system; the army said this was a communist view.

Most charges were supported by only one informant, but one charge included two informants. It read: "At the University of Chicago Law School one informant says that Sherman is a radical, but not so radical as to be a Communist (a second informant says that the first informant signed a petition in favor of pardoning the Rosenbergs)." I am not sure if the statement in parentheses was intended to imply that I was more radical than the first informant said or was intended to condemn me by virtue of my knowing the first informant.

Finally, one charge was that I had been invited to the home of a man in Berkeley, "whose mother often had Negroes to her home." Why did it jeopardize U.S. security to have "Negroes" to your home?

Some men had even more extraordinary charges against them. One soldier was charged with advocating recognition of China. My favorite, however, was the charge that a soldier "intimately knew" Mrs. Jones, who it was said "was a Communist in the Peace movement, who was now lying low." In fact, Mrs. Jones was his mother-in-law and she had died eight years before he met his wife—so she was lying very low.

After many months, I was suddenly given an Undesirable Discharge, reduced in pay from Private 2 to Private 3, and denied all GI benefits. I joined a class action law suit against the army, which was fought for eight years till it reached the Supreme Court. We won the case. I was eventually given a General Discharge under Honorable Conditions and received all of my GI rights. For eight years I had requested education benefits each month and been refused. Finally, I was paid. The money was not much, but it was a victory against McCarthyism. Since McCarthyism defended inequality, I felt it was a victory against inequality.

Unions Against Inequality

In America, there are antagonism and conflicting interests not only between men and women, the majority and minorities, but also between corporations and their employees. Thus, there are not only organizations to fight inequality representing women and organizations representing minorities, but also organizations fighting inequality that represent employees, namely, trade unions.

In the late 1940s and early 1950s, unions came under attack by government witch-hunters who claimed that many militant union leaders were communists and unpatriotic. Unions were also attacked, and new antilabor laws passed, by a Republican Congress. The Taft-Hartley Act of 1947 weakened unions in many ways. For example, they prohibited one union from striking to support another union on strike. They also instituted an anticommunist oath for union officers. If a union leader signed the oath and was then found to be a communist, he could be sent to prison for perjury. In those days of anticommunist hysteria, some union leaders went to jail as communists solely on the basis of testimony against them by informers who received pay for making these allegations.

In the face of such witch-hunts, coupled with the Cold War ideology that considered any militant defense of labor to be communist and evil, the Congress of Industrial Unions (CIO) tossed out its ten most militant left-wing unions in 1949 and merged with the American Federation of Labor (AFL) in 1953. The new AFL-CIO compromised with big business, received some gains for its workers in return for pledges not to strike, and supported the Cold War.

As a result of the decline in militancy, coupled with the antiunion labor laws, the unions steadily lost strength. Union membership fell from 36 percent of all nonagricultural workers in 1955 to only 13 percent in 2003. This decline has drastically reduced the bargaining power and influence of labor. As a result, real wages have declined from the 1970s to the present.

This decline does not mean there are no more conflicts between labor and capital, only that labor's side has been weakened. For example, in 2004 the three largest grocery store chains tried to end all health benefits for their employees. Their employees went on strike. The strike lasted many months and caused great hardships for the employees and their families. Eventually, the strike was settled but with a large decline in benefits for the employees, though they did retain some health benefits. New employees would get no benefits.

What lessons does the strife-torn history of U.S. labor relations have for the analysis of society? Any social analysis should ask: How does the power, organization, and consciousness of the opposing group interests, such as employers and employees, affect the main issues of our society? For example, how do the strength and views of opposing groups affect the wage bargain, bargaining over health insurance and working conditions, laws on minimum wages, public views on the desirability of unions, or the amount of unemployment compensation and welfare payments?

The coming of global capitalism had a devastating effect on U.S. trade unions. It was shown in the section on unemployment that American jobs—and high-paying jobs in Europe—have migrated overseas. Those employees who have gotten new jobs have mostly done so in the low-paying service areas. Service jobs, such as restaurant and food service workers, are not performed by thousands of employees in one place. The greater isolation of many service jobs makes them far more difficult to organize. These factors have contributed to the decline of union strength in the United States and in Europe.

Legal Institutions and Inequality

Chapter 6 described the first period of U.S. law a pre-capitalist period. It showed how pre-capitalist law evolved into the second period of laws, which benefit industrial capital. There were also programs put into law during the 1930s to give some benefits to the poor and middle-income employees to keep them happy with industrial capitalism.

Starting in the 1930s, during the Great Depression and throughout World War II, there was a great increase in the power of government over the economy. At first, this meant the creation of many programs to help the average person. These included unemployment compensation, social security insurance for old age, minimum wages, maximum hours, and eventually workers' compensation for injuries on the job, plus Medicare. After World War II and during the 1950s, however, the law came to include antilabor laws and political oppression.

After a reduction of constructive government programs during the 1950s, there was another wave of improved programs during the 1960s. The reform programs of the 1930s were known as the New Deal. The reform programs of the 1960s were known as the Great Society. Both waves resulted from massive progressive movements of the population and their elected representatives. The Great Society especially focused on the war on poverty, including the expansion of Medicare and other entitlement programs. These reforms did not succeed in eliminating poverty because they were never expanded enough. They did, however, succeed in sharply reducing poverty for the elderly. The programs did bring down the overall poverty rate for a while, but it has risen again since then (see Collins and Yeskel, 2000).

There were also new legal problems emerging under global capitalism. The great importance of international trade and investment led to a period that could be called "global capitalism" in the economic sector. This new economic stage was reflected in the law. This period, particularly from the 1970s to the present, witnessed the relative decline in the powers of individual nations and the rise in power of the global corporations and global agencies. Legal disputes centered more and more on the use of the new technology, such as the worldwide communication network.

How is it possible to avoid pirating of songs and movies on the Internet? What are the rights of individuals to free speech on such a net? The new technology produced many new types of intellectual property, not foreseen in earlier law. Each of these legal issues over worldwide rights to new kinds of commodities meant disputes about billions of dollars. The point that new technology leads to new organization of the economy and new laws has been driven home more dramatically than ever before.

Crime and Inequality

The criminal laws protect capitalist institutions against those who would violate private property or contract rights. The criminal laws are enforced by legalized violence by the government, that is, prisons and executions. Under capitalism, if a man or woman steals a loaf of bread, he or she is guilty, regardless of the need of the person or of his or her family. There have been societies, such as the early communal societies that lasted 100,000 years, that allowed anyone to take a loaf of bread as they needed it without paying. In the prehistoric communes anyone would be thought criminal who would prevent a starving man or woman from taking whatever he or she needed to stay alive. Under the legal institutions of capitalism, a hospital may turn away a sick person with no money. There are now many proposals for a universal health care system in the United States. Under a system of universal health care, it would be a crime for a hospital to refuse care for anyone. Refusal of bread to a starving person or health care to an ill person are the logical legal consequences of a process built on our present system of private property.

Over two million people in the United States are in prison, the largest number per capita in the entire world. In 2003, one in every seventy-five U.S. males was in prison. Those in prison included one in ten of all African-American males between the ages of twenty and thirty-four. Most prisoners are poor.

Crimes by the poor are usually punished with much harsher sentences than are crimes by white-collar or more affluent citizens. The report of the President's Crime Commission concluded that "the poor are arrested more often, convicted more frequently, sentenced more harshly, rehabilitated less successfully than the rest of society" (President's Commission on Law Enforcement and the Administration of Justice, 1968: 87). This 1968 statement remains true according to every investigation (for example, Reiman, 1990).

The effects of differences in economic status stand out very clearly in law enforcement practices. Inequality in the legal process is caused by economic inequality. The actual inequality, however, is mostly concealed in the formal equality under the law. Both the unemployed worker and the billionaire have the same formal rights under the law, but the actual treatment is very different.

The extremely rich executive officers of Enron Corporation, who took billions of dollars in illegal schemes in that corporation, used every trick by many highly paid lawyers to fight against their punishment.

The poor African-American worker, who comes to the attention of the police, gets a different treatment. For example, a video showed that Rodney King, a poor African-American, was beaten by the police purely because of prejudice. Of course, the poor had the same formal, legal rights, as a billionaire, but very few rights in reality. Prejudice and monetary interest tend to make many police and judges go easy on rich whites, while being rough on the poor.

There are enormous differences in the experiences of the rich versus the poor when dealing with the justice system and the courts. The most important reason is that the millionaire can employ the best possible lawyer.

The wealthy can keep even an open-and-shut case against them stalled in the courts for many years. Yet the poor lose many cases against them—

whether brought by the police, the landlord, or the bill collector—even when they are completely in the right under present laws and economic institutions, simply because they have no money with which to fight the case.

The vast majority of the lower-income victims of the legal process lack the financial resources to hire a good lawyer or to get out on bail. Therefore, most (70 percent of all those arrested in the United States) are forced to plead guilty in order to avoid lengthy detention before their case comes to trial. Thus, in order to avoid a long pretrial time in jail and the probability of a long jail sentence, they settle with the prosecutor for a shorter jail sentence even if they are innocent. Moreover, in the pretrial period, the rich are able to be released on bail, while the poor are unable to raise a considerable bail. Furthermore, the poor are more likely to have a high bail set because they are not "respectable" citizens and have no economic stake to keep them from fleeing prosecution.

Government and Inequality

Government spending and taxes not only influence the level of aggregate production and employment, but they also affect income distribution. Taxes take about one-third of the gross domestic product to support local, state, and federal government. So it matters very much who pays the taxes. The corporations and the rich have enormous tax breaks. For example, a bill passed in October 2004 gave an astonishing list of tax cuts and tax breaks to corporations amounting to a total of 137 billion dollars (for details, see Andrews, 2004). The U.S. Senate voted in favor of the corporate tax breaks 69 to 17, showing the strength of the friends of vested interests when it really matters for profits. On the other hand, the middle class and the poor have very few tax breaks and must pay a large percentage of their income in taxes. The reason for this difference is that almost no tax breaks are available to those earning wages and salaries, but a great many tax breaks are available to anyone receiving profit income.

On the spending side, one question is, how much of government spending ends up as profits in the hands of large corporations? Another question is how much have the social programs for the poor and low wage earners been cut from their previous levels by the budgets designed by the Bush administration? For example, there have been cutbacks in school lunches for poor children, tax deductions for the middle class, and funding for the Public Broadcasting System—plus an unwillingness to have healthcare for the 45 million uninsured Americans.

Government also makes labor laws governing the relationship between capital and labor. After the end of World War II, labor laws were changed. These changes, especially the 1947 Taft-Hartley Act, provide more power for corporations and make it far more difficult for unions to organize. Although other factors were also important, the legal changes were one of the major factors that caused the percentage of workers in unions to steadily decline since that time.

During the 1950s, the era of repression called McCarthyism, the government attacked liberals in every sphere, but most of the witnesses who were attacked by the Un-American Activities Committee were trade unionists from militant unions. Not only did repression succeed in weakening these unions, but forced some of them to accept a merger with the conservative American Federation of Labor. After that, union militancy against business ceased for a long time. Some unions resumed their militant activity by the 1970s, but some have never recovered.

Government continues to play its traditional role of protector of private property. People who are poor and desperate often violate the laws of private property. As our society has acquired a permanent group of people living in poverty, government has replied to crime, not by raising low incomes, but mostly by increasing the severity of punishment. The United States has over two million people in prison, a higher percentage of the population than any other country. As discussed above, crimes by corporate executives are treated far less severely.

Thus, criminal law is one channel by which the government controls the population and defends the vested rights of the rich, because the rich have the most influence in government. Besides the government, the mechanisms of control in a mature capitalist country include the media, religious institutions, and all educational institutions. Furthermore, an enormous amount of money is spent by lobbyists to influence candidates and parties. This technique does have some effect, though not as much as the contribution of money by the rich and the large corporations to candidates and parties to help determine who gets elected.

To understand the actions of the U.S. government, it is also important to remember that usually only half the people vote, even in presidential elections, and far fewer in purely congressional, state, or local elections. It should be noted that 59 percent of those eligible voted in the hotly contested election of 2004. Of those who do not vote, most are poorly paid, minorities, and/or unemployed. Thus in most elections, only the higher income half of the population needs to be convinced.

A precise notion of how race, gender, and class differences affect U.S. politics can be seen in the voting patterns of the 2004 presidential election between the more liberal John Kerry and the more conservative George W. Bush. The data are for those who actually voted according to exit polls (see Perry, 2004). Because of their different conditioning by family, church, intense advertising and media, education, and lifestyle, men and women voted somewhat differently on average. Men voted 53 percent for Bush and 46 percent for Kerry, whereas women voted 49 percent for Bush and 50 percent for Kerry. A higher percentage of women than men voted for Kerry because Kerry was perceived as a better candidate on women's issues.

In racial and ethnic terms, whites voted 57 percent for Bush and 43 percent for Kerry. Latinos voted 45 percent for Bush and 54 percent for Kerry. Asians voted 34 percent for Bush and 64 percent for Kerry. African-Americans voted 14 percent for Bush and 86 percent for Kerry (Perry, 2004). These numbers show that Bush received a majority of votes by the white majority, but Kerry received more votes from minorities because Kerry was perceived to be friendlier toward minorities.

Finally, in terms of class differences as reflected to some degree in income, there were five groups in the exit polls: below 20,000 dollars; 20,000 dollars to 40,000 dollars; 40,000 dollars to 60,000 dollars; 60,000 dollars to 75,000 dollars; and over 75,000 dollars. The percentages voting for Bush were 46, 47, 51, 53, and 57 percent, respectively. Thus, Bush's vote rose steadily from the lowest income group to the highest. Kerry's percentages of the vote in each income group were 51, 52, 48, 46, and 45 percent. Thus, Kerry's vote percentage fell from the lowest to the highest income group (Perry, 2004). Obviously, Bush was perceived as more of a friend of the rich, while Kerry was perceived as more of a friend of the poor. The perceptions were the result of life experience plus all of the conditioning mentioned above.

The Media and Inequality

The media tend to convince people, because of the emphasis in most of the stories that they write, that nothing can be achieved by participation in politics because it is all corrupt. If most people are convinced that nothing can change, how can change ever occur? If everyone believed the media all of the time, then inequality would never be reduced. In reality, however, crises lead to protest regardless of the media, and protest leads to political change. If the media cannot be changed, then only traumatic experience in crises can convince people that basic institutional change is desirable.

The paradox of modern U.S. democracy is that there are better and better communications, but there is less and less knowledge of politics and society by most people. Every poll on major issues shows appalling ignorance of basic facts. One reason is the increasing concentration of ownership of the media. The information media are owned and controlled by a few large corporations. The interest of these large corporations is to provide sensationalism in order to attract listeners; they have no interest in educating people about the facts of political and economic life.

For instance, the Fox network is owned by a small group of very rich conservatives. As a result, most people who primarily relied on Fox for their news thought that Iraq had weapons of mass destruction long after official reports had disproved this myth. In spite of the reports exposing these myths, a large majority of self-identified Bush voters polled believed that Saddam Hussein provided "substantial support" to Al-Qaeda, and 47 percent believed that Iraq had weapons of mass destruction before the U.S. invasion (see Wirzbicki, 2004).

Most people watch television several hours a day; thus, control of television is often said to amount to control of most minds. It is certainly true that when there is no internal crisis and no foreign crisis, the media, as well as the other institutions of the society, have a large measure of control in shaping the social outlook.

Only if there is an internal crisis, such as a major depression, or if there is a foreign crisis, such as a war, can the influence of the media be overridden by people's experiences. During the Great Depression, everyone saw its effects, so a broad progressive movement came into being, regardless of media views. Most of the media were very conservative at the time, but they could not prevent people from seeing the effects of the Great Depression on their lives. During the Vietnam War, the media downplayed the difficulties of the war for a long time. Many people, however, had deaths among their own families or friends, so the antiwar movement spread rapidly after a time.

Although the media do have incredible power, it is good to remember

that the media themselves emerge from certain political-economic institutions. Institutions are themselves the result of struggles by groups
of people. Human struggle, therefore, can change their media in the
long run. To make the point dramatically, consider the fact that the only
media existing in Medieval Europe were the Catholic Church and all of
its priests. Thus, the media influence people in every society, but it is
also true that people sometimes change the basic institutions, which
change the media.

Today, one antidemocratic trend in the media is their tendency to
convince people that nothing can be changed, there are no alternatives,
and all politicians are corrupt. While there is some truth in the allegations of corruption, their complete overexaggeration leads people to
withdraw from participation in democracy. Contrary to the media, it is
important to remember that reforms do happen and revolutionary change
has occurred. For example, this book is a story of enormous change
from one alternative society to another in a number of cases.

Of course, the media are not the sole cause of less democracy, but
they play an important role. The media do not conspire to be antidemocratic and probusiness, but they are driven by profits and by advertising.
Since corporate giants own the media, their prime concern is making
profits from the media by sensational stories.The corporate owners of
the media, however, are also interested in favorable treatment of their
businesses and the political objectives of those businesses. Those who
benefit from the present economic institutions are the ones who strongly
defend them. If they own the media, they use it to support the present
institutions. The media get rich and democracy gets poorer.

By definition, democracy means the rule of the people, that is, the
people make the basic decisions. But in the United States it appears that
most decisions are made by a small number of giant corporations and
the politicians that they put into power. Some social scientists argue that
the way to more democracy is reduction of economic inequality plus
greater democratic control of the media.

Increasing concentration of media ownership means that the media are
controlled by fewer and fewer corporations (the entire historical trend is
mapped in detailed data in McChesney, 1999). In 2003 the Federal Communications Commission (FCC) passed new rules allowing more concentration of ownership by one firm, both in the percentage of television
outlets controlled and in the ownership of other media (newspapers and

radio) in the same market. Hundreds of thousands of people complained, but the FCC held to that decision under pressure from media giants.

Why worry about concentration of ownership of the media? There is a myth that the Internet will set us free. The Internet is mostly unregulated, free market capitalism. So concentration is increasing among the companies that control it, with fewer and larger providers. Millions of people in the lower -income group know nothing about the use of the Internet and cannot afford it. The Internet may be increasing inequality.

There is a myth in the media that there is no conflict among classes in the United States and that almost everybody is "middle class." Yet there is widespread discussion of conflict among classes every day in the media under different names, with opposing liberal and conservative views. Most liberals describe the class warfare of the corporations and their rich owners against their employees by pushing wages lower, against the consumer by pushing prices higher, and against the public interests in many ways, such as poisoning the environment.

Many conservatives claim there is no conflict between corporations and their employees, consumers, or the public. They do spend a lot of time describing an alleged conflict between what they call the "liberal, intellectual (effhead) elite" and "us common people." These conservatives argue that a liberal intellectual elite controls the education system, the corporations, and the government. The liberal intellectual elite push many causes that are allegedly harmful to the great majority of Americans. In these descriptions, most ordinary Americans are portrayed as white males. Those allegedly harmful causes include affirmative action, which they claim tries to take away jobs and education from white males. Conservatives claim that another cause of the liberal elite is gay marriage, which they argue destroys the ordinary marriage of the majority. This myth about a harmful and all-powerful intellectual elite is presented by so much of the media that it is a basic belief of millions of people. This leads people to vote for conservatives, who stress these issues, against their own economic interests (for details, see Frank, 2004).

Why do the commercial media help maintain the existing economic institutions? Because they are a part of those institutions. As noted above, they are owned mostly by giant conglomerates. They are run to make profits and they tend toward the lowest culture and the most extravagant overstatement of sensational items. They give little time for hard news and in-depth analysis.

The judicial system has interpreted the First Amendment to mean that the corporations can do as they please on the Internet, selling or putting ads all over it. Everyone has the formal freedom to use it, but it costs money. Those with money can use the Internet and gain access to all of its power. The poor cannot afford a computer or a Web connection, thus the poor cannot use the Internet.

The interpretation of the First Amendment has changed in the past three decades. The First Amendment was put into the Constitution to protect the speech of heretics and critics of the government. But now it is used to defend corporate giants and the wealthy. It has been accepted by the courts that the wealthy can make campaign contributions of as many millions as they wish as a right of free speech. It has also been argued, as a right of free speech, that the government should not regulate the ownership of radio and TV stations. The courts have presumed that freedom of speech is compatible with any degree of concentration in the media.

These new uses of the First Amendment are contrary to case law before the 1970s, but the new interpretation of speech rights as money rights is consistent with the emergence of global capitalism. The argument for protection of money rights under the First Amendment assumes that government is the only problem for free speech, while giant corporations are no problem.

It is assumed by some conservative lawyers that income and wealth are equal and everyone can make equal political contributions. On the basis of such arguments, the Supreme Court has allowed candidates to spend as much as they wish on their campaigns.

Health Care and Inequality

The U.S. health-care system reflects an unequal society. The rich get very good health care, most people get mediocre health care, and a large number of people get no health care. Health care for everyone has been held back by the vested interests of the insurance companies and other global giants, the health maintenance organizations, and the rich. The rich do not want to pay taxes toward health care. As an example of the power of American vested interests in the age of global capitalism, the United States spends the highest proportion of gross domestic product of any country in the world on health care (14 percent according to Navarro, 1993). Yet the United States does not provide good health care to its citizens, since over 40 million Americans or 17 percent of the population have no health-care benefits and the number without health care has risen in recent years (see Navarro, 1993).

Why is the health-care system so bad for most people? The problem is that most people have very little political power, while those with power have very little interest in extending health care to everyone. The people without health care are poorly paid employees and the unemployed. But poorly paid employees and unemployed workers have little economic power and little political power. Those who have immense economic power do not need public health care and resent paying taxes to maintain it. The owners of industry not only have vast economic power, but this economic power is used to control political outcomes (as discussed in the earlier section on government).

Rather than having a universal publicly owned health-care system, much of the health care industry in the United States is directly controlled by giant corporations, including the insurance companies. These very large corporations make enormous profits from health care and want to keep it that way (the data on the health industry is discussed in detail in Navarro, 1993).

Conclusions

Under global capitalism the gap has widened between rich countries and poor countries. Hundreds of thousands in the poorest countries are dying of starvation (the data are spelled out in Griffin, 1987.) In the United States under the system of global capitalism many things have changed. Yet there is still inequality between men and women, inequality between the majority and minorities, and inequality between owners of corporations and employees, as well as inequality between small businesses and giant corporations. This inequality is enforced by both the civil law and the criminal law. This inequality is supported by the message of the media. This inequality is reflected in the health-care system, the educational system, and other social organizations.

Suggested Reading

All of the data on inequality in this chapter are from government agencies, especially the Federal Reserve Board. The data (from government agencies) on individual inequality are reported in clear, simple language by Collins, Leondar-Wright, and Sklar, *Shifting Fortunes: The Perils of the Growing American Wealth Gap* (1999); and in Collins and Yeskel, *Economic Apartheid in America* (2000). On global inequality, see the useful data in Yates (2004).

The history of the fight over sexist discrimination is covered by Deckard (1983); while women's fight to get the vote is in Flexner (1975).The history and theory of racial discrimination are in Reich (1980). There are many good writers in a book edited by Susan Feiner, *Race and Gender in the US Economy: Views from Across the Spectrum* (2002). An exciting and militant African-American view is presented in Manning Marable, *Black Liberation in Conservative America* (1997).

The best discussion of the U.S. criminal law process is in Jeffrey Reiman, *The Rich Get Richer and the Poor Get Prison* (1990). An entire issue of the journal, *Monthly Review,* is called "Prisons and Executions: The US Model" (2001). The evolution of the legal system continues in Chase (1997). Jay Feinman (2004) explains how conservative lawyers have undermined American rights.

All of the facts about the diseased condition of American health care used in this chapter come from the excellent, but brief and popularly written book by Vicente Navarro, *Dangerous to Your Health* (1993).

The history of the labor movement continues in Boyer and Morais, *Labor's Untold Story* (1970). The role of the media and its relation to global capitalism is told in a startling way, but with full documentation, in Robert McChesney, *Rich Media, Poor Democracy: Communication Politics in Dubious Times* (1999). The myth of the intellectual elite controlling everything is exposed in an important, but delightful and humorous book about political ideology by Thomas Frank, *What's the Matter with Kansas?* (2004).

– 11 –

Economic Instability and Environment in the United States Under Global Capitalism

This chapter, like the previous two chapters, focuses primarily on the United States under the international system of global capitalism. The chapter mainly considers economic instability and environmental destruction.

Economic Instability

The business institutions of capitalism—combined with the educational system, the supporting governmental system, and the media—create an ideology favorable to newness and innovation. Many times more technological change has occurred in the past two hundred years of capitalism than in all of the preceding thousands of years of earlier political-economic systems.

On the other hand, the growth is not continuous, but comes in spurts. The usual growth pattern over time is one of economic boom and bust, combined with financial bubbles and bursting bubbles. Millions of people in the advanced capitalist countries are unemployed for some unpleasant periods of time. Since the ideology says that unemployment is the fault of the individual, this has a devastating impact on self-respect, leads to more mental illness, more divorce, more crime, and even more suicide. Almost everyone in a capitalist society is subject to doubt and uncertainty over jobs and savings.

In the most recent recession from 2000 to 2003, millions of workers lost their jobs, and millions were involuntarily reduced to fewer hours a week. In addition, about 40 percent of the population had their savings invested in the stock market by themselves or through retirement funds. When the stock market crashed in 2000, trillions of dollars were lost, including most of the savings of millions of people.

What leads to these cyclical outbreaks of a mysterious economic disease that causes the economy to decline, workers to be unemployed, and businesses and individuals to go bankrupt? In every economic expansion, profits tend to go up faster than wages. As productivity increases, employees turn out more and more product. Under capitalist institutions, the increased product belongs to the corporation. So profits rise automatically in an expansion, but employees' contracts are fixed. So employees must always play catch-up, trying to get their share of the higher product.

For this and other reasons, the distribution of income shifts toward the wealthy and the business owners. This affects consumer demand. Employees have to spend all of their income to maintain their usual standard of living. Business owners, however, save a large part of their profits and managerial salaries. Therefore, business owners do not spend all of their income on consumption. As their income rises in an expansion, the rich spend less and less of it on consumption. Employees cannot spend more on consumption because their income is limited. Eventually, these limits on consumer spending cause a decline in the percentage of business output that can be sold in the market.

At the same time, many kinds of expenses rise faster than business revenues. For example, the price of raw materials rises rapidly in every expansion. Interest rates rise in every expansion, especially toward the end of expansion. Producers of final goods find their costs rising faster than their revenues. At the same time, the amount they can sell and their prices are constrained by the limitations of consumer demand.

In every business expansion profits rise rapidly at first as demand rises and costs are still low. But as the expansion progresses, consumer demand is limited as discussed above. At the same time, costs, such as raw materials and interest payments, are increasing faster and faster. Therefore, business profits reach a certain point in the expansion and then begin to decline. The profits are squeezed by both the limits on demand and the rising costs. As business profits decline, the outlook for investors becomes gloomy. When profits decline and the outlook for further profits is gloomy, investment starts to decline. Investment normally serves as the main fuel of the economy under capitalism. Thus, the decline in investment results in fewer jobs.

Declining jobs cause a vicious circle. Fewer jobs mean less consumer demand, which leads to less profit expectation. Lower expected profits lead to less investment. These cumulative processes end in a contraction of the economy. After a more or less long time, most of the processes reverse themselves and a new recovery is under way.

In addition to the processes described so far, the cycle is made much worse by financial speculation and the stock market. For example, the stock market rose throughout the 1990s and the media declared that it would rise forever. Millions of small investors were lured into the prospect of an eternal gold mine. But the stock market bubble reached a peak in 2000, and then burst. It continued to decline for three years, even though physical production rose after a one-year recession.

Millions of small investors had their savings wiped out when they were forced to sell at very low prices to pay for their current needs. These small investors were far larger in numbers than the few very big investors. But the big investors control most of the stock in the market. The big investors were able to weather the storm and the value of their stock rose again as the recovery occurred.

The decline of the stock market causes both real losses and lower savings shown on paper. This greatly reduces the amount that these people are willing to spend on consumption. All of the losses of consumers— losses of wages or stocks or other losses—reduce their spending. The reduced consumer spending makes corporations postpone investment and lay off workers.

Psychological Insecurity

All of this instability leaves employees anxious about their jobs and small investors anxious about their investments. Thus, economic instability leads not only to actual job losses and investment losses but also to psychological insecurity. "Psychological insecurity" is a fancy way of saying that unemployed people are worried, depressed, feel helpless, and often cannot eat, sleep, or make love.

Ours is a society in which everyone competes against everyone else— and this competition is highly praised by some people. But if everyone is out for himself or herself, then there is little or no community spirit. Each person is forced to compete against others for jobs, for mates, and for attention. Money and material goods are put far above all desires to help the community. Rather than a community spirit, many people feel alone and helpless.

To combat feelings of insecurity and helplessness, some people turn to drugs, such as marijuana, while many others turn to religion. In a search for meaning and psychological security, over 90 percent of U.S. citizens are religious in the sense that they believe in a supernatural being called God. Interestingly, over 90 percent of the members of the prestigious National Academy of Sciences believe there is no supernatural being or god of any sort. Because there is little community spirit under our present economic institutions, there is little trust. Most employees do not trust the giant corporation for which they work. Most voters do not trust the lawmakers. Most people do not trust the newspapers they read or the television newscasters. Although some people overcome the pressures that push people apart, many people feel so much alone that they are subject to mental illness, fights with their family, and may commit crime as a way out of poverty and unemployment. Top executives feel under pressure to make as much money as possible for their corporations and for themselves. Therefore, some corporate executive officers use any means—including illegal means—to make money.

Unemployment and the Global Economy

Global corporations choose the cheapest labor supply for their operations. Thus, the global corporations have moved some of their operations away from the higher wages in the more developed capitalist countries to the cheaper wages in the less developed countries. This movement of jobs has lowered wages of the workers in the more developed countries. It has, however, done very little to raise wages in the less developed countries because they started with a very large pool of unemployed.

It used to be that in each country, employees were fired in depressions until there was a huge reserve army of labor. Those reserves were then hired when a new expansion began. Under global capitalism, this reserve army consists of all the unemployed workers in the whole world. Therefore, a firm in an advanced European capitalist country may hire a worker in India to do certain computer jobs. After finishing the work, the Indian employee sends the results on the Internet back to that corporation. Thus it is much easier than in earlier eras to shift among the workers in the reverse army of unemployed around the world to those who will take the cheapest wages.

In the United States, this has meant continuous loss of manufacturing jobs overseas for many years. It has resulted in the unusual and, in fact, unique phenomenon that the first two years of recovery from the 2000 recession resulted in no decrease of unemployment. There is no historical record showing a similar situation of significant growth of the economy with no simultaneous growth of employment for two whole years. In fact, President George W. Bush is the first president since Herbert Hoover in the Great Depression to preside over a four-year period where there were fewer jobs at the end of his term than there were at the beginning.

Insecurity and Inequality Among Corporations

We all know that many people are poor and some are insecure, but business enterprises are often viewed as secure and rich. Certainly, the giant corporations are very rich and have some security, but most businesses are small and very insecure. In the United States the lifetime of the average business is only two years. Therefore, most businesses start up with high hopes and end with losses in a remarkably short time. During every economic expansion, hundreds of thousands of new businesses come into being, but about the same number go bankrupt or simply out of business in every recession.

While most enterprises remain small, some grow to enormous size through mergers and other means of growth. The boom of the 1950s and 1960s, like all boom periods, inspired many business mergers. These mergers happen because conditions look very profitable for giant enterprises. The third wave of mergers was from 1953 to 1969. Remember that the first wave of mergers in the beginning of the twentieth century was mostly mergers among competitors (called horizontal mergers). The second wave, mainly in the 1920s, was mergers of manufacturers with suppliers and sales outlets (called vertical mergers). The third wave, mainly in the 1950s and 1960s, was mostly mergers of many types of businesses with little relation to each other (called conglomerate mergers).

One reason for conglomerate mergers was that antitrust laws made the horizontal and vertical mergers illegal (when the laws were enforced, which was seldom in this period). The laws, however, said nothing about conglomerate mergers because it was assumed that conglomerate mergers had no effect on competition.

International mergers between corporations in different countries constitute a fourth wave, which may be called global mergers. Global mergers reached an all-time high toward the end of the expansion of the 1990s. In 1985, there were 1,923 mergers among corporations in the world, estimated at $165.8 billion dollars in value. In 1999, there were 9,946 mergers among corporations in the world, estimated at 2.4 trillion dollars in value!

In addition to mergers, the late 1990s saw growth by direct investment in foreign countries. In 1999, the European Union (EU) countries made two-thirds of all new foreign investments in the global economy. Also, the EU made more investments in the underdeveloped countries than did the United States for the first time since World War II. Thus, the EU has passed the United States in the annual amount of direct foreign investment. So another source of insecurity for corporations is the fact that there are shifts in which countries and geographical areas of the world have the most economic strength.

Although the EU is expanding faster, the United States is still increasing the percentage of its investments and profits that come from abroad. In 1997, U.S. corporate investments abroad provided 5.4 percent of all private sector gross production, 16 percent of all exports, and 26 percent of all imports. In 1997, total U.S. investment overseas amounted to over 3 trillion dollars.

By 2000, however, investment by foreigners in the United States amounted to over 6 trillion dollars. This investment by foreigners was 22 percent of all investment in U.S. businesses and residences. Thus, foreigners now own more in the United States than the U.S. firms and citizens own abroad.

In policy terms, the conservative position on mergers and monopoly power is that large size does no harm. When the system produces a larger size firm because that firm is the most efficient, competition eventually gets rid of any monopoly power conferred by large size. Therefore, nothing should be done about monopoly power. This conservative position, that nothing should be done about monopoly, was dominant in the nineteenth century, so nothing was done about monopoly until the 1890s.

The liberal position is that giant corporations have monopoly power. Monopoly power causes higher prices and less output. Therefore, giant firms should be broken into smaller, more competitive firms. But conservatives argue that the smaller units will be less efficient. They claim that the firms merged for efficiency in the first place, so smaller size would mean less efficiency.

As an answer to conservatives, some liberals have argued that the giant firms could be left large and efficient, but that they should be regulated by government agencies to see that they behave in a competitive manner. These agencies regulate prices and profits. Conservatives claim that any such regulations must reduce competition and efficiency. Radicals have argued that these firms usually manage to get their friends appointed as regulators, so no real change is made.

The position of strongly anticorporation economists was that state, local, and federal governments should take over firms that used their giant size and monopoly power to make immense profits. These anticorporate economists argued that the public should run the monopoly firms for the public interest (as the post office is run). Some anticorporate economists also argued that employees should participate in running the firm.

The most striking thing about the global merger wave was the enormous size of the mergers, which often included mergers between two enormous giants! In the first half of 2000 alone, there were mergers of firms with a half a trillion assets.

All of the old arguments about control of giant monopoly firms in each country have been replaced by new arguments about the control of the global firms in the global economy. The large firms have become global corporations, with branches in every country. These branches may focus on manufacturing commodities or they may focus on selling the commodities or do both. Now there is increasing concentration of economic power in the whole world. In other words, a relatively small number of corporations have an increasing share of the whole world economy. This gives them power in every country. One use of that power is to get laws passed that help them to make still more profits, such as more tax breaks.

Some degree of monopoly power on the world market does not mean an end of competition. These huge corporations compete against each other for a share of the market with ferocity, using all kinds of methods. But they usually do not compete by offering lower prices; rather they do more advertising, claim higher quality, and provide additional services. Moreover, they all agree on getting laws to protect global capitalism. There is no international agency with the power to control global monopolies, so the power of these firms continues to grow.

Environmental Destruction

Some of the well-known problems of the environment are caused by present-day economic institutions. One problem is the destruction of the ozone layer by human activity and by manufacturing byproducts. Destruction of the ozone layer leads to global warming, which causes rising oceans and other massive environmental problems. Here is a list of some other key problems:

Humans have caused the extinction of many species of plants and animals, some of them crucial to our ecosystem. Acid rain, caused by industry, destroys forests, destroys farm crops, and directly harms people. Poor containment of nuclear reactor radioactive material causes injury and death for miles around it.

Logging for profit has caused loss of forests, especially tropical forests, which are the source of much of our air supply, and are also desirable for their beauty and recreational importance. Destruction of vital wetlands causes species that rely on that environment to die and may also reduce our water supply in those areas. Soil erosion means less crops and less living space. Fertile land has been changed to desert by reckless management. Pollution of lakes and rivers means an end to many species of fish, on which our food supply relies.

Lowering of the level of ground water means that we have less to drink. Pollution of coastal waters harms not only swimming but also fishing. Destruction of coastal reefs ends many species of fish and also removes a source of protection of the shore. Oil spills have terrible consequences for both fish and human beings. Overfishing in some areas results in a lack of future food from those areas. Toxic wastes from industry make the environment lethal for animals, plants, and human beings.

Pesticide poisons used in agriculture have sometimes caused harm to consumers. Exposure to job hazards harms thousands of employees.

Urban congestion not only means hours sitting in a car but also pollution of the air. Other industrial sources add to the air pollution, sometimes making it difficult to get a breath of clean air in cities such as London or Beijing or Los Angeles.

The crisis of our environment is not produced by nature, which was fine for billions of years. It is the interference of human beings under particular kinds of economic institutions that causes the problems. Moreover, it is not technology that is the problem because there are perfectly well-known technological ways to cure any problem caused by industrialization.

The cures to things such as water pollution or air pollution are clear to all engineers. For example, if all automobiles were run on solar energy, most of the air pollution in Southern California would end. Unfortunately, our institutions dictate that many of the cures will not be used because they are expensive and hurt the profit of some business. It is the economic institutions that may prevent the cure from being used.

Of course, technology is not neutral. A switch from gasoline engines to solar energy in many areas would greatly change the degree of pollution. The question is what determines whether that change will be made. The answer is that our system of political-economic institutions determines what will be valued most and who will make the decision.

While our technology is shaped by our economic institutions, it is also true that new technology changes our institutions. For example, one cannot imagine global capitalism with sailing ships and pony express to deliver mail. Global capitalism becomes possible when there is instantaneous communication around the world and very fast transportation. So technology and economic institutions influence each other.

It is certainly true that increased use of energy, increased industrialization, increased urbanization, and increased population all directly cause environmental problems in our current society. But the reason they cause environmental problems is not inherent in any one of them. Rather, the form of technology, urbanization, and industrialization, as well as the role they play in the environment, are determined by the political-economic relationships of the society. Let us examine each of these issues.

As to the issue of population, before capitalism, most earlier societies had high birthrates. Yet they also had high death rates, so population grew very slowly. When capitalism began in England and brought industrialization in the cities, the new cities did not have very good sanitation by present standards, but it was much better than what most people had in the countryside. The better sanitation produced a lower death rate—and people lived longer. This caused a rapid growth of population.

More advanced capitalism not only lowered the death rate still further, but it also reduced the birthrate. The birthrate fell because in the countryside, children had been an economic asset in farming at an early age. In the cities, however, after a good education was required for most jobs, children became a burden on parents in the economic sense. Children continued to be born and raised out of love. The number of children per family fell slowly, but it inevitably did fall under the circumstances.

Moreover, women slowly moved into paid jobs and achieved a more equal status and a higher degree of education than in any earlier society. Women wanted to develop their own lives and did not want to give birth to a child every year for ten or fifteen years. Because of the need for smaller families, contraception came into normal use. Therefore, in advanced capitalism, population growth slows and may even decline because death rates have fallen less than birth rates. Many countries in Europe, even Catholic Italy, now have declining population.

Many of the colonial and neo-colonial countries, however, have not been allowed to industrialize and have not achieved a high level of income. Most of the people still live on the farm. Where low-productivity farming and poverty remain the norm, the earlier stage of high growth of population continues. Thus, the population problem of the neocolonial countries is caused in part by the lack of advanced industrialization.

Another problem of industrialization has been pollution from the burning of coal and similar materials for energy. Coal production was 200,000 tons in 1750, but rose to 701 million tons in 1900. Similarly, world manufacturing production rose by 80 times from 1750 to 1980, thus requiring more and more energy. Dirty fuels such as coal could be replaced by alternative sources, such as clean solar energy. But coal is cheaper and the profit motive under institutions of capitalism ensures that the cheaper fuel will be used, regardless of pollution.

Very little pollution is created by simple farming, but cities pour

179

out huge amounts of pollution. In the United States, 2.5 percent of the people lived in cities in 1800. By 2000, however, half the people lived in cities and most of the rest lived in small towns. The worst pollution occurs in cities of the neocolonial world. This pollution occurs because (1) there is vast poverty and starvation, so people are unwilling to spend any resources to stop pollution, and (2) the global corporations have so much control that they can easily stop antipollution laws.

The environmental problems are massive, systemic problems. Therefore, they cannot be cured by the voluntary abstention of some individuals or voluntary industry rules, which are seldom followed. Many regulations have been passed against corporate environmental destruction. But many regulations are not enforced or only enforced in a slight, cosmetic way. The reason is that politicians are influenced by donors to appoint regulators who come from the very corporations that are being regulated.

Moreover, most of the environmental problems involve many countries or are worldwide, so national regulations are insufficient to control them. The most obvious example is global warming, where an international agreement spells out some of the steps to be taken to control the problem. But the treaty on global warming, referred to as the Kyoto Protocol, has not been ratified by the United States because of the lobbying of corporations. Corporations calculate that the proscribed activities will be very profitable. What is needed are enforceable international agreements.

Insecurity and Inequality Amid Plenty

The magnificent achievements of apparently miraculous technological improvement under capitalist institutions suggest that all of our problems must have been solved by now. Yet, the earlier sections of this chapter and the previous chapter have revealed periodic mass unemployment, poverty and inequality, discrimination, and environmental destruction. To understand these problems, we must recognize that technology does not stand alone, but interacts with our current institutions in each area.

Advanced agriculture could produce enough food for everyone in the world to have a more-than-adequate diet; the Green Revolution and use of biotechnology have made this possible. Yet millions of people go hungry every day. There are accurate and unpleasant figures on how many people will die of hunger each day in the world. By one estimate, over 30,000 children under the age of five die daily of hunger and preventable diseases. Even in the wealthy United States, many people go to sleep hungry every night.

Clearly, the problem is not the lack of wonderful technology to produce, but the economic institutions under which people live or die. Under these institutions, the food may be available, but a person may not have the money to buy it. So the problem of hunger is a problem of income distribution rather than the lack of production.

Our spectacular technology could produce adequate housing for everyone in the world. In reality, seven people may live in a tent with a dirt floor in Afghanistan or Burundi. Even in the rich United States, a great many people live in single, rat-infested rooms or live outside with no roof overhead.

Advances in equipment and techniques of health care have been astounding, but millions and millions of people around the world have no health care. Even in the affluent United States, over 40 million people have no health insurance. Uninsured people wait until things get so bad that they must go to a hospital emergency room to wait in line with many others for hours and they often go too late or are taken for care too late.

Our wonderful technology does not exist by itself in a vacuum. It is incorrect and very misleading to say that institutions are determined by technology in a one-way street. It is also incorrect and misleading, however, to say that our institutions determine our technology on a one-way street. Rather, technology (such as computers) always interacts with our institutions (such as the health-care system). A useful metaphor is that the traffic between institutions and technology is a two-way street. A given technology, such as the Internet, will influence the development of our institutions. But it is also true that given institutions (such as health care under capitalism) may prevent the highest-level technology from being fully used by anyone but the very rich and powerful. This evolution in which high-level technology is used by the rich, while low-level technology is used by the middle class and the poor, produces many questions as to where the society is going.

Suggested Reading

As in earlier chapters, the best source on the environment is Foster (1984). A full, detailed discussion of the mechanisms causing instability and the data on business cycles are given in Sherman, *The Business Cycle: Growth and Crisis in Capitalism* (1991). The data on global mergers come from a complex, but useful article by Frederick Pryor (2001). Jared Diamond, in *Collapse* (2005), provides a dramatic and powerful description of how environmental destruction by humans can be a major factor in social collapse and, moreover, explains how the environmental destruction is caused by human institutions and associated ideology.

– 12 –

Rise and Fall of the Soviet Union

The Soviet Union began with a revolution in 1917 and ended with a counter-revolution in 1991. Since it affected everything else in the twentieth century, this amazing episode reveals much about social evolution.

What Caused the Soviet Revolution?

Until 1917, the Russian Empire was ruled by a monarch, the tsar, with the support of the great landowners. The serfs were emancipated in 1861, but the land remained with the landlords. Every village, as a whole, had the responsibility to make payments to the landlord for the cost of the emancipated serfs and the use of the land. There was little democracy and the path of peaceful, gradual reform seemed blocked, leading many to consider revolution. Parties advocating basic change were outlawed and forced underground. Among these parties was the Communist Party, which was then called the left wing of the Social Democratic Party, often called the Bolsheviks. Here, it will be called Communist to avoid confusion.

The peasants were poor and had no land to call their own because they owed a huge debt to the landlord. The city workers were also poor, and received low wages. Although there were some domestic capitalists, most of the corporate profits went to German, French, and British capitalists. Soldiers were drafted, paid little, and kept for an indefinite time. Then, in 1914, World War I began and made conditions worse.

The tsarist government was so weak and inefficient that it was tossed out by a revolution in February 1917 and replaced by a government representing the capitalist group. The new government, however, refused to give land to the peasants. When their demands were not met, many peasants revolted and took over land by force.

The city workers had little food to eat, as the countryside was chaotic, so the city workers formed councils (the Russian word is *soviet*) to resist capitalist corporations, to obtain higher wages, and to achieve more control over their lives.

During World War I, the Russian government was so poor that the Russian army had little ammunition. As the Germans advanced into Russia, the Russian soldiers had to use bayonets against German guns. The angry soldiers formed their own councils (soviets) and would not take the orders of officers unless their soviet representatives agreed.

As the war was being lost and people were close to starvation, by October 1917, the councils of the city workers were dominated by the radical Communist Party. The Communist Party also became the largest party in elections in most cities. In October the Communist Party—and its allies among the radical peasants—revolted, tossed out the old government, and formed a new, radical government. It was supported by the soviets of the workers and of the soldiers, so it was called the Soviet government. Notice that, at the time, Russia was using a different calendar. Thus, they celebrate the so-called October Revolution on November 7.

The Communist government gave all of the land into the possession of the peasants. As capitalists fled the country, they gave all power over the business enterprises to the councils elected by the workers of each enterprise. For the soldiers, the Soviet government made peace with the Germans, giving away a big chunk of the Russian empire to achieve peace. Thus, the Communist government was popular among many workers, peasants, and soldiers. Of course, it was hated by the landlords, native business people, and foreign capitalists who had lost their holdings.

Why Was There a Dictatorship?

In 1917, more than 80 percent of Russian people could not read, so the kind of open, national communication and debate needed for democracy was not possible. The parties that led the revolution had opposed monarchy, so they had been forced underground until the revolution. Therefore, they had no long tradition of democratic politics in the country or within their secret party organization.

The Communists took power during a war, which is never favorable to democracy. Then there was a civil war as the landlords and native capitalists tried to regain their economic power. The civil war was long and bloody and allowed no exercise of democratic politics. At the same time, armies from sixteen capitalist countries, representing the interests of the foreign capitalists who had lost their factories, invaded the Soviet Union and supported the anti-Communist forces of the landlords and native capitalists in the civil war.

Even when they won the civil war after incredible violence and devastation, the Communist government was not popular with some groups because of the extreme poverty that still existed. Others opposed the dictatorial political structure. Finally, some of their opponents desired to go back to a regime of landlords. There was also foreign economic pressure against the Soviet Union. The economic force was used by many capitalist countries to try to force the Soviet Union to go back to capitalism.

Because many groups wanted to get rid of the Communists, a democratic vote might have taken power away from them. The Communists were not ready to give up power, so they did not take the risk of a democratic election.

Finally, the Communist government was dedicated to rapid economic growth, partly because they feared the rise of German military power. In order to get rapid growth, the dominant party group led by Stalin, forced all of the peasants into giant collective farms. These huge farms could be controlled by the central government, even though in theory they were democratic cooperatives. The farms were forced to sell agricultural products at fixed, cheap prices to the government. In addition to the economic motivation for collectivization, the Soviet leadership also worried that millions of independent farm owners would be a base for capitalist sentiments and political opposition to pubic ownership.

The government then used these goods bought at low prices from the collectives as raw materials for industry. The food was also used to feed industrial workers. Finally, the food and raw materials extracted from agriculture were sold abroad so as to import machinery. These policies did result in rapid economic growth in the 1930s. The economic achievements were impressive to many people at a time when the rest of the world was in the Great Depression.

These drastic economic policies, however, also changed the dictatorship from a temporary war expedient to a permanent institution. The Communist Party had started out as the proponent of democracy against monarchy, but now all of its leadership had a vested interest in a continued dictatorship.

Why Did Central Planning Emerge?

By the end of the civil war in 1921, most of the Soviet economy had come under control of the government or of the workers in each enterprise. There was no market system. Money became worthless because of extreme inflation. In order to prosecute the war, the government gave economic commands not only to government-owned enterprises but also to worker-run enterprises. These orders were all for individual cases, mostly emergencies, with no overall plan.

For a while in the early 1920s, the Soviet Union experimented with an economy of small farms and decentralized control of businesses. They allowed each enterprise to do its own planning and sell things in a market system. By the late 1920s, however, terrible conditions forced a rethinking. As we saw earlier, all the small farms were gathered together into huge collective farms. All businesses were taken over into centralized control.

The reasons for the centralization were partly the lack of good managers in the enterprises and partly the decision to avoid a return to a market system. Rather than allowing a market system, they wanted strict control of all enterprises in order to ensure that no wasteful goods would be produced. They wanted to focus all production activity on the most rapid expansion to make the economy grow as fast as possible. They believed that a rapidly growing economy was the best defense against foreign enemies.

With giant farms controlled by the government to a large degree and business enterprises controlled directly by the government, it was necessary to have central planning of economic activity as soon as possible. In 1928 a series of five-year plans for the economy began. The plans were drawn up by a group of planners sitting in Moscow. They relied on information gathered from all of the farms and businesses. Since that information determined the future of each enterprise, it was often in the interests of the enterprise not to supply all of the information or even to send false information.

When the planners had gathered their information, they then had to prepare a number of alternative plans, all of them feasible, but with different results. These alternative plans were submitted to the prime minister and his cabinet. Based on conflicting interests, this top political level finally chose one variant of the plans, usually the most ambitious one. After it was enacted into law, it was given to each enterprise as a set of commands. Often, the plan for one enterprise for one year (which was all it received at one time) amounted to fifty thousand pages. It had to be followed by the manager because it was the law. The scope of discretion lay only in carrying out the orders. The Soviet system might be thought of as one enormous enterprise giving orders to all of its managers in every field.

How Did the Soviet Regime Perform During Its Existence?

During the early 1920s, the chaos of recovery from the war meant that the economic growth was painfully slow. After the five-year plans began in 1928, however, there was remarkably rapid growth throughout the 1930s. The growth was concentrated in a very large increase in production of durable goods to build more factories. What suffered was production of consumer goods, since much of their resources were shifted over to heavy industry. Thus the population paid a heavy price for the rapid growth of industry. Moreover, political repression was necessary to carry out this unpopular policy. Therefore, dictatorship was a long-run cost of the drastic measures used to maximize growth.

The large industrial production of the 1930s, however, did help the Soviet Union defend itself against the fascist onslaught during World War II in the early 1940s. There was also some economic and military help from the United States during the war. The war was won, but German fascism had destroyed about a third of Soviet industrial capacity and had killed twenty million people. So many men had been killed that for some years, several women often competed for one man. Scarcity of labor also made the Soviet government oppose birth control.

The system of central planning did prove itself a useful tool for a very rapid economic recovery from the war devastation in the late 1940s and early 1950s, when the Soviet rate of economic growth was higher than that of any other country. Soviet planning gave it the ability to have full employment, so the Soviet Union did have full employment for the rest of its existence.

Full employment, full use of industrial capacity, and a very high rate of investment gave the Soviet Union a comparatively high rate of investment in industry. Full employment of all workers and resources by central planning produced a high rate of growth for many years and a positive rate right up to the end of the Soviet Union in 1991. Some of the output was used to support education, so the Soviet Union went from an illiterate country to one with a very high rate of literacy. It produced large numbers of engineers and other professionals. It used its output for adult education, compulsory child education, and a university education that was free and gave large stipends to the average student. Its education system was one of its strongest institutions.

Some of the growing output was also used for health care. There was free health care for all and a strong program of examinations and preventive medicine. When this author traveled in the Soviet Union, a Soviet nurse came into my hostel room at 6:00 A.M. without knocking, woke me from sleep, rolled up my pajama sleeve, gave me a shot, and said "Flu, comrade." This incident illustrates both its preventive medicine and its dictatorial nature. The worst weakness of the health system was favoritism toward the elite for the services of scarce specialists. Rationing of health care was by political influence, not by the use of money. General health care went to everyone, but specialized health care went more to the political elite.

Many of the elite also managed to get their children into universities, regardless of test scores. Favoritism to the children of the elite has also been widespread in the United States (as was documented at the University of California), but the favoritism has been mostly the result of the use of wealth rather than political influence.

The Soviet growth rate was higher than that of the United States for most years from 1945 to 1975 because of the favorable factors stated above. From 1975 to 1991, however, the Soviet economy grew more slowly than that of the U.S. economy. Growth did remain positive every year until the end of the Soviet Union in 1991, but it grew slower and slower every decade.

The reason for the slower growth was that the Soviet economy had many problems that had always existed, but now became increasingly severe as the economy became more complex. Every Soviet citizen discovered in painful ways that growth was lower in the 1950s, still lower in the 1970s, worse in the 1980s, and still worse in the 1990s. Since the Soviet Union was founded on the claim that its economic system was far better than the capitalist system, this ever slower rate of growth worried everyone, made many people pessimistic about the system, and caused political unrest.

Why did the Soviet growth rate decline? The Soviet system of central planning (under political dictatorship) did very well in the initial task of building industry and in the task of reconstruction after World War II. These tasks were clear and could use existing technology. But economic success created a very complex economy. Planning for a modern, complex economy would require vast amounts of information. Although the planned Soviet economy rose faster than the U.S. economy until 1975 and continued to rise to the end in 1991, the problems of insufficient information in a structure directed by dictatorship caused an inexorable decline in the growth rate after a certain point.

The information that the central planners had in the Soviet Union was not complete and often distorted by the interests of the sender. After the early 1970s, consumers demanded a greater variety and a higher quality of products, while firms needed to make more and more complex choices of technology. These problems required vast amounts of precise information and enormously powerful computers with perfect programming, but these were not available.

Let us begin with the simplest technical problem. A complex problem with tons of data requires an ultra-fast computer and a good program. The Soviet Union did not have a good enough program or enough good computers to solve the problems in any reasonable time. Without super-computers and perfect programs, central planning had to fail even if the planners had perfect data. Therefore, poor planning was one source of the worsening performance of the economy.

Even with a perfect plan, one still had to get managers to follow the plan. There were strong incentives for managers, including bonuses and promotions. But the incentive systems tended to be distorted. They were distorted for several reasons. The incentives relied to some extent on artificial prices set by the government. The shortage of labor encouraged the managers to hire the best workers away from others by illegal means and not to fire any worker (no matter how bad).

The shortage of raw materials encouraged managers to hoard unnecessary amounts of materials. If the plan was set in purely quantitative terms, then managers tended to ignore quality control to an amazing degree. For example, if a manager is judged by the total weight of the steel girders produced for building bridges, then performance of the firm looks better if all the girders produced are very heavy. Therefore, some Soviet managers produced steel girders that were far too heavy to be used for any bridge.

Managers also took a very short-run view because they were paid by the month and were often transferred. Therefore, a manager would not introduce a whole new system of technology, even if it was a great improvement, if it would mean short-run reduction of production. By the time the new system started producing efficiently, the manager was likely to be elsewhere, having been demoted for a short-run decline.

Perhaps the biggest problem caused by giving the wrong incentives to managers was that in attempting to get short-run results, managers were afraid to invest in major changes in technology. Of course, there were some technological advances under Soviet planning, such as the first satellite in their space program (called Sputnik). But a lack of incentive to take chances by innovation in most industries most of the time meant that the Soviet Union fell behind most advanced economies. As noted above, the slowing growth rate became lower than the American rate after 1975.

Dictatorship intensified these problems and caused other major ones. Science suffered repression from the dictatorship, so it was unable to make innovative breakthroughs in many areas. Scientific directors were appointed by a political dictatorship that nourished corruption. Dictatorship also meant that appointments of managers and their promotions might depend on bribery, not ability. Finally, dictatorship meant that it was very dangerous to criticize a manager, no matter how bad he or she might be.

What lessons can be learned from the story of Soviet planning? First, how well would central planning perform in a democratic country? This question cannot be answered because the Soviet Union was a dictatorship.

Second, what were its strengths? What did Soviet planning accomplish? It carried out the initial industrialization of a backward economy and it ran a functioning economy for sixty years. Central planning also set up universal health-care and education systems. The Soviet Union recovered rapidly from World War II, and it laid the foundations for a mass consumer economy from 1945 to 1975.

Third, what were its weaknesses? Why did it slow down and fail? In an economy of complex technology and complex consumer wants, there were insufficient information and insufficient computers. The wrong incentives were given to managers. Dictatorship suppressed criticism and innovative ideas. A large modern economy cannot be run with extremely centralized planning and a dictatorship.

Reform

All of these problems led to attempts at reform. What were they? For a long time, there were attempts to reform the system by decentralizing the huge planning apparatus in order to give more scope for innovation to every manager. There were schemes to make profits more important and mere quantity much less important. Finally, there was the idea that the central plan should only be a guidepost, not a set of commands. The Soviet managers would be guided by the incentive to make profit in a competitive market. The manager would keep some of the profit as a bonus, while the rest would go to the government to reinvest.

One problem of reform was that, if the central plan had no power to command, all the instability of capitalism would reappear. But if the plan was to prevent instability, then it had to command and that meant no decentralization. Thus, the Soviets could not agree on the right balance between planned stability and individual innovation.

Moreover, the dictatorship had complete control of the economy; so many officials based their power on central planning and its enforcement. To abolish much of central planning meant that these officials lost their power over the economy. But any successful reform needed the cooperation of all the top- and middle-level officials. So they were able to stop every reform that might result in loss of power.

Why Was There a Counterrevolution in 1991?

By the 1980s, everyone recognized that the growth rate had fallen very low and something had to be done. The present structure of the economic institutions was holding back technological progress (as had

191

happened in the late Roman Empire and in late feudalism). Soviet President Mikhail Gorbachev suggested two kinds of reforms: decentralization and democratization.

Gorbachev called for decentralization of economic decisions to the enterprise level in many respects, with bonuses based on performance going to both the managers and the workers. Firms would be coordinated by the market rather than central planning.

Gorbachev succeeded in changing the basic law on enterprises to decentralize decisions from planners to firms. The new law gave far more power to enterprise managers to make many kinds of decisions on payments to workers, what to produce, and how to produce it. The law took effect on January 1, 1988. While the new law increased decentralization, it did not indicate how the system would be coordinated. It greatly weakened central planning, but did not provide a new system to replace it. The Gorbachev forces wanted the enterprises to compete in the market and be judged by their profit-making—though there would be constraints on the market to protect workers and consumers.

Because of intense factional fighting—with objections from both the left and right described below—such a complete change to a market-coordinated system of state enterprises was never put into effect. Thus, the reforms were left hanging halfway between systems. The result was weak planning with no market to replace it, so there was much economic dislocation. There was a loosening of payment constraints to workers, so there was inflationary pressure and shortages of many items. Consumers were unhappy and managers were unhappy. Moreover, the old taxes on enterprises were ended, but no new system was created, so there was a growing budget deficit—this made it difficult to pay state workers, who also became unhappy.

To protect the decentralization law already passed and to have the power to pass a more comprehensive change, Gorbachev reformed the election system so as to allow much greater freedom. His speeches indicated that he did not merely want democracy to protect the reforms, but also believed in democracy as the heart of socialism. Gorbachev said that socialism stood for democratic control of the society and the economy.

Gorbachev thought that the conservatives would be defeated in elections and that his reformers would get an overwhelming majority. This expectation was a big mistake! More freedom in elections and in speech let the genie out of the bottle. Most people were angry about the halfway reforms and the dislocations they caused, for which they blamed the government and Gorbachev. All kinds of groups appeared, many wanting to change to capitalism. Since the Cold War between the Soviet Union and the United States still continued, at that time, there was heavy foreign pressure in favor of the forces supporting capitalism.

The struggle became violent, revealing three groups among the elite. One group of conservative Communist Party officials wanted to preserve the old system (and their power) at any cost. These conservatives were a small minority. Second, a group of reformers wanted to drastically improve the old system. These reformers were led by Gorbachev. Advocates of reform included a large minority of the elite. Most of the population also sympathized with reform.

Third, another group of the elite wanted to change the system to capitalism. This group was led by Yeltsin and included a large majority of the elite (for reasons discussed below). Yeltsin's group never told the population that they wanted capitalism. Most of the populace was confused and deliberately misled into doing little. Most people were convinced into voting against the reformist government because of the poor situation. The majority certainly did not like the conservatives, so they voted for Yeltsin's party and its vague promises of a better system.

What happened in this struggle? First, the Communist Party hardliners, favoring the old system, tried a coup against Gorbachev and any reform. They were not successful because few people supported the hardliners. The economic situation, however, was deteriorating and needed change, while the government was shown to be weak by the near success of the coup. Then there was a coup by the pro-capitalist groups in the government. It was successful and they seized power, dismantled the Soviet Union into a number of independent countries, and moved in devious ways toward capitalism.

Why did so many of the elite agree to a peaceable change to capitalism that ended their old powers? Once it was clear that the government was weak and the old system was collapsing, most of the officials and managers rushed to grab the vast economic assets of the government for themselves. As they privatized the immense spoils of the factory system, they rather quickly changed their ideological color and supported the march toward capitalist institutions. This change in the ideas of part of the elite added strength to the movement to replace the Soviet system with capitalism.

The pro-capitalist party got to power by convincing the population with slogans of major reform of the old socialist system. Then rather than reform, they ended that system completely. Criminal elements had such a big role in the new system that it was sometimes called mafia capitalism. In truth, for the next ten years it is more precise to say that it was no system at all. Central planning was destroyed, but very little capitalism was built. The result was a ten-year decline in output and living standards.

Lessons of Soviet History

The Russian revolution of 1917 was caused by the fact that economic progress was held back by the rigid and obsolete institutions of an empire that still reflected mainly the interests of the landowners, modified by the interests of foreign capitalists. Within the crucible of World War I, this tension between economic institutions and economic progress led to social conflicts, which eventually ended the old regime.

The counterrevolution of 1991 in Russia was caused by the fact that economic progress was held back by the rigid and obsolete Soviet institutions, including dictatorship and extreme use of central planning. Once again, the tension between economic institutions and economic progress produced social conflicts, which eventually led to the end of the old regime.

The Soviets claimed to be very democratic because there were no capitalists to control the economic and political processes, so the publicly owned economy was run by all of the citizens. The reality was that a one-party dictatorship controlled both the political structure and the economy, leaving no room whatsoever for democracy. This undemocratic political and economic structure could not meet the needs of the modern economy or the modern Russian citizens.

Suggested Readings

The best books on the background of the Soviet revolution and the early years of Soviet history are by Isaac Deutscher and are both very insightful and beautifully written in a style that is always exciting and sometimes lyrical. The place to begin is Deutscher's book on Soviet history written as a biography of Stalin (Deutscher, *Stalin,* 1965a). A profound insight into Soviet politics is his moving biography of Trotsky (Deutscher, *Trotsky*, 1965b). An excellent description of the exciting events of the Soviet Revolution of 1917 is in Rabinowitch (2004), but a much more interesting history of the Soviet Revolution is in the classic by John Reed, *Ten Days That Shook the World*.

The history of Soviet economic development and problems is given in Andrew Zimbalist, Howard Sherman, and Stuart Brown, *Comparing Economic Systems: A Political-Economic Approach* (1988). The best book on the decline and fall of the Soviet Union is: David Kotz with Fred Weir, *Revolution from Above: The Demise of the Soviet Union* (1997).

– 13 –

Beginnings of
Economic Democracy

The world today is dominated by global capitalism, but as evolution continues, that may change some day. There have been many attempts to increase democracy, both political and economic. This chapter will examine some of these attempts.

Evolution of Democratic Institutions

Before getting to the present, it is useful to look at the evolution of democratic institutions as one thread in the evolution of society.

Let us summarize some of the information discussed in detail in earlier chapters. Chapters 1 and 2 showed that in the earliest societies, the economic and political unit was the extended family, usually of twenty-five to thirty-five people. In such a society, decision making was usually done at a meeting of all of the adults. It was often by consensus along lines strongly given by tradition, so the issue of the democratic process did not arise as a separate matter.

Chapter 3 showed that most slave societies were empires ruled by emperors, with no democracy. A few Greek cities, however, did use democratic forms. As a result of many sharp struggles, monarchy was overthrown and all "citizens" could vote. Citizens, however, did not include the large number of foreigners who were permanent residents. Citizens did not include the large part of the population—a majority at some times and places—who were slaves. Citizens did not include the half of the population who were women.

Ancient Athens was an example where all the forms of democracy were followed, including free speech and voting, but where most people were excluded. This example was followed by the U.S. South before the Civil War, which also claimed to be a democracy, but excluded all slaves and all women. The real economic and political power in ancient Athens—and in the U.S. South before the Civil War—was exclusively with the slave owners. It was also normal in ancient Athens for citizens with large amounts of money to buy the votes of other citizens. So there was very little democracy in the political sphere, where it was extremely limited and distorted by power and money. There was no democracy at all in the economic sphere, where slavery was the rule.

Chapter 4 showed that under feudalism, there was very little democracy. The lord governed the serfs both as political ruler and as economic manager. There was some democracy when the peasants had to make collective decisions among themselves. The lords also sometimes asked the king for greater rights for themselves, but their democratic requests did not extend to the peasants.

Toward the end of feudalism, two revolutions—the British Revolution of 1648 and the French Revolution of 1789—swept away the final remnants of feudalism in those countries and initiated a capitalist economy with a limited democratic political process. From 1789 to the present, there has been a slow tendency, with some backward steps at times (as in the period of fascism), toward an increase in the forms of democracy. At the expense of long and bitter struggles, barriers were removed for voting by those without property, by minorities, and by women. There is no space to follow this process all over the world, so it is examined here only for the United States, which was one of its leaders.

Political Democracy in the United States

In the United States, the Revolutionary War of 1776 tossed out British colonial rule, in which the ultimate power had rested with British colonial governors. The new U.S. government initiated a political process that produced an elected president and legislature, but no king. Like ancient Athens, it had all the forms of democracy, but excluded large groups of people from the process.

Immediately after the U.S. revolution, people without property were excluded from the political process in many states, slaves were excluded in the Southern states, and women were excluded in all states. It required many battles until the 1840s before people without property could vote in all states. It took a century of struggle from the 1820s to the 1920s before women could vote and participate. It took the Civil War for the former slaves to be emancipated and given the vote. Additional obstacles kept the former slaves from participating fully in voting for almost a hundred years. Finally, the Civil Rights movement of the 1950s and 1960s demolished the remaining obstacles to the political procedures of voting for African-Americans.

Every American school child knows some of that history and is then told that "we have democracy" now. There are only a few remaining undemocratic forms, such as the Electoral College, a system that in 2000 gave the presidency to George W. Bush, even though Al Gore received more votes. Nevertheless, the United States does have most of the forms of democracy in the sense that almost all adults can vote and most people can freely express their political opinions. "Formal democracy" means that a country has all the forms of democracy. A country with formal democracy, however, may not have a fully "effective democracy," where effective is defined to mean that everyone can really participate on fairly equal terms.

Suppose there is a town with 10,001 adults, all of whom can vote and say what they please. They elect a city government with their votes, so there is formal democracy. Ten thousand adults, however, are very poor, while one man is a billionaire. The billionaire owns all of the businesses in town, including the local newspaper, radio station, and television station. The billionaire gives much money to candidates he wants and none to others. In the newspaper, radio, and television, he carries stories and editorials favorable to the candidates he wants and against the other candidates. His candidates always win. This town has a formal democracy, but little or no effective democracy.

There are still obstacles to a fully effective democracy in the United States. Because there is some democracy, but it is limited, it is more precise to speak of the degree of effective democracy, rather than just saying there is or is not democracy.

The Degree of Effective Democracy

There are two main kinds of problems for American democracy that reduce its degree of completeness and effectiveness. First, the economic power of a relatively small number of wealthy people and giant corporations prevents political equality in participation and in influence. Second, the formal democratic process applies only to the political sphere of legislatures and the executive branch. Even formal democracy does not extend to the economic sphere. For example, most chief executive officers (CEOs) of corporations are elected only by the stockholders, but employees and consumers and the public have no say in the matter.

Let us examine the first problem, how economic power limits political democracy. The problem of economic influence must be thoroughly distinguished from that of dictatorship. Germany in the 1930s had a dictatorship (fascism) that abolished most formal democratic rights. The United States in the 1950s had a considerable degree of repression (McCarthyism) that greatly reduced democratic rights. But the question here is: what restricts democracy under capitalist institutions when all formal rights are granted?

The United States has full formal democracy, but severe limits on effective democracy. Effective democracy requires a high level of participation, which is lacking. For example, in the American presidential election of 2000, only half the eligible voters actually voted. Most of the non-voters were in the lower-income half of the nation, including a large part of the middle class and all of the poor. Therefore, the election process was very strongly biased toward the interests of the more affluent voters. Moreover, the two main parties spent a total of three billion dollars in 2000, in addition to which the political action committees spent a lot more. In brief, money rules and effective democracy is very limited. By what mechanisms does this happen?

First of all, begin with the fact that the main political parties spend enormous sums. Where does this vast river of political spending come from? The answer is that all of the large contributions come from the wealthy and, by indirect means, from the big corporations. Note that labor unions contribute less than a tenth of what corporations do.

Second, lobbying has the reputation of being the main cause of bribery, corruption, and distortion of the democratic process. In spite of dramatic examples, lobbying plays a relatively minor role compared with other mechanisms. But it is the bridge between the legislator and a corporation or organization that supplies money or supporters or even writes a bill for a legislator.

Third, corporate culture tries to condition every professional and other employee to its own view of the world through a pervasive atmosphere of loyalty and common interests with the corporation. This pervasive influence every working day is one reason most people never question whether any other way of life, let alone a different economic system, is possible.

Fourth, our views are shaped in part by the educational system, but the educational system is shaped to some extent by the money contributions of wealthy individuals and corporations to private and public colleges. In public colleges, it is also shaped by the political influence, which reflects economic influence. Many of the big donors sit on boards that rule the colleges and universities, so that these boards are often composed of old, white, rich men.

Education prepares an educated workforce for the economy and is a road to upward mobility for some people. The percentage of students going to college, however, increases with family income. Thus, the degree of inequality is reproduced from generation to generation. Also, most teachers of social science teach the dominant ideology, so it is further reinforced.

Fifth, religion helps shape some people, such as the religious rightwing political movement. Moreover, religious leaders spend much time collecting money from wealthy donors. The wealthy donors have an enormous influence on church policies and teachings, while the church teachings have a strong influence in conditioning people to follow the existing order. On the contrary, it is worth noting that a small number of religious ministers preach a radical doctrine of applying the ethical views of religion to everyday struggles for a better life for most people.

Sixth, the media have a powerful effect on people's minds. Most of the media are owned by a few giant corporations. In conformity with the corporate interests that provide their bread and butter, the media convey the message that there is no alternative to the present economic system, and they imply that it is useless to vote because all politicians are corrupt.

Seventh, as income declines, so does political participation. The low participation is revealed in the lack of voting and lack of political action among low-income and lower-middle income groups. The reason is simply that poor people have less time to themselves, less information about politics, and a greater feeling of helplessness and resignation. Most people do not become pro-capitalist, but they are often convinced that nothing can be changed, so they simply do not vote.

As a result of all of these mechanisms, most elected officials are happy to do the bidding of the rich. A disproportionate number of the rich themselves are elected; for example, a quarter of U.S. senators are millionaires. Given the composition of the elected politicians and the powerful forces that affect them, it is not surprising that governments do as the rich desire to a large degree. Thus, government gives tax breaks to the rich, gives harsh sentences to the poor who take private property, protects environmental polluters, and gives lucrative contracts for military spending or for rebuilding of conquered nations. For example, before the war with Iraq, deals were made in secret with no competition with some firms (one of which had been led by Vice President Cheney). These contracts were to do various construction jobs in Iraq after the war at high rates of profit that were guaranteed in the contract.

The picture painted above makes it look like money rules politics completely, but that is not true. First, there are other groups such as farmers, business employees, and independent professionals. Each of these groups has its own interests and each of them fights for those interests against the corporate elite. Second, there are many factions among the different corporations who have opposing interests on some matters, though they all have very basic interests in common. Third, many politicians follow corporate interests most of the time, but they have their own autonomous interests as well. If a political position is very unpopular, a politician may be forced to oppose it even if all of his or her money comes from those in favor of it.

Struggles for Economic Democracy

The previous sections showed that a very long struggle has finally resulted in almost complete formal political democracy in the United States (and in most of the capitalist world). In practice, however, this has meant an ongoing struggle among groups in which the corporate elite, who control the economy, have always won the important battles due to their economic power. It was shown that their power is not absolute, but very strong.

In addition to this problem of the exercise of economic power over the political process, there is also the related question of having a democratic process of decision making within business enterprises as well as in politics. Chapters 7 and 8 showed that under capitalism a relatively small elite control the economy by their private ownership and control of businesses. Most people are employees who can be hired and fired, promoted or demoted, and told what work to do, with no say in the matter. In brief, the owners and the managers may act as dictators in the workplace.

Economic democracy means that the people rule the economy, not just politics. Examples of economic democracy may be found in many types of institutions and processes. The following investigates the ways in which economic democracy has been extended in some times and some places in the United States. The rest of the world has seen much greater and more successful movements for economic democracy, but there is room here to examine only one country on this point, so the focus is on the United States.

Cooperative Forms of Economic Democracy

One form of economic democracy is the voluntary cooperation of many people in forming an enterprise, to be governed by its members, rather than by stockholders. A very large number of different types of non-capitalist enterprises may be formed. There are consumer-organized cooperatives, business-organized cooperatives, and worker-organized cooperatives.

By 2004, about 10 percent of all workers were employed by cooperatives of all kinds and by other nonprofit enterprises. For example, there are large health organizations, such as Kaiser, that are nonprofit. The focus here, however, is on democratically run enterprises, beginning with cooperatives.

Consumers have organized many groups to buy goods at a low wholesale price and then resell them to their members without a profit. Consumer cooperatives are not capitalist institutions because there are no private owners and there is no private profit. Rather, a cooperative is formed by many people and each person usually has one vote in the cooperative. In this way, consumers have organized themselves democratically to buy and market some goods, for example, a store selling food. One type of consumer cooperative is subscriber-controlled radio stations, such as KPFK or KPFA. To a large extent, National Public Radio and the Public Broadcasting System for television are financed by their subscribers—though other types of financing also play a major role, as discussed below.

Another type of cooperative is the condominium in the housing market. The most usual type of condominium structure, especially in large buildings, is a structure in which the apartment owners each cast one vote for a board of directors. The board then selects a management enterprise to give it professional management. The management company collects the monthly fees and does all day-to-day direction and decision making. Few homeowners see this as a democratically run enterprise, but only as a useful way to own an apartment without worrying about building management. While most condominiums are bought by relatively affluent citizens, there are also some nonprofit enterprises providing housing to the poor.

The largest single consumer cooperative group is helped by an agency of the U.S. government, the Rural Electrification Administration. It helps farmers and rural villages get electricity when private firms find it unprofitable. It has had a long and successful history.

Some groups of small businesses organize themselves into cooperatives to get the advantages of size. For example, there are cooperatives of chicken farmers to market chickens and cooperatives of grocery stores to facilitate the retail sale of food.

There are many cooperatives designed to raise enough money for various projects. This has led to credit unions, which collect savings and make loans. In the United States, over 79 million people belong to cooperative credit unions. In addition, employees have often gotten together to provide insurance for the group, but some of these small insurance activities have grown into giant corporations.

Besides consumer and financial cooperatives, there are also many producer cooperatives. In a producer cooperative, each employee is also an owner. The employee owns a share of the enterprise. In fact, all stock in the enterprise is owned by its employees. In most cooperative enterprises, each employee/owner has one vote on how to run the enterprise. No one may have more than one vote, no matter how much of its stock they own. They democratically elect a board of directors. The board of directors appoints a manager for day-to-day decisions.

There are a considerable number of such enterprises in the United States in which the employees own all of the stock and therefore control the enterprise through a board of directors. Who gets the profit in these employee-owned enterprises? The profit is reinvested or is distributed among the employees. Of course, if all employees get both wages and profits, there is very little difference between the two streams of income. As far as employees are concerned, they perceive little or no difference between the two types of income. The legal differences and the tax differences, however, may be considerable.

There is a wide variety of forms of employee-based cooperatives. For example, taxi drivers have gathered together to form a taxi company run by its drivers. One example is the Denver Yellow Cab Company. This company was originally privately owned, but it was bought out by its employees. They designed their structure to be based on one vote by one driver. Drivers collected their own fares, but contributed a certain percentage to the company for operating expenses. Any profit at the end of the year could be paid out to every member. Otherwise, profit might be reinvested for expansion purposes. This employee-owned firm began and continued as a quite profitable enterprise.

In the meat-packing industry, the Rath Packing Company was on the edge of bankruptcy when it was taken over by its workers. They did this to protect two thousand jobs. Of course, after they took over, it was still on the edge of bankruptcy. This is often the case with such takeovers—and they often remain in great financial difficulty. The Denver Yellow Cab Company was unusual in that it was profitable. The cab drivers wanted independence and democratic procedures. The drivers achieved this independence by risking their own money plus a large bank loan.

In the 1960s, partly for job protection, but partly to achieve more democracy, about twenty cooperatives were formed by forestry workers in Oregon and adjoining states. The employees in the cooperatives received certain wage levels plus fringe benefits plus profit bonuses at the end of the year. Many cooperatives were also formed in the plywood manufacturing industry. These cooperatives owned the whole enterprise, gave equal votes to every worker, and every worker got equal pay per hour of work.

Another quite different type of cooperative is the so-called Employee Stock Ownership Plan (ESOP). In these cases, employees take over a firm through a very particular type of corporation, set up by Congress. Employees in the ESOP own the corporation through their ownership of stock, so it remains very similar to ordinary capitalist institutions. Some important ESOPs have been the Avis car rental company and United Airlines.

Under the legal rules, it is possible to make an ESOP very similar to a workers' cooperative, except for the difference made by leaving control tied to the amount of stock ownership). Other ESOPs are clearly very far from workers' cooperatives. Basically, some enterprises manage to sell most of the stock to employees, but to retain control of all decisions. One way to do this is to put all the employee stock into a trust, and then have management gain control of it.

Several arguments have been given in favor of employee cooperatives. First, they increase democracy over firms run by private owners. Second, cooperatives result in more income equality in the society. Third, cooperative ownership results in more incentive for the individual professional worker or manual worker.

On the other hand, many controversial issues have been discovered. After a workers' cooperative has been formed, are unions needed any more? If employees become rebellious against their own elected management, should strikes be allowed? How much financing can a cooperative get from the banks? Does bank interference reduce democracy? In more general terms, can cooperatives be maintained when the rest of the society is capitalist? Should the whole society be run by workers' cooperatives? Should wages be equal for all workers in a workers' cooperative or should wages differ by skill or by performance? Should individual groups of workers on the shop floor be allowed independence? These are difficult questions. To their credit, many cooperatively managed firms raise these questions and debate them among the employee/owners.

The Public Road to Economic Democracy

In addition to employee ownership, democratic control may be exercised by democratically elected governmental bodies. Control may also be exercised by the representatives of democratically elected bodies, such as publicly owned universities.

Some of the media have been run through democratic ownership of various types. Many writers have argued that the media are a likely place for democratic control for two main reasons. One reason is that there can be no effective political democracy without a media free of control by giant corporations. Second, the media are highly concentrated in ownership by a relatively few corporations, so democratic control of some media will reduce income inequality as well as inequality of power.

There is a myth that the private ownership of the media is "natural" in some sense and there is no alternative. This myth may be shown to be false by considering American media of the 1930s. At that time, public radio broadcasting predominated. Many stations were nonprofit and run by universities. In the 1930s many educators tried to establish a non-profit and noncommercial radio broadcasting system. There were over a hundred broadcasting stations established by universities. Thus, educators were the pioneers in radio broadcasting. In the early 1930s, only the name of a private advertiser was mentioned. It was unthinkable in America in the 1930s that anyone would sit through a commercial advertisement!

Many of the universities that owned radio stations were public universities whose leaders were appointed by democratically elected governors and legislators. Private industry at first thought that radio would be unprofitable. How could one make a profit by broadcasting when no one had to pay for the broadcasts?

There was a long fight for public radio and against private radio. Private radio broadcasting—and later private television broadcasting—were seen as antidemocratic by most educators because a few corporations would control the flow of information.

The U.S. Public Broadcasting System (PBS) and the National Public Radio (NPR) system are publicly owned institutions that have made major contributions to the development of radio and television broadcasting. Part of their revenue comes from the public treasury by law and part comes from individual subscribers as in a cooperative. This structure illustrates the very important point that public and cooperative control need not be mutually exclusive, but can be mixed in different percentages in different industries and at different times.

Another very important area of democratic ownership has been the public utilities sector. There were many fierce battles in the early twentieth-century United States, with reformers and unions on one side, and big business on the other side. Many towns and cities decided that they should own the public utilities that they used. One example of the many publicly owned utilities is the Department of Water and Power in Los Angeles. This agency sells all of the water and electricity in Los Angeles. Customers pay according to their useage. The record shows that it has been very efficient and more successful in terms of production and profits than private firms.

It should be stressed that it is not just big cities that manage their affairs this way. Even out on the Great Plains, the Nebraska Public Power

District is a public corporation and a political subdivision of the state. Through collective ownership and a democratically elected board, the citizens of the Cornhusker State enjoy reliable service and some of the lowest electrical utility rates in the country.

In the early twenty-first century, the private energy firms of California were involved in a crisis. The crisis included manipulation of prices to make vast extra profits, as well as exaggerated shortages to make even more profits. After extracting as much profit as possible, some firms sent a larage amount of their earnings out of state and threatened to go bankrupt. During this crisis, the Los Angeles public water and power agency went about its business serenely with no problems. Thus, the Los Angeles public department has proven itself to be more efficient than the private firms. At the same time that it makes high revenues, it is able to charge lower prices because it is nonprofit and publicly owned.

Almost all public utilities, such as water, gas, and electricity, are natural monopolies because it makes no sense to have more than one supplier in a town. The reason that only one supplier can be efficient is that the cost of infrastructure and initial investment is enormous, so the cost per unit is much less if there is only one supplier. For example, the water company supplies water through certain pipes. It would be ridiculous for a competitor to lay down additional water pipes to serve the exact same areas.

The lack of possibility for competition is true of cable television suppliers. A natural lack of competition in the interest of efficiency is also true, to some extent, of telephone lines. Since all of these are monopolies by nature, to leave them to a single private firm without regulation is to ask to be extremely exploited by monopoly prices. The monopolies can be regulated. The regulators, however, are often bribed in various ways to do as the corporations say. Therefore, according to its advocates, public ownership by the city or other local government entity is the best way to ensure efficiency and low cost.

At the regional or state level, an interesting example is in North Dakota. In that state, during the period of control by the populist movement of angry farmers at the end of the nineteenth century and in the early twentieth century, it was decided that control of the financial system was too important to leave to private, capitalist enterprise.

Farmers and small business needed loans with low interest rates and the banks were unwilling to provide them. So the state of North Dakota set up the Bank of North Dakota, which was wholly state owned and state controlled. It still exists today and continues "to encourage and promote agriculture, commerce and industry" in North Dakota. At the national level, the delivery of much of the mail is done by the U.S. Post Office. The democratically elected U.S. government owns and controls the Post Office. It sells its services to anyone who pays for them. So it is an enterprise under democratic control of all American voters through their representatives. Various businesses would like to take over the post office as a private enterprise, and to make large profits. The private profit would be made from what customers would pay in higher prices and what postal employees would have taken from them through lower wages. Thus, there has been a long struggle by postal employees and consumers to defend the post office against those who would take it over for profit reasons.

Another example at the American national level was one in which democracy lost. The nuclear energy industry was developed by the American government, which poured huge amounts of money into its research to build an atomic bomb during World War II. After the war, the government poured more money into developing the peaceful use of nuclear energy. Once the government had gone to the enormous expense of research and construction of a nuclear industry, it was not maintained under the democratic control of the public. Instead, this rich bonanza was given away for free or at very low prices to private entrepreneurs, who expected to make large profits out of it.

At the global level, some reformers have advocated ownership of the international airlines by an international, democratically governed agency. It is argued that one integrated global airline would be much more efficient and give better service. The airlines are presently in economic trouble, so they might be bought cheaply.

One problem with any global regulation or ownership is that there is no democratic global government. The United Nations is both weak and largely undemocratic in structure. There was a very slow evolution towards a global government in the twentieth century. After World War I, the League of Nations was formed, but it had very limited powers. Also, some countries, such as the United States, refused to join it. After World War II, the United Nations was established.

The United Nations was much stronger in theory than the League, but it is far from democratic. The power to police the global community is mostly held by just five nations. Those five often disagree, so it is weak as well as undemocratic. Many people, including Albert Einstein, began, immediately after the United Nations was organized, to advocate making the United Nations into a strong and democratic global government, but that has not happened so far.

Economic Democracy in Health Care and Education

In American education, the elementary school is public and free. The secondary school is public and free. Thus, there is economic democracy in elementary and secondary education. Students must go to school, but they may choose a private school.

There are public universities in most states, so there is also economic democracy at that level. Public universities used to be free, but conservative lawmakers have been adding fees, so they are now less equal and more difficult for lower-income students to attend. Most graduate programs cost a lot of money, even in public universities. Thus, although there is some economic democracy at the university level, there are still a great deal of inequality and obstacles to lower-income students. There is a movement to make all public education available to every qualified student and completely free.

Conservatives argue that all education should be left to market supply and demand. Liberals argue that free education not only benefits the student, but is a very profitable investment for society because it provides a much larger pool of educated specialists.

Most health care in the United states is provided through profit-making insurance companies. It is an undemocratic system that leaves over 45 million people without health insurance, but costs a higher percentage of gross domestic product than is the case in any other country. There is also Medicare, a health-care system supplied by the democratically elected government to older citizens, so there is economic democracy in that sector of the health-care industry.

Canada has economic democracy in all of its health care, as do most other industrialized countries. All Canadians receive free health care from a system funded by their democratically elected government. This system increases both democracy and equality. It also reduces the sick days off work for the average employee.

In health and education and many other sectors discussed above, one can look carefully through a strong microscope and see emerging in embryo the beginning of what may be a new, democratic economic system. If historical experience is any guide, however, it will be resisted by the elite and will be won, if it is, only by a long struggle.

Conclusions

First, the United States has all the forms of political democracy. It is, however, predominantly capitalist in its economic institutions. Capitalism sets narrow limits to political democracy because those with wealth usually hold almost all of the power through the use of that wealth in the political process.

Second, capitalism is undemocratic in the economic sphere. A few large stockholders are dictators in each business enterprise and employees have no power at all.

Third, one form of economic democracy is the cooperative firm. In such a firm, the employees own all the stock and make off the decisions through an elected board of directors. There are some successful examples of this form in the United States, and it has been practiced on a wide scale in a number of other countries.

Fourth, another form of economic democracy is ownership and management by an elected legislature through an appointed agency. This has been practiced with some success in the United States and on a large in a number of other countries. There are also many examples of mixed cooperative and public ownership throughout the world.

Fifth, the elite oppose evolution from capitalism to economic democracy, so any such evolution would be long and turbulent.

Suggested Readings

The fascinating story of early broadcasting and university participation in it is described in depth in McChesney, *Rich Media, Poor Democracies* (1999). The relationship of democratic political institutions to capitalist economic institutions is best described in Bowles and Gintis, *Democracy and Capitalism* (1986). A powerful and clear argument for a change to more democratic economic institutions is given in David Schweickart, *There Is An Alternative* (2002).

The development of employees' cooperatives is told with excellent scholarship in Christopher Gunn, *Workers' Self-Management in the*

*United Sta*tes (1984). He followed up with a book covering nonprofit enterprises as well as cooperatives, Christopher Gunn, *Third Sector Development: Making Up For The Market* (2004). The vehement arguments for and against a system of cooperative enterprises are presented clearly in Robin Hahnel, *Economic Justice and Democracy: From Competition to Cooperation* (2005).

A good, scholarly book on public ownership is: Yair Aharoni, *Evolution and Management of State-Owned Enterprises* (1986).

– 14 –

Lessons from the Story of Evolution

The main point of this book is that the story of evolution offers hope to us all. Human social evolution has followed a tortured path from its earliest beginnings to the present with some awful conflicts and terrible happenings. But it does show that there have been drastic changes and could be more drastic changes ahead. Good changes are not inevitable, but they are possible. The present situation is a great deal better than the conditions of the earliest humans, who lived very short and often unpleasant lives. The story of evolution shows that if one does not like the present situation in some important respects, it is possible for humanity to make further drastic changes in its institutions and to build a better world.

The other main point made by the book is that the process of social evolution is not mysterious. One need not be baffled by the world and its changing situation, nor need one attribute events to some supernatural cause. The book has explained the dynamic process by which society changes, so no one should fear it. The process of change is understandable and it is controlled by we human beings working under certain given historical circumstances.

It is true that there are no laws of social evolution if you mean something like a law of physics. But there are some useful lessons to be learned about the mechanisms of evolution from the points made in this book.

First, every aspect of society is connected with every other one by a tangled web of connections, so society acts as one organic whole. For example, if one wants to understand drug addiction, merely looking at each drug user as an isolated individual does not help much. How do social conditions create the kind of tensions that lead to drug addiction? How does the kind of market exchange and profit seeking in our present society affect the drug sellers? It is misleading to look at any social problem as if it is isolated from society.

As another example, in many chapters this book investigated the history of the struggle for women's rights. In every era, it was shown how the struggle for those rights interacted with politics, basic economic institutions, ideology, and every aspect of society. The same interconnections with all aspects of society were found in the case of racism, as, for example, the relationship of racism with slavery. In short, every individual story told in this book was shown to be part of the social whole in each historically given human society. The story is one of connected human beings in a society, not isolated individuals.

Second, social evolution can be compared with biological evolution. Charles Darwin's theory of evolution shows that the internal stresses and conflicts of nature cause biological evolution. So, to explain the changes in species, there is no need to drag in outside forces, such as an inevitable Fate, or God, or any supernatural being. (The best book on Darwin is Stephen J. Gould, *Ever Since Darwin* 1977). Similarly, the story in previous chapters has shown that the internal dynamics of the social processes themselves explain social evolution. In other words, we and our institutions determine our own fate and there is no inevitable fate beyond humanity. Aside from this general principle, the actual processes of biological and social evolution are entirely different.

Third, sometimes societies go for a very long time without any change in their institutions, technology, or culture. For example, early human communal societies lasted around a hundred thousand years without much basic change. When there is no change, investigation shows that the culture, the economic institutions, and the technology all fit well together. In this case, there are no tensions leading to a change in basic institutions.

Fourth, sometimes societies change drastically into totally new relationships in a relatively short period. For example, after being mostly unchanged for a hundred thousand years, the Neolithic revolution changed some societies from communal to slave or serf relationships in a few thousand years. This process included changes in technology, in every social institution, and in the dominant ideological view.

In a similar example, after a thousand years of feudalism in England, feudalism changed to capitalism with a transition of about three hundred years. After long periods of increasing tensions, the British, French, American, and Russian Revolutions each took place in a few years. After the horrors of slavery lasted for generations, the U.S. Civil War ended slavery within a few years.

Each of these societies had completely different institutions and economic systems. As a result, each society had very different social and economic laws of operation and development. Any good analysis of any aspect of society must be very specific as to which type of political-economic system it is discussing. This understanding of the differences between systems and its application to each social problem is the principle of historical specificity.

Fifth, why do relatively sudden changes occur from an old type of society to a new type of society? This book has illustrated two necessary conditions for such a dramatic change in fundamental human relations. One necessary condition is the clash between institutions and economic and environmental progress. A second condition is that this clash leads to human conflicts, which alone can lead to change.

The first condition occurs when the economic institutions no longer fit with the present technology. This lack of fit between institutions and technology means that economic and political institutions no longer encourage economic advancement, technological innovation, and a sustainable environment. When economic institutions start to hold back the economy, tensions mount and major evolutionary change may occur.

For example, at the end of the Roman Empire, technology was stagnant and the economy declined because of slave institutions. Similarly, in 1789 in France, the remnants of feudalism were a burden on the economy and were holding back economic progress. Another example was revealed in the Great Depression of the 1930s, when the economic institutions of American capitalism led to decline and stagnation in the U.S. economy.

Rigid, unchanging economic institutions not only may hold back technological change, they also tend to produce environmental calamity. For example, when profit motives induced overhunting with the use of guns in the old American West, millions of buffalo were wiped out in a short time and much of the Native American way of life in that area disappeared. Similarly, in 2005, when profit motives led to the end of most of the wetlands in the Mississippi delta, this removed one important barrier to flooding, so it was one cause of the disastrous flood of New Orleans that was initiated by a hurricane. Attempts to reduce taxes under the existing political system, influenced by business interests, also caused too little money to be spent on fixing the dikes of New Orleans, another cause of the disastrous affects of the hurricane.

Sixth, tensions between economic institutions and economic progress (including environmental stability) are not the only necessary conditions for change to a new society. The fact that economic institutions are outmoded and are causing immense damage to the economy and the environment does not automatically mean that they will change. There is usually resistance to change in economic institutions by the ruling elite.

In most cases where drastic change in economic institutions has been urgent, the ruling elite have tried to defend the existing system because it is the source of their power and wealth. The average person may fight in favor of change against the old ruling elite. If the forces in favor of change are successful in these momentous struggles, wars, and revolutions, then an evolutionary change to a new society may occur. The new society will then have new institutions that fit the level of technology, as well as a new politics and culture that fit with both of these.

In the present United States, capitalist economic institutions are still leading to economic advance, but they also have caused some enormous problems leading to social conflict. Briefly, the main problems and conflicts discussed in previous chapters (chapters 7 to 11) were as follows:

In addition to the Great Depression of the 1930s, the economic institutions of capitalism have brought the economy to a halt and decline every few years, causing great human misery. In spite of the resistance of the elite, many reforms were made in the 1930s. Reforms, such as the minimum wage and the unemployment compensation system, were designed to alleviate the suffering from recessions and depressions.

American capitalist institutions have also led to extreme and worsening economic inequality. The middle class has been greatly reduced. The top one percent hold most of the power and wealth, while the bottom 60 percent have no wealth and little power.

American capitalist institutions mean that enterprises must put profit before environment. For example, short-run profit seeking has led to cutting down of many forests, air pollution, and sickness as in my city of Los Angeles, pollution of drinking water in many rivers and lakes, and the turning of farmland into dusty wasteland. There is continual conflict between the environmental movement and business.

American capitalism has continued some of the prejudice and discrimination against African-Americans inherited from slavery. This discrimination is profitable for many reasons, including lower wages to African-Americans and division of the labor force in each large company along racial lines that make unions much more difficult. Similar profit considerations have led to continued discrimination against Latino-Americans, inherited from the conquest of the Southwest from Mexico. Large profits are also made by corporations from the lower wages paid to women employees as well as the divisiveness of sexist prejudice by male employees. All of these divisions, caused by profit-seeking institutions, have led to strife by race, ethnicity, and gender.

Last, but not least, there was a drive for expansion under past economic institutions for slaves, serfs, and land. Under capitalism there was imperial expansion that used force to get colonies that would produce profit. Under global capitalism, it is more rational to use peaceful corporate expansion to gain profit. In exceptions, such as Iraq, capitalist governments decide, based on both rational calculations and irrational ideologies, that force will bring more prestige, power, and profit.

Thus, the second necessary condition for major evolutionary change is that structural tensions must lead to problems causing social conflicts. The conflicts may appear as religious conflicts, as in the English Revolution of 1648 that ended feudalism in England. The conflicts may appear as racial conflicts, which was one major factor in the U.S. Civil War that ended slavery. The social conflicts may also appear as class conflicts, as in the French Revolution of 1789, which ended feudalism in France. In each of these cases, the conflicts resulted from economic institutions that were inappropriate to continued economic and social advance. The conflicts resulted in each case in a new economic system that allowed further progress.

Of course, in some cases the structural tensions and human conflicts may result in a defeat for the forces of progress and a triumph for the vested interests. When those who wish to preserve present economic and political relations are victorious, the result is further stagnation. The chance for progress, however, does exist if the struggles of the common people are successful.

– Appendix –

History of
Evolutionary Thought

Hunter and gatherer societies saw no change from year to year, so they all believed there would never be a change in their basic way of life and institutions. Their ideology was one of no change and no evolution (based on evidence from similar societies in recent times studied by anthropologists).

Among the ancient Greeks, there were a few philosophers who believed that everything—including institutions—keeps changing. Others said that nothing ever changes. The debates were based on pure speculation, not factual research.

In medieval Europe, change in technology or institutions was extremely slow. Therefore, medieval people believed the religious dogma that said nothing would ever change. Nothing would change because God had decided it should be that way.

In the early nineteenth century, when there was rapid technological change, there were many speculations about social evolution. Yet few were based on facts because few facts were known. The common theme in many of them was that humanity was passing through a series of pre-ordained historical stages. They believed that progress from the lowest stage to the highest stage is inevitable.

In the mid-nineteenth century, Karl Marx formulated a well-developed evolutionary theory, based on the limited facts known at that time. Marx's theory depended on internal dynamics and did not assume inevitable progress. Marx found that the elite live off of the exploitation of the

217

direct producers in each society. He believed there would probably be a revolution. In that revolution, the basic producers—white-collar and blue-collar workers in our present jargon—would take over the society and dismiss the elite as useless. Marx stated forcefully that the capitalist elite were exceedingly important in making remarkable economic progress at an earlier time. Now, however, the capitalist elite have become an obstacle to further progress.

Charles Darwin also published his theory of biological evolution in the mid-nineteenth century. Darwin had a profound effect on all evolutionary thinking. Darwin showed that evolution takes place by natural selection of new species to fit the environment. Therefore, in Darwin's theory, there is no need to assume actions by a supernatural god. This was such a revolutionary view that Darwin did not publish it for forty years till he was less afraid of retribution. Some of Darwin's most revolutionary views were never published in his lifetime.

Herbert Spencer was influenced by the debates on Darwin's theory of biological evolution, but used a misreading of Darwin to defend the elite. Spencer found that evolution is producing a better and better elite on the basis of a struggle that leads to the biological survival and dominance of the fittest. This confusion of biological and social evolution has been repeated by many conservatives.

In most of the nineteenth century, the social sciences were a unified whole of which evolutionary theory was a part. But the social sciences split into different fields in the late nineteenth century. By the early twentieth century, the theory of evolution vanished from most of the social sciences and was relegated to the separate field of anthropology.

Even in anthropology people such as Franz Boas pointed out all of the vagueness to be found in the nineteenth-century writers. To improve the scientific content, they set aside broad evolutionary theory and concentrated on factual knowledge about specific societies at a given level. So social evolutionary theory almost disappeared from academia for decades.

Outside of the academic mainstream, those who were influenced by Marx continued to use a unified social science with evolution being a central focus. Another exception appeared in the writings of Thorstein Veblen in the early twentieth century. Veblen was the most famous non-mainstream American economist of the twentieth century. He had a unified theory including economics, sociology, psychology, and history. He wrote in many books and articles that economics must become an evolutionary science. He also argued that economics must be part of a unified social science. But the mainstream economists largely ignored Veblen and attacked Marx.

In the 1940s, Leslie White and his followers in anthropology resuscitated evolutionary theory. They said that detailed studies of individual societies are good factual material, but are not enough. White's main idea was that humans were constantly gaining command of more and more energy, such as coal and electricity, through science and technology. This upward trend in energy per human was the basis of social evolution. White and his followers made some mistakes of the type common in the nineteenth century, such as the idea that progress is inevitable. Nevertheless, they did pioneer a new start of evolutionary theory with far more rigor and facts than before.

In the 1950s and 1960s, the outstanding Marxist archaeologist, V. Gordon Childe, tried to combine the theory of social evolution with factual knowledge of what he found in the Middle East and facts about other areas as well. His well-written studies had some impact on the general population, but anthropologists were very hesitant to accept any idea from someone in the tradition of Marx during the Cold War.

In the 1960s, the best writer on the process of evolution from communal to class-divided societies was Elman Service (1967), who wrote a book that is still very useful and a pleasure to read. For many decades beginning with the 1970s, the strongest voice for an evolutionary approach was Marvin Harris, who was chair of anthropology at Columbia University for a long time.

In the 1970s, 1980s, and 1990s, anthropologists and archeologists came to take social evolution for granted. They argued, however, over every detail presented by any general work on evolution, striving to see that every fact was exactly correct and proven. What has emerged is a theory of social evolution that is far stronger, but far more complex, than the pioneering theories of the 1950s and 1960s. The theory of evolution is still mostly absent from economics, where the main theories continue to be static and eternal in their assumptions.

Suggested Readings

By far the most interesting and readable history of thought on social evolution is by Marvin Harris (2001). Harris makes it all alive and interesting. Almost all of the authors mentioned below are cited and discussed in his book. Harris discusses all the social sciences in the nineteenth century, then focuses on anthropology in the twentieth century. In addition to his scholarly extensions of evolutionary theory, Harris wrote some amusing and insightful applications, such as the books, *Cows, Pigs, and Witches* (1974) and *Cannibals and Kings* (1977).

Another outstanding, scholarly book on the history of social evolutionary thought, with a focus on anthropology, is by Thomas C. Patterson (2001). This book is unique in that it explains why evolutionary thought evolved the way it did in the United States in relation to how our society evolved. Both Harris and Patterson make clear that the theory of social evolution has itself evolved, but not in a straight line. V. Gordon Childe wrote many books, some of them still fun to read, such as *What Happens in History* (1957).

The contemporary Marxist theory of social evolution is discussed in Howard Sherman, *Reinventing Marxism* (1995). The similarities and differences in the evolutionary theories of Marx and of Veblen are discussed in William Dugger and Howard Sherman (2000). For a collection of the best works on social evolution from the early nineteenth century to the present, see Dugger and Sherman, eds., *Evolutionary Theory and the Social Sciences* (2003).

References

Aharoni, Yair. 1986. *Evolution and Management of State-Owned Enterprises.* Cambridge, MA: Ballinger Publishing.

Alvarez, Walter. 1998. *T. Rex and the Crater of Doom.* New York: Vintage Books.

Ambrose, Stephen. 2001. *Nothing Like It in the World: The Men Who Built the Transcontinental Railroad, 1863–1869.* New York: Simon and Schuster.

Anderson, Perry. 1974. *Passages from Antiquity to Feudalism.* London: New Left Books.

Andrews, Edward L. 2004. "How Tax Bill Gave Business More and More." *New York Times.* October 13: 1, 14.

Aston, T.H., and C.H.E. Philpin. 1985. *The Brenner Debate.* Cambridge: Cambridge University Press.

Bolles, Edmund Blair. 1999. *The Ice Finders: How a Poet, a Professor, and a Politician Discovered the Ice Age.* Washington, DC: Counterpoint.

Bowles, Samuel, and Herbert Gintis. 1986. *Democracy and Capitalism.* New York: Basic Books.

Boyer, Richard O., and Herbert Morais. 1970. *Labor's Untold Story.* New York: United Electrical Workers.

Burton, Maureen, and Reynold Nesiba. 2004. "Transnational Financial Institutions, Global Financial Flows, and the International Monetary Fund." In Philip O'Hara, ed., *Global Political Economy and the Wealth of Nations: Performance, Institutions, Problems and Policies.* New York and London: Routledge, 147–69.

Ceram, C.W. 1951. *Gods, Graves and Scholars.* New York: A. Knopf.

Chase, Anthony. 1997. *The American Legal System: The Evolution of the American Legal System.* New York: New Press.

Chernow, Ron. 1998. *House of Morgan: An American Banking Dynasty and the Rise of Modern Finance.* New York: Grove Press.

———. 1999. *Titan: Biography of John D. Rockefeller.* New York: Vintage Books.

Childe, V. Gordon. 1957. *What Happens in History.* New York: Penguin.

Collins, Chuck, and Felice Yeskel. 2000. *Economic Apartheid in America.* New York: New Press.

Collins, Chuck, Betsy Leondar-Wright, and Holly Sklar. 1999. *Shifting Fortunes: The Perils of the Growing American Wealth Gap.* Boston: United for a Fair Economy.

Dahlberg, Frances, ed. 1981. *Woman the Gatherer.* New Haven: Yale University Press.

Deckard, Barbara Sinclair. 1983. *The Women's Movement.* New York: Harper and Row.

Deutscher, Isaac. 1965a. *Stalin.* New York: Oxford University Press.

————. 1965b. *Trotsky*. 3 vols. New York: Vintage Books.

Diamond, Jared. 1997. *Guns, Germs, and Steel*. New York: W.W. Norton.

————. 2005. *Collapse*. New York: Viking.

DuBoff, Richard. 1989. *Accumulation and Power: An Economic History of the United States*. Armonk, NY: M.E. Sharpe.

Dugger, William M., and Howard J. Sherman. 2000. *Reclaiming Evolution*. New York: Routledge.

Dugger, William M., and Howard J. Sherman, eds. 2003. *Evolutionary Theory and the Social Sciences*. 4 vols. New York and London: Routledge.

Feiner, Susan, ed. 2002. *Race and Gender in the US Economy: Views from Across the Spectrum*. Englewood Cliffs, NJ: Prentice Hall.

Feinman, Jay. 2004. *Un-Making Law: The Conservative Campaign to Roll Back the Common Law*. Boston: Beacon Press.

Flexner, Eleanor. 1975. *Century of Struggle: The Women's Rights Movement in the United States*. Cambridge: Beklnap Press of Harvard University Press.

Fogel, Robert, and Sydney Engerman. 1989. *Time on the Cross*. New York: Norton.

Foner, Eric. 1988. *Reconstruction*. New York: Harper and Row.

Foner, Philip. 1947–1994. *History of the Labor Movement in the United States*. 10 vols. New York: International Publishers.

Foster, John Bellamy. 1984. *The Vulnerable Planet: A Short Economic History of The Environment*. New York: Monthly Review.

Frank, Thomas. 2004. *What's the Matter with Kansas? How Conservatives Won the Heart of America*. New York: Metropolitan Books.

Galbraith, John Kenneth. 2004. "The Iraq War." *Guardian*, July 15. n.p.

Genovese, Eugene. 1976. *Roll, Jordan, Roll: The World the Slaves Made*. New York: Vintage Books.

————. 1989. *The Political Economy of Slavery: Studies in the Economy and Society of the Slave South*. Middletown, CT: Wesleyan University Press.

Gosselin, Peter. 2004. "Poor and Uninsured Americans Increase for Third Straight Year." *Los Angeles Times*, August 27: 1, 7.

Gould, Stephen Jay. 1977. *Ever Since Darwin*. New York: W.W. Norton.

Griffin, Keith. 1987. *World Hunger and the World Economy*. London: Macmillan.

Gunn, Christopher. 1984. *Workers' Self-Management in the United States*. Ithaca, NY: Cornell University Press.

————. 2004. *Third Sector Development: Making Up for the Market*. Ithaca: Cornell University Press.

Hahnel, Robin. 2005. *Economic Justice and Democracy: From Competition to Cooperation*. New York: Routledge.

Harris, Marvin. 1974. *Cows, Pigs, and Witches*. New York: Random House.

————. 1977. *Cannibals and Kings*. New York: Random House.

————. 2001. *Rise of Anthropological Theory*. Updated ed. Walnut Creek, CA: Alta Mira.

Hilton, R.H., ed. 1976. *The Transition from Feudalism to Capitalism*. London: Verso.

Iritani, Evelyn. 2004. "New Trade Pact Could Cut Clout of U.S. in Asia." *Los Angeles Times*, November 30: C1, C6.

Kotz, David, with Fred Weir. 1997. *Revolution from Above: The Demise of the Soviet Union*. London: Routledge.

Marable, Manning. 1997. *Black Liberation in Conservative America*. Boston: South End Press.

McChesney, Robert. 1999. *Rich Media, Poor Democracy: Communication Politics in Dubious Times*. Urbana: University of Illinois Press.

Mintz, Sidney. 1986. *Sweetness and Power: The Place of Sugar in Modern History*. New York: Penguin Books.

National Bureau of Economic Research. 2004. "Foreign Investment." News release, June 30.

Navarro, Vicente. 1993. *Dangerous to Your Health*. New York: Monthly Review.

Patterson, Thomas C. 2001. *A Social History of Anthropology in The United States*. New York: Berg.

Perry, Rebecca. 2004. "Late Exit Poll Data." *Los Angeles Times*, November 4: 1, 23.

Pollin, Robert. 2004. *Contours of Descent: U.S. Economic Fractures and the Landscape of Global Austerity*. New York: Verso.

Power, Eileen. 2000. *Medieval People*. New York: Barnes and Noble.

"Prisons and Executions: The US Model." 2001. *Monthly Review* 53, no. 3 (July–August).

Pryor, Frederick. 2001. "Dimensions of the World-Wide Merger Boom." *Journal of Economic Issues* 35, no. 4: 825–40.

Rabinowitch, Alexander. 2004. *The Bolsheviks Come to Power*. Chicago: Haymarket Books.

Ransom, Roger. 1989. *Conflict and Compromise: The Political Economy of Slavery, Emancipation, and the Civil War*. Cambridge, UK: Cambridge University Press.

Ransom, Roger, and Richard Sutch. 1977. *One Kind of Freedom: The Economic Consequences of Emancipation*. New York: Cambridge University Press.

Reich, Michael. 1980. *Racial Inequality, Economic Theory, and Class Conflict*. Princeton: Princeton University Press.

Reiman, Jeffrey. 1990. *The Rich Get Richer and the Poor Get Prison*. 3rd ed. New York: Macmillan.

Rosenberg, Samuel. 2003. *American Economic Development Since 1945: Growth, Decline and Rejuvenation*. New York: Palgrave-Macmillan.

Schweickart, David. 2002. *There Is an Alternative*. London: Rowman and Littlefield.

Service, Elman. 1967. *Primitive Social Organization*. New York: Random House.

Sherman, Howard J. 1968. *Profits in the United States: An Introduction to a Study of Economic Concentration and Business Cycles*. Ithaca, NY: Cornell University Press.

———1991. *The Business Cycle: Growth and Crisis in Capitalism*. Princeton: Princeton University Press.

———. 1995. *Reinventing Marxism*. Baltimore: Johns Hopkins University Press.

Stiglitz, Joseph. 2002. *Globalization and Its Discontents*. New York: W.W. Norton.

Tigar, Michael, and Madeline Levy. 1977. *Law and the Rise of Capitalism*. New York: Monthly Review.

Wirzbicki, Alan. 2004. "Divide Seen in Voter Knowledge." *Boston Globe*, October 22: 1, 13.

Wood, Ellen Meiksins. 2002. *The Origins of Capitalism*. London: Verso.

Woodward, C. Vann. 1974. *The Strange Career of Jim Crow*. 3rd ed. New York: Oxford University Press.

Yates, Michael. 2004. "Poverty and Inequality in the Global Economy." *Monthly Review* 55, no. 9 (February): 37–48.

Zimbalist, Andrew; Howard Sherman; and Stuart Brown. 1988. *Comparing Economic Systems: A Political-Economic Approach*. 2nd ed. San Diego: Harcourt-Brace-Jovanovich.

Zinn, Howard. 1999. *A People's History of the United States*. New York: HarperCollins.

Index